RESITUATING
WRITING

RESITUATING
WRITING

Constructing and Administering
Writing Programs

Edited by

JOSEPH JANANGELO *&* KRISTINE HANSEN

New Perspectives in Rhetoric and Composition

CHARLES I. SCHUSTER, SERIES EDITOR

BOYNTON/COOK PUBLISHERS
HEINEMANN
PORTSMOUTH, NH

Boynton/Cook Publishers
A subsidiary of Reed Elsevier Inc.
361 Hanover Street
Portsmouth, NH 03801-3912

Offices and agents throughout the world

We would like to thank those who have given their permission to include material in this book. Every effort has been made to contact the copyright holders for permission to reprint borrowed material where necessary. We regret any oversights that may have occurred and would be happy to rectify them in future printings of this work.

Library of Congress Cataloging-in-Publication Data
Resituating writing: constructing and administering programs/edited by Joseph Janangelo and Kristine Hansen.
     p.cm. — (CrossCurrents: new perspectives in rhetoric and composition)
     Includes bibliographical references.
     ISBN 0-86709-366-8 (pbk.)
     1. English language—Rhetoric—Study and teaching. 2. Writing centers—Administration.   I. Janangelo, Joseph.   II. Hansen, Kristine.   III. Series: Cross Currents (Portsmouth, N.H.)
PE1404.R44   1995   95-31501
808'.042'07—dc20   CIP

Editor: Peter Stillman
Cover design: Jenny Jensen Greenleaf

Printed in the United States of America on acid-free paper
98 97 96 95   DA   1 2 3 4 5 6

We dedicate this book to

Daniel and Lucille Hansen

*Yola Janangelo, Peter Janangelo Sr., Peter Janangelo Jr.,
and Farrell J. Webb*

Contents

Foreword

With this volume of scholarly essays, the concept of writing program administration as a significant expression of academic scholarship comes of age. As the essays in this volume make plain, the work of composition directors is worthy of promotion, tenure, salary compensation, and the respect of administrators and scholars alike. Unlike other administrative positions within the university that are often at one remove from a disciplinary specialty, such as chairs, chancellors, and deans, writing program administrators (WPAs) must possess both administrative skills and broad-based, up-to-date knowledge of highly specialized disciplinary theory and practice. No WPA can work effectively without knowing the theories and practices that underlie basic writing, invention, pedagogy, collaborative learning, writing across the curriculum, assessment, portfolios, computer classrooms, radical pedagogy—the list could be extended indefinitely.

Of course the Council of Writing Program Administrators has already made this claim, particularly in the Portland Resolution, a document available from the Council, which offers a full articulation of the responsibilities and roles of the WPA. The essays collected here by Joe Janangelo and Kristine Hansen offer a concretization of the Portland Resolution and are authored by a veritable who's who in current writing program administration. Moreover, Janangelo and Hansen have put together a landmark book: This is the first time, to my knowledge, that essays exclusively by WPAs about writing program administration appear in one volume.

To read this book is to glimpse the extraordinary topography of writing instruction from the perspective of those responsible for shaping it. Janangelo opens with a brilliant Derridean analysis of writing programs, exploring the conflicting values and valences of composition as difference, *différance*, and deferral. One major theme of Janangelo's essay is that WPAs "menace with a message," a theme I will return to shortly. Hansen's analysis of the adjunct faculty issue presents both the problems and, in my view, the best set of strategies I've seen yet about how to improve working conditions, morale, and prestige for part-timers within composition programs. For Hansen, the key is to bring "administrators into a relationship with the part-time faculty because relationships are the venue for ethical action." From there we move to consideration of what happens when the composition classroom goes electronic as Faigley and Romano consider a host of virtual realities and the innovative possibilities that graduate instructors devise to computerize writing, possibilities that have "the potential to overturn the privileging of the essay in a writing classroom." Nist and Raines conclude Part I with a call for the Council of Writing Program Administrators and faculty generally to recognize the fundamental importance and value of writing programs and writing program administration in the two-year college, that is, in their words, "to move from communication and accommodation to cooperation and collaboration."

Part II opens with Lynn Bloom's essay on the creative aspect of administering writing programs "which can transform a routine endeavor into a creative enterprise with enormous benefits for students, faculty, institutions —even the entire profession." Ellen Strenski invokes a force field metaphor to explore this same subject, arguing that "an entrepreneurial model offers explanatory hope and power," especially when applied to hiring, training, and retaining writing instructors. Like many others in this volume, both Bloom and Strenski emphasize the importance of risk taking and experimentation. Molly Wingate shifts our focus to writing centers and their not always clear relations to English departments and university power structures. Striking a note we see in many of the essays, Wingate argues that "by entering into positive and proactive forms of collaboration with its host institution, a writing center can find, and even make, opportunities for change." Concluding Part II, Susan McLeod asserts that Writing Across the Curriculum directors who are building transdisciplinary programs "need to invent a new role for themselves— that of change agent." Clearly, then, the unifying theme of all these essays is the importance of WPAs possessing the vision, knowledge, and ethos to alter institutional philosophies and practices.

In an essay that celebrates the coming-of-age of writing program administration scholarship, Christine Hult, past editor of the *WPA* journal, opens Part III by stating eloquently that the "scholarship of administration . . . is the systematic, theory-based production and oversight of a dynamic program." Her extended analysis of this innovative kind of scholarship should be required reading by every review committee evaluating the work of WPAs. Edward White, past director and in many ways founding father of the WPA Consultant Evaluator Program, follows with a knowledgeable and insightful analysis of the hows and whys of program evaluation. As White makes clear, "the value of the WPA program lies in its sensitivity to the uniqueness of local situations and its resistance to over-simplification." Finally, in an essay that challenges our basic assumptions about the institutional identity of the WPA, Barbara Cambridge and Ben McClelland, both past presidents of the Council of Writing Program Administrators, argue that the power of the WPA derives from a concept of shared governance and collaborative decision making. Drawing on a wide array of scholarship about administrative models, Cambridge and McClelland "suggest a more radical redefinition of the WPA, a redefinition that involves changing the basic architecture of leadership and the responsibilities of the WPA."

That this is an extremely important and ground-breaking collection of essays seems to me obvious. From their various perspectives, the authors in this volume explore the seldom-discussed category that Ernest Boyer characterized as the scholarship of application (21–23). As Boyer and the authors in this volume make clear:

> To be considered scholarship, service activities must be tied directly to one's special field of knowledge and relate to, and flow directly out of, this professional activity. Such service is serious, demanding work, requiring the rigor— and the accountability—traditionally associated with research activities." (22)

Boyer's formulation accurately describes the work of WPAs: They are scholars and researchers whose disciplinary rigor is made manifest in their daily work. They are creators of programs and policies who are directly accountable to students, faculty, administrators, and the public.

The theme that I wish to emphasize here, however, is the WPA as, in Susan McLeod's words, a "change agent." Too often, the role of WPA is seen as someone who maintains the status quo and forestalls crises. This conception was brought home to me as I read the case studies and the responses to those studies that formed the centerpiece of the 1994 WPA/ADE Summer Conference at the University of Mississippi. My initial impression was of a potential sense of doom, of some kind of looming administrative crisis that WPAs must ameliorate. You walk into your office on Monday morning, for example, to find a boiling mass of students and instructors infuriated about portfolio evaluation. Or the provost calls to tell you that an armada of parents is in her office complaining about one of your instructor's decision to require Nancy Miller's essay "My Father's Penis" for his two English 101 sections. "Bad idea," she declares. Thus conventional wisdom would suggest that composition directors manage best when they avoid crises and steer their programs through calm waters and sunny weather.

Janangelo's invocation of limbo, Susan McLeod's description of WAC coordinator as foreigner, Wingate's account of renewed vigilance and power sharing, Cambridge and McClelland's challenge to WPA as unitary and hegemonic authority—what these essays describe is a willingness to roil the waters. Granted, all administrators sleep better when the winds are calm and the sea is as smooth as a lemon parfait. Real progress and programmatic reform, however, do not occur in temperate times but in turbulent ones. It makes sense: Complacent composition programs exist in stasis. Such Panglossian optimism, however, is often unjustified. Composition instructors may not complain about work conditions, but the reason may be that they are demoralized or because the departmental administration is unresponsive. A lack of complaints concerning sexual harassment may be attributable to a departmental atmosphere that condones such behavior and treats complainants as troublemakers. Neither undergraduates nor instructors may be unhappy about the composition curriculum that emphasizes workbook practice and prescriptive usage, but that may be because they are theoretically and pedagogically unaware of the past thirty years of work in the discipline. Complacency, fear, demoralization, confusion, exhaustion, timidity: Such attitudes make for a calm writing program that seems at ease but may well be foundering intellectually, educationally, and institutionally.

What such departments—indeed what most departments—need is an occasional crisis. They need a gypsy moth invasion, an influenza outbreak, an unexpected eclipse of the sun. In proposing my principle of crisis creation, I do not mean to suggest that the best administrators are those that cause programmatic bedlam; rather, I want to argue that unforeseen problems or even the occasional nudging along of a crisis can be an administrator's most effective means for accomplishing significant reforms. Such crises are genuinely scary and can cause real damage: Departmental emergencies as we all know can lead to a whole host of afflictions too familiar to catalog here. But as the Chinese proverb reminds us, within every crisis is the opportunity for change.

Like any WPA, I have had my share of crises, some destructive but others productive. Let me describe just one. For years before my arrival at the University of Wisconsin–Milwaukee, freshman composition had been governed by a proficiency test—a 90-minute, blind topic, pseudoargumentative essay that all students had to pass before they could attain junior status. Instituted in the 1970s because of grade inflation, the test did offer a check on student writing. Some undergraduate students took it because they earned a grade of B- in our courses; others because of transfer grades or cut scores on a 100-item multiple choice usage exam. The correlation between success on this exam and success in our courses was low, and it led to our writing instruction being held hostage by a dubious testing procedure. Thus although instructors taught invention, revision, and intellectual complexity, the proficiency exam rewarded quick and superficially correct formulaic writing of the five-paragraph theme variety.

A series of exigencies developed. The proficiency exam kept thousands of students from graduating. It could not be equivalent to a second-semester composition course that emphasized critical reading and sustained and revised argumentative writing. The fail rate dipped and soared between 22 and 37 percent. In multiple ways, the proficiency test had outlived its usefulness, but university faculty and administration were too wedded to the concept of an exam-driven curriculum to be willing to find other solutions.

My solution, with the support of dean and instructors, was to establish meaningful standards for the exam, so meaningful that 70 to 80 percent of the students taking it failed. I did this by defining the criteria for passing the exam in terms of earning a "C" or better in our second-semester course. Since few students can write a thoughtful, meaningful, well-developed, and exemplified argumentative essay on a blind topic in 90 minutes, most of them failed. Needless to say, students, parents, and the central administration expressed outrage as burgeoning numbers of undergraduates were denied junior status and graduation. The university was besieged; minority students wrote to the press; previously congenial advisers nuked my office.

The ensuing crisis was the worst I experienced in my ten-year administrative career. Yet it was also the most productive; it resulted in genuine reform. After two years of committee deliberations, the proficiency exam was eliminated, replaced by a course requirement. The dean was willing to accept this requirement because as a result of an earlier grade crisis, I had instituted a portfolio assessment program that brought real rigor and meaningful grade distribution into our curriculum. That reform became the keystone to our second-semester course where all students (1400 to 1800 per semester) produce portfolios that are holistically scored by instructors other than their own. Thus the grading crisis met the proficiency exam crisis and created a course requirement, a significant and important step forward in improving the education of our students and the credibility of our writing program. Needless to say, however, this new and better program is now producing additional crises of its own.

Let me take a step back for a moment to generalize. In order for crises of whatever magnitude to initiate productive change, certain preconditions must be met. Drawing on my experience skirting on the edge of chaos, I offer a few principles:

1. Do not create a crisis. Crises must emerge from curricular and programmatic flash points. That way, they contain the seeds of significant change.

2. Do not be afraid to take risks, even when—perhaps especially when—they lead to crises. Most academics, and certainly most administrators, prefer caution and conservatism. In my estimation, a little bit of the daredevil is worth cultivating, especially once you have established yourself as an able, flexible, well-regarded administrator.

3. Bring others into your crisis. The true catastrophe occurs when an administrator stands on the edge of a precipice alone. Unlike other situations, where it was me against the world, the slowly unfolding proficiency exam crisis drew support from both key campus administrators and from the teaching staff.

4. Have a plan. My tendency is to rage at circumstances; but it is much more important to sketch out provisional solutions and work toward them. If a problem ruins your sleep, develop some kind of practical option by breakfast.

5. Make sure you have power. Ed White has written about the need for WPAs to use power selectively and judiciously. As he makes clear, the "only way to do the job of a WPA is to be aware of the power relationships we necessarily conduct, and to use the considerable power we have for the good of our program" (White 12). I agree; WPAs must be willing to use their office to achieve results, even if that means they end up expending their symbolic capital and moving out of administration.

6. Try to limit yourself to one good crisis at a time—and no more than one a year. A good crisis can take a lot of a person's time and erode a great deal of equanimity. They are best scheduled annually.

I offer the preceding sketch of crisis creation as a gloss on this volume. The essays that follow express the collective wisdom of thoughtful and experienced administrators engaging on their own terms with crisis, change, and opportunity. Their work is a testament to the basic principle that writing program administration is not comprised of sitting remotely in an office allocating resources and scheduling classes; it is, rather, scholarship in the most significant sense of the word.

Charles I. Schuster

Works Cited

Boyer, Ernest L. *Scholarship Reconsidered: Priorities of the Professoriate.* Princeton, NJ: The Carnegie Foundation, 1990.

White, Edward M. "Use It or Lose It: Power and the WPA." *WPA: Writing Program Administration* 15.1–2 (1991): 3–12.

Preface

Recent years have seen the emergence and increased visibility of a new generation of professional writing program administrators (WPAs). Sometimes self-
taught, yet now often formally trained in graduate schools, these individuals see
their work as central to the academy and worthy of increased institutional support and respect. Eager to engage in scholarly activity that centers around their
work, WPAs have created a professional organization, the Council of Writing
Program Administrators, which sponsors outlets for scholarship, including the
journal *WPA: Writing Program Administration*, the annual WPA Conference,
and sessions on writing program administration at the conferences of CCCC,
NCTE, MLA, and AAHE. In addition, the Council offers an annual Summer
Workshop to provide both experienced and inexperienced WPAs with ideas and
strategies to help them become more effective on their own campuses, annual
grants of up to $2000 to fund research projects related to writing program ad-
ministration, and a Consultant-Evaluator Program to assess writing programs
and advise administrators on how to strengthen them. Each of these testifies to
the growing recognition of writing program administration as a serious field of
inquiry and to the field's maturing sense of identity.

Despite this increased visibility and professionalization, however, writing
programs and writing program administrators are still anomalies on most campuses. Both the program and the administrator have no (or at best very few)
counterparts in the rest of the academy. The writing program is different from
other academic programs in that it typically offers no major, serving general
education needs only. The program thus offers a small number of courses but
multiple sections of each course. The courses are frequently staffed by a
largely transient "faculty" of graduate students, part-time employees, and adjuncts, who differ from each other greatly in their professional interests, time
constraints, preparation and training, and levels of commitment to teaching
writing. Given this type of program and teaching staff to supervise, the WPA
must daily confront the paradox of designing and overseeing the instructional
quality of courses that are required because they are thought to be important,
yet are also often perceived as low in status by students, other faculty and administrators, and sometimes even by the people who teach them. Because the
very existence of college writing programs is perceived by many as a sign of

deteriorating skill and poor instruction in primary and secondary schools, the "different" status of the writing program is often seen as a disability. As a result, the writing program often has been described of late as "marginalized" or even "ghettoized." Laboring under the stigma that such labels bring, the WPA must simultaneously fill all of the following roles: administrator, teacher, scholar, teacher trainer, curriculum planner, evaluator, innovator, arbitrator, emissary, mentor, career counselor, public relations specialist, and politician. The WPA's differences from other administrators and scholars in the academy often lead to his or her work being misunderstood and improperly evaluated. Yet enacting all of these different administrative roles is necessary to permit writing programs to function as well as they do.

In this book the collected essays explore the various manifestations and meanings of difference in college writing programs, arguing that difference does not have to be a liability; in fact, it can be made into a strength. Beginning from the premise that miscommunication about our differences is debilitating to students, teachers, and administrators—indeed, to the whole process of education—the authors of these collected essays aim to improve understanding and promote dialogue about writing programs and their administrators. We aim to articulate the differences that compose and constrain writing programs and to present those differences as positive rather than negative, as enabling rather than stigmatizing. We want to resituate writing programs in the academy—not just physically (because we would like to take them out of the basements and other inadequate quarters they so often inhabit) but conceptually as well—to take them from the margins and locate them at the center of undergraduate education. We hope to take them out of the purely service category they have occupied for so long and permit them to take their place with other respected units in the academy. We hope to help writing program administrators view their assignment as one that calls for their best intellectual efforts as they theorize and implement a vision of writing instruction, and to view their leadership position as one that calls for an ethical example as they lift their voices in behalf of teachers who are manifestly different from others in the academy.

To that end, we have invited people to contribute essays whose own differences—in institutional locations, administrative roles, academic training, experience, philosophy, and temperament—enable them to provide the breadth of discussion that no single-authored text could. Their different backgrounds and, in some cases, their differences of opinion with each other combine here in collective wisdom and experience that give this book its strength. We hope that readers who are similarly diverse will find in it themes, suggestions, and provocations applicable to their own situations. In conceptualizing this text, inviting contributors, and responding to them, we have tried to consider the needs of at least three audiences who we hope will find the book helpful.

The first audience is writing program administrators, at whatever career stage you might be in. For you, we hope the book provides ideas to strengthen your own programs and positions on campus. The second audience we hope to reach is graduate students who are preparing for careers in composition and rhetoric. Currently, many new PhDs accept tenure-track jobs that carry with them often unmentioned heavy administrative loads; even individuals who try to defer writing program administration until after tenure find that they are assigned responsibilities that call for them to contribute much time, thought, and energy to administration. We want you to enter the profession more fully informed of the resources available to help you succeed. The third audience we hope will read this book is other administrators—department chairs, deans, vice-presidents, and provosts. We hope to persuade you that writing programs and their administrators are founded on intellectually solid bases, formed by theory and by experience. We hope the book will provide a basis for fruitful dialogue among WPAs; between WPAs and the graduate students and writing faculty they are responsible to mentor; and between WPAs and the administrators who hire, supervise, and evaluate them.

We have divided this book into three sections that we believe touch on the diversity of the WPA's activities. In the first section, "Philosophical Issues and Institutional Identities," Joseph Janangelo discusses philosophical theories that illuminate the writing program's difference from other, more familiar academic units; he argues that writing programs should use their "unnamable" status to their advantage—to retain their suppleness and their ability to constantly re-create their identity. Kristine Hansen, in discussing the ethical dimension of writing program administration, suggests a method for enfranchising part-time faculty and presents a vision of a new kind of profession and professional. Lester Faigley and Susan Romano provoke us to acknowledge the changing identities and missions of writing programs in the context of the new, technologically supported literacies at which many of our students excel. Finally, Elizabeth Nist and Helon Raines provide an important correction to the supposition that literacy instruction in higher education happens exclusively or even mainly in four-year institutions. Their chapter describes the students, faculty, and curriculum at two- year institutions, which now teach approximately half of the postsecondary students in writing, and it proposes ways for greater collaboration between two- and four-year institutions.

In the second section, "The WPA Within and Across Departments," four veteran WPAs suggest ways of building liaisons with other members of the campus community. Lynn Bloom outlines ways a WPA can work creatively and collegially to change traditional notions of what writing programs and their administrators must now do to be current. Ellen Strenski shows how a WPA can meet her institution's evolving needs by judiciously recruiting new instructors and carefully retraining experienced teachers of writing. Molly Wingate examines productive and unproductive forms of collaboration and shows how a writing center can collaborate with other academic units to make a positive contribution in campus politics. Susan McLeod describes the various metaphors for the writing-across-the-curriculum director, warning of the pitfalls in some of the roles WAC directors might cast themselves and explaining how the WAC director can become a change agent by modifying faculty's classroom practices and theories about writing.

The book's final section, "Professional and Scholarly Identities," reflects on how writing program administrators can conceptualize their work both to make it possible to accomplish and to make its differences understandable and appreciated by the constituencies who judge WPAs. Both Christine Hult's and Edward White's essays describe how the WPA can present to evaluators and higher administrators the most persuasive case they can for the work they do and the programs they direct. In discussing what she calls "the scholarship of administration," Christine, longtime editor of *WPA: Writing Program Administration*, argues that administering a writing program is a complex scholarly activity, requiring the WPA not only to discover and publish knowledge in traditional forms, but to apply, integrate, and teach knowledge in the daily work of keeping a dynamic program functioning. Ed, the former head of the WPA Consultant-Evaluator Service, exposes the fallacies inherent in using positivistic methods to evaluate a writing program's success and describes more responsible and valid forms of assessment. Finally, Barbara Cambridge and Ben McClelland, past facilitators of the WPA Summer Workshop, suggest a radical new idea, namely that the WPA should not be the single symbol or icon of the writing program; in fact, the webs of relationships the WPA is located in and the clusters of roles the WPA performs suggest that the position ought to be reconceptualized as a network of partnerships.

This book was made possible by the faith and assistance of many important people. We thank the authors of the individual essays who listened to us in a dingy Cincinnati hotel room when the book was still a vaguely sketched idea. We are grateful that you believed in us; we thank you for the opportunity of working with you. We thank Peter Stillman of Heinemann–Boynton/Cook for also believing in the project and offering us the contract that made it real. Sharon Adams and Ruth Liljenquist, of Brigham Young University, offered timely, valuable, and always pleasant assistance with the details of getting the manuscript in the right format, ready to be submitted for printing. The BYU English Department and College of Humanities provided a leave of absence that allowed Kristine to devote the time needed to complete this book. Both BYU and Loyola University–Chicago supplied funding that contributed to our ability to complete the project.

Most of all, we thank Chuck Schuster, whose encouragement and advocacy of the book were the catalyst that made everything possible. Thank you for mentoring us through every aspect of its creation. Finally, we thank dear friends and family members whose moral support kept our spirits up and whose help on the domestic front enabled us to focus our energies more effectively.

Joseph Janangelo
Kristine Hansen

RESITUATING WRITING

Part I

Philosophical Issues
and Institutional Identities

1

Theorizing Difference and Negotiating Differends
(Un)naming Writing Programs' Many Complexities and Strengths

Joseph Janangelo
Loyola University—Chicago

As I consider the complex relations that simultaneously compose and constrain writing programs, two sets of questions come to mind. The first set is voiced by Samuel Beckett and serves as the opening for his novel *The Unnamable*. The questions are:

> Where now? Who now? When now? Unquestioning. I, say I.(3)

Beckett's questions, which address the enigma of identity, strike me as pertinent to the challenges of self-definition, self-justification, and self-preservation that continually face writing programs.

To better appreciate these challenges, we might consider the set of questions Carol Hartzog raises in *Composition and the Academy*:

> What kind of discipline is as slippery as this? Why are so many people spending so much time trying to explain what it is—and to dignify it within the academy? (70)

Like Beckett, Hartzog asks questions about self-definition. Yet she relates our discipline's identity issues to its relationship with the academy, a more powerful Other. Unlike Beckett, Hartzog does not just raise questions. She goes so far as to pose a possible solution—one which positions itself as a truth and a dare to writing programs. "Given all that I have seen and heard of these programs," she writes,

I would say that many of them are trying to become something they are not: familiar academic units that cause little trouble. Ironically, that's just what they used to be, harmless and unobtrusive freshman writing programs that simply ticked over from year to year, generally without notice. Now they cause notice. Now, in trying to become respectable and vigorous citizens of the academy, they're threatening to upset common notions of citizenship. If they can't slip quietly into position as normal departments, maybe they shouldn't try to do so. (70–71)

I would argue that "causing notice" in the academy is something that writing programs do best (Bamberg, Ide, Flora & Lindemann, Miller, Witte and Faigley). By the sometimes "tortured virtue" of our anomaly status within our institutions, we represent a different and unfamiliar presence in the academy.

What makes matters more complicated is the fact that our difference is not homogenized within our programs themselves. In fact, writing programs rarely represent a unified "different" voice on campus, but a site where many different voices (student, staff, faculty, and administration) converge and conflict in constant conversation. Much like Beckett's *Unnamable*, every constituency in a writing program is trying to "say I"—to be heard and dignified, and to have a definitive "say" in their program's ongoing definition of self.

In this essay, I will attempt to name and theorize several animating differences of intentions, opinions, and epistemologies that may constrain, compel, or enable writing programs. I will use Jacques Derrida's theory of *différance* which "marks not only the activity of 'originary' difference, but also the temporizing detour of deferral" (*Margins* 14), as a primary lens for interpreting these factors. I will also use philosopher Jean-François Lyotard's theory of "the differend"—a case in conflict in which issues in dispute "cannot be equitably resolved for lack of a rule of judgement applicable to both arguments" (xi)—to discuss the lack of dialogue and mutual understanding that often contributes to a writing program's difficult relationship with its "home" institution. Elaborating on a set of questions in Derrida's *Margins of Philosophy*, my chapter's next section seeks to answer the questions, "What differs? Who differs? What is *différance*?" (14).

What is *Différance*?

According to Derrida, the term *différance* is "immediately and irreducibly polysemic" (*Margins* 8). As a noun, it encompasses both the sense of deferring—"the action of putting off until later"—and the sense of differing—"to be not identical, to be other" (8). In *Positions* Derrida gives his clearest definition of this slippery term:

> First, *différance* refers to the (active and passive) movement that consists in deferring by means of delay, delegation, reprieve, referral, detour, postpone-

ment, reserving. . . . Second, the movement of *différance* as that which produces different things, that which differentiates, is the common root of all the oppositional concepts that mark our language. . . . (8–9, italics in original)

It is by describing our tendency to hold and enact oppositional concepts from the academy that I begin my discussion of writing programs and difference.

Who Differs?

To begin with, writing programs may oppose and contradict the traditional methods of professional recruitment and appointment used in the academy. While an English Department might logically seek a PhD in Victorian Literature to teach its nineteenth–century literature classes, the same equation of advanced degree equals expertise may not apply to writing instructors. For example, I taught for four years as a UCLA Writing Programs "lecturer."[1] At that time, the program included forty-three lecturers with degree status ranging from MA to ABD to PhD. Our backgrounds ranged from linguistics to business, and from literature to folklore. In fact, there was only one person among us with a PhD in rhetoric and composition—a degree that, following traditional academic criteria, could be seen as the one of choice and qualification to teach college-level writing.

In this sense, this program enacts a difference from other academic units in the academy by representing a hybrid presence on campus. That writing program, like many others, constitutes a space where instructors' ages, backgrounds, and career paths—what I call our "deliberately checkered pasts"—reflect many different experiences, types of training, and levels of education—some of which may not be considered traditionally "academic" or even tenure-track(able).

What Differs?

Another difference writing programs tend to enact is to undermine traditional hegemonies within the academy—hegemonies which privilege research over teaching, and which value graduate teaching over undergraduate instruction. In deliberate difference from, and contradiction of, these hegemonies, writing programs position themselves as places where "unauthorized discourse" (Miller 187)—the written and spoken words of undergraduates—becomes the center of teachers' scholarly and pedagogical activity.

At this point, I am still configuring *différance* as a noun. Within this noun, we see disagreements about *what* is worth studying (the discourse of student authors or that of "published" authors) and *who* is worth hiring—a specialist with a focused, advanced degree or a pedagogically effective "generalist"? To my mind, these disagreements are best understood by considering *différance* in its other aspect—as a verb—and by bringing that verb into conversation with Lyotard's concept of the differend.

Assessing Differends
and the Troubling Enigma of *Différance*

As stated earlier, Derrida also configures *différance* as a verb. He calls it "the name we might give to the 'active,' moving discord of different forces, and of differences of forces" (Derrida, *Writing* 18). This moving discord is illustrated when writing instructors work together, yet teach differently within a program (see Strenski, this volume) and when the program itself, cognizant of those different pedagogies, perpetuates the "convenient fiction" (see Faigley and Romano, this volume) of offering a common curriculum.

This moving discord can also manifest itself in other ways. For one, think of the aforementioned writing program with forty-three lecturers of diverse ages, backgrounds, and training. These individuals' different epistemologies, constituencies, and concerns can constitute an ongoing heteroglossia of "centrifugal, stratifying forces" (Bakhtin 272). These forces may enact the competing intentions and visions that exist within the program's members themselves.

As challenging as it is, this aspect of *différance*—the phenomenon of competing voices differing from one another within a program—is multiplied many times when considering a writing program's tenuous, often uneasy, relationships with other departments in its institution. Yet a writing program, however insular, can never be a self-contained, autonomous entity. As Derrida writes:

> The play of differences supposes, in effect, syntheses and referrals which forbid at any moment, or in any sense, that a simple element be *present* in and of itself, referring only to itself. (*Positions* 26)

One way of explaining the concept of "syntheses" is to think about introductory composition courses that are expected to play integral, yet often underfunded, roles in freshman experience programs. Another would be to think about writing centers which serve the entire campus community. One way of interpreting the term "referrals" is to think about writing-across-the-curriculum courses which exist in explicit reference to other departments' courses. Perceived in these ways, both terms express the intricate interweaving of writing programs and other academic missions and units.

I see this interweaving of difference—a writing program existing as a service to its institution, while having its own potentially subversive goals—as a phenomenon

> which permits the different threads and different lines of meaning—[read here "of epistemology"] or of force—to go off again in different directions, just as it is always ready to tie itself up with others. (Derrida *Margins* 3)

These complex interweavings—which raise questions about whether a writing program should "tie itself up" with an English or Humanities Department or affiliate itself with other departments—also inspire curiosity about why a writing program can choose to be sometimes supportive, and sometimes subversive, of its institution's stated missions and goals. The decision to be subversive, which I wish to address next, is best explained by examining the argument put forth by Jean-François Lyotard in his book, *The Differend: Phrases in Dispute.*

Defining the Differend

As mentioned earlier, Lyotard defines the differend as "a case in conflict, between (at least) two parties, that cannot be equitably resolved for lack of a rule of judgement applicable to both arguments" (xi). When this definition is applied to writing programs, the fact that there is disagreement over an issue (e.g., methods of literacy instruction, undergraduate curriculum, graduate student training, program administration, writing assessment) does not mean that one side is right or wrong. Instead, it means that each party's very different traditions and values keep them from understanding or appreciating the other's somewhat mysterious and unfathomable perspective. As Lyotard admits, "A wrong results from the fact that the rules of the genre of discourse [read here as "rules of behavior, of pedagogy, of epistemology"] by which one judges are not those of the judged" (xi). Since the "rules"—of discourse, of pedagogy, or protocol—are often very different both within writing programs (e.g., see Strenski, this volume) and between writing programs and other departments, we encounter the differend's two inevitable truths, namely: "the impossibility of avoiding conflicts" and "the absence of a universal genre of discourse to regulate them" (xii).

This lack of a "universal" code of assessing the contributions of writing programs plays itself out in the activities of recruiting (Janangelo) and tenuring of a writing program administrator (see Hult, this volume). In short, just as a writing program's faculty may present a peculiar profile to its institution, a candidate for tenure as a WPA can become something of a personnel anomaly to a review board. This person may complicate tenure procedures by presenting a *vitae* of contributions and achievements that can look, at best, illogical and unfamiliar and, at worst, insignificant and inscrutable to an evaluatory panel of senior colleagues with more traditional backgrounds and expectations.

To portray the ways that the work of a WPA can elude professional categorization, I will create a scenario. Let us imagine that two colleagues—two assistant professors named Sun and Liza—are being reviewed for tenure. Sun is on a literature track. He has a PhD in modernist fiction, and has published extensively on Virginia Woolf and John Dos Passos. Liza is a WPA and has also published extensively, though not in such focused areas of inquiry. What's more, her PhD is also in modernist fiction, and she has published on William Faulkner but also on computers and composition, writing centers, and writing program administration. She has even written a textbook on freshman composition, and published such in-house texts as instructors' guides and teaching assistant training manuals. I would suggest that the task a committee faces in reviewing Liza's dossier will be very different than when reviewing Sun's.

By not showing the same equation between advanced degree and its connection to job title or scholarship, by blurring traditional areas of scholarly specialization (Liza's publishing on Faulkner and writing centers) and by questioning the hallmarks of scholarship (think of her textbook and in-house work), Liza presents her institution with a different and difficult case to review. If she is reviewed by the same criteria as Sun, she may not fare so well. Yet if Liza wishes to suggest different evaluation criteria to her institution, how can she do it in terms that they will recognize and understand? Hence, the phenomenon of the differend makes itself known as Liza, with some pride, and some frustration, presents her colleagues with a tenure case that cannot be judged or valued by the same criteria they use to assess the work of other faculty (see "Case Study" and Hult, this volume).

In this sense, a WPA incarnates the differend. She is often someone who eludes existing categorizations and domestication. This avoidance of domestication is perhaps the most frightening aspect of the differend. It plays itself out on campus through the question, "What will or can an institution do with a tenured WPA who tires of her administrative activities?" By claiming, and even showing, expertise in strange clusters of accomplishments (e.g., publications in autobiography, composition theory, and film), a WPA's scholarly achievements may appear to be indiscriminately juxtaposed and overdiversified. Whatever their juxtaposition, they will almost certainly complicate and challenge the academy's traditional notions of "scholarship" and "specialization"—even in writing instruction.

Furthermore, just as the decision about what makes a WPA worth hiring or tenuring is fraught with sometimes naive and "sometimes willful misunderstanding of what it means to study and teach writing" (Trimbur and Cambridge 15), questions about what kinds of writing should be taught by a program (personal narrative, the exploratory essay, the research paper) are also not easily validated according to the traditions of the academy. These traditions vigorously support and protect what can be perceived as the rational, paternalistic discourse of linear, thesis-oriented prose by using traditional assessment measures of student writing (Faigley, Owens). Through student and teacher evaluation measures, these traditions often discourage and punish the nurturing or enactment of unauthorized discursive practices. This sense of the differend—these disagreements over which literacy activities to protect and which to punish—is highlighted when a writing program chooses to resist fulfilling its institution's and faculty's expectations about which services it should perform. This resistance plays itself out most dramatically in the frustrated hope of writing across the curriculum.

Interrogating Writing Across the Curriculum and the Complexity of Linkages

I call the writing across the curriculum (WAC) movement a "frustrated hope" because, outside of writing programs, it is often perceived, largely by default, as a way of teaching students how to replicate traditional paternalistic forms of academic discourse. These forms regularly privilege western European rhetorical traditions, and are sometimes perceived as nondialogic with, and exclusionary of, contrastive rhetorics (Severino) or alternative discourses (Mahala).

Yet, instead of fulfilling the academy's wish to train students to write proficiently in traditional, familiar ways, a writing program often enacts the differend by subverting institutional expectations—by countering positivist beliefs that a writing program exists simply to teach students how to "write better" in traditional ways. Instead of teaching students to replicate the traditional forms of academic discourse, writing programs' faculty may raise students' suspicions and ask them to scrutinize these forms in terms of language and gender biases, the desirability of linear discourse (Kaplan & Moulthrop), the value of single authorship (Ede & Lunsford), and of the applicability of traditional assessment tools to evaluate the success of process-oriented instruction (Harris, Tezerini, White; see also White, this volume).

Because we bring different beliefs to our discussions of writing across the curriculum (some of our colleagues may want us to teach students to "write well" in the old ways, when we want to show them how to explore the potentialities of what writing well could mean apart from the current structures and strictures of academic discourse), our different epistemologies often give us few grounds for mutual agreement or understanding. This lack of agreement is intensified when a WAC specialist asks senior colleagues in other departments to reconsider the gender and social biases inherent in their assignments, or to reevaluate their pedagogy in "the light" of those reconsiderations. Thus what Lyotard writes of the differend between Platonic poetics and Socratic dialogue could be said of a conversation between a WAC director and colleagues in other departments: "We are incapable of coming to an agreement concerning the rules of the dialogue, whose principal rule is that the agreement concerning the referent [to be read here as "student writing"] ought to be obtained for ourselves by ourselves" (25–26).

As departments and writing programs vie for authority concerning who should have a definitive "say" (Beckett 3) over what counts as good writing and what constitutes the most effective methods of writing instruction, the disagreements and different vested interests announce themselves. As Lyotard concedes, the

> conflict is a differend, since the success (or the validation) proper to one genre [read here as "one discipline"] is not the one proper to others . . . [and]

the multiplicity of stakes [ideas about what should be taught], on a par with the multiplicity of genres, turns every linkage [e.g., every WAC course] into a kind of 'victory' of one of them over the others. (136)

Lyotard portrays these conflicts as struggles in which the silenced party (e.g., a writing program that provides support to "content" teachers) regrets its "neglected, forgotten, or repressed possibilities" (136). Yet this sense of regret is diminished as writing programs become increasingly vocal about instigating change.

Sometimes enacting a political activism that some scholars find troubling, dangerous, and invasive (Hairston), some more politically vocal composition faculty illustrate Hartzog's statement that, by and large, writing programs are not content to remain "harmless and unobtrusive" (71) entities in the academy. Rather than seeing ourselves as only marginal, remedial, ghettoized spaces where students' textual errors are identified and then either corrected or disciplined, we increasingly see ourselves as a dynamic, theoretically informed, uniquely positioned "site for dismantling particularly troublesome versions of hegemonic discursive 'common sense'" (Miller 187). Most especially a writing program's WAC courses, but also many of its "own" courses as well, will involve *teaching* the textual features of particular discipline-specific discourses while *exposing* those discourses' "privileging mechanisms and discriminatory practices" (Miller 195). Thus WAC activists highlight the fact that we "never teach (or write) neutrally," and that each literate activity serves to either "maintain or undermine an [oppressive, exclusionary] establishment" (Miller 195).

In championing and defending "other" discourses and "other" visions, a writing program can also cause discomfort within its institution by aligning itself as an advocate for marginal voices including undergraduates, graduate students, women, ethnic minorities, gay students and teachers, and part-time faculty. For example, a writing program administrator may sometimes choose to speak out on behalf of her part-time employees (see Hansen, this volume), even though the administration may expect (and even have hired) the WPA to keep those teachers quiet, functional, and invisible, if not happy. Just as WPAs risk alienation and misunderstanding from their institutions by privileging pedagogy over traditional scholarship and by regarding student texts as worthy of extended scholarly inquiry, we also risk being perceived as troublemakers when we speak out on behalf of marginal voices in the academy.

When writing programs combine our militant sensibilities with a tendency to intrude on senior colleagues' disciplinary territory through WAC activities—by adding to their burdens and asking these individuals to assume what may be viewed on campus as the writing program's responsibility to mentor student writing—we can see how a writing program can be accurately perceived as a trouble-making, even burdensome, presence on its campus. This sense of a writing program as a troublesome and quarrelsome unit—staffed with individuals who either cannot or will not only teach students to "write well" and who make demands on senior colleagues who have already proven their worth and value to an institution—brings a new resonance to the concept of the differend. It is one in which a writing program resists achieving consensus and relishes causing conflict about what constitutes good writing, good learning, and good teaching. This resistance is, in some ways, natural since the differend never seeks to resolve an issue that is in dispute. Rather, "It concerns (and tampers with) its ultimate presuppositions" (Lyotard xv).

Tampering with the academy's "presuppositions"—with its philosophies, pedagogies, practices, and protocols—has, so far, been the life work of writing programs. Hartzog points out some of the "conceptual disagreements" (xiii) between composition and the academy, and within the field itself. While some voices in the academy, and in composition, anticipate the day when the field will develop into a formal discipline, others hope that our field, by virtue of its interdisciplinary nature and eclectic faculty profile, will resist such definition—which they see as a calcification—and keep calling into question the idea and value of disciplinary practices and boundaries. Certainly, this expression and enactment of resistance to achieving disciplinary status have caused trouble for many writing programs faculty who see our work as stigmatized and who wish we had the recognizable profile and (perhaps overestimated) privilege, power, and prestige of an English Department.

In answer to this lack of prestige or power, Hartzog suggests that we should not regard our difference from departments as intrinsically disabling. She thinks that

> writing programs may not be doing something wrong when they fail to be recognized as proper academic units: they may in fact bring into question our common understanding of academic structures and procedures, our very notion of academic legitimacy . . . [for although] many of them rest uneasily within the academy . . . in that very uneasiness, I would argue, lies strength. (71)

To me, the words "may not be doing something wrong" offer an important qualification. For although "strength" (the power to re-imagine, reconceive, and reinvent the academy) may lie in "uneasiness" (the position of being perpetually vulnerable and uncomfortable, of feeling somewhat unwelcome, and having to continually think critically about how to justify one's existence and growth), I would suggest that the academy's potential recognition of writing programs' value will not be predicated on our programs bringing a romanticized notion of difference into our interactions with our institutions. No meaningful collegial exchange or lasting curricular change can be gained by a writing program imagining itself as a center of pedagogical and moral goodness whose duty is to function as a renegade unit on campus. It is fallacious for a writing program to assume an aggressive, antagonistic stance or, worse, an isolationist stance toward its institution, which it regards as emblematic of the racist, sexist, and classist tendencies inherent in the academy and the world.

Instead, I believe that "strength" could be promised in creating a dialogical vision of difference—in identifying and showing what a writing program can add to an institution by virtue of our difference, and by suggesting the kinds of differences that our evolving presence can make on campus over time. It is toward this goal of dialogizing writing programs' difference—preserving the integrity of what makes us unique, while making our uniqueness supple, responsive, and attractive to our institutions—that I direct the rest of this essay.

Seeing Difference as Supplement/ Putting Difference in Dialogue

Writing programs have seen themselves, with some truth and some ire, as being treated as mere service components of the academy. We have seen ourselves as ghettos, centers of remediation for undergraduates; handmaids to our institutions, sites where graduate students are trained and women teachers are exploited (Tuell); and adjuncts to other departments, in which writing-across-the-curriculum courses and writing centers "support" other disciplines' "content" and visions. We have perceived the support that we have given to our students and institutions go largely unrecognized and unrewarded. We have also seen our difference from other academic units perceived as less valuable and unworthy of equal respect or treatment. In this section, I wish to offer another definition of service—to make writing programs' difference more comprehensible, more decipherable and, if possible, more desirable to all parties involved. I will do so by discussing Derrida's theory of supplementarity and applying it to aspects of writing program administration and pedagogy.

Derrida argues that supplements exist because things are not complete in themselves. Their presence signifies "the result of a lack which must be *supplemented*" (*Writing* 290, italics in original). For instance, one might create a supplement to a dictionary as new words come into being, or to a history text as new "facts" are discovered or admitted. Citing an "originary lack" on the part of the signified (read here as "the academy"), literary critic Jonathan Culler's definition of the supplement can be used to explain a writing program's existence on campus, and its relationship to other academic units:

> The supplement is an inessential extra, added to something complete in itself, but the supplement is added in order to complete, to compensate for a lack in what was supposed to be complete in itself. (103)

When we acknowledge the multiple "lack(s)" inherent in the academy—in terms of its inadequate attention to literacy instruction, the mentoring for undergraduates, and equitable treatment for women, people of color, lesbian and gay students, and part-time faculty—we can see the need and justification for a supplement. Thus what Derrida writes of the sign is equally true of the academy: ". . . there is something missing from it: a center which arrests and grounds the play of substitutions" (*Writing* 289). Thus, "this sign is added, occurs as a surplus, . . . to supplement a lack on the part of the signified" (289).

Derrida also notes that there is at once an enriching and subversive power to supplements. Let me speak first of enrichment where "the supplement adds itself, . . . is a surplus, a plenitude enriching another plenitude, [and becomes] the *fullest measure* of presence" (Derrida, *Of Grammatology* 144, italics in original). In considering writing programs as supplements—sources of peda-gogical/epistemological surplus within the academy—I would argue that these programs enrich our institutions by providing a versatility and breadth of knowledge that is not available to other disciplines. Because our expertise lies in writing—a shared and essential medium of communication among people and among disciplines—writing programs are epistemologically positioned, if not institutionally situated, to function as unifying agents in the academy by providing pedagogical perspectives on the complexity of composing, perspec-tives that imbue all disciplines. In this sense, writing programs can support the liberal arts perspective of emphasizing and envisioning points of consonance, rather than dissonance, within the disciplines. This inclusive perspective can help institutions resist curricular atomization.[2] Writing programs can also en-rich our institutions by providing empathy and socially transformative strate-gies to groups whose difference (age, ethnicity, physical challenges, and "at risk" status) makes them feel less than welcome in the academy. By mentoring freshmen and other lower-division students, and by training graduate students, writing programs, by virtue of the number of students we serve and teachers we prepare, may play potentially important roles in changing educational ex-pectations and performance in the twenty-first century.

Along with potential enrichment, Derrida also envisions the supplement as a site for subversion and social critique. For when the supplement works,

> It adds only to replace. It intervenes or insinuates itself *in-the-place-of*; if it fills, it is as if one fills a void . . . by the anterior default of a presence. . . . As substitute, . . . it produces no relief, its place is assigned in the structure by the mark of an emptiness. (*Of Grammatology* 145, italics in original)

Producing "no [or little] relief" to the literacy crisis—and agitating over gen-der, social, human, and professional inequities—the subversive aspect of the supplement becomes apparent as writing programs sometimes engage in up-start, trouble-making activities.

Perhaps writing programs were born to be upstarts. Even a program's acts of empathy—amplifying marginal voices in the academy—can cause trouble. This is especially true when a program transforms its empathy into political action by asking for better treatment of adjuncts and graduate students, by ask-ing senior colleagues for more pedagogical support, or by asking administrators for an increased budget, for more ladder faculty positions, for smaller classes, and for more sophisticated, expensive, and valid procedures for student assessment. By and large, writing programs and their personnel rarely hesitate to "mark" and proclaim the philosophical and pedagogical "emptiness" (Derrida, *Of Grammatology* 145) we see at work in the world and in our institutions. There is no doubt that many writing programs would like to become more powerful change agents in the academy and world. Problems arise, however, when we speak as though we are the best change agents possible—and have the *definitive* plans for reform. It is toward rectifying this mistake—where writing programs' immature, sometimes undiplomatic, rhetoric alienates colleagues and administrators and undercuts our political effectiveness—that I direct my chapter's concluding section.

Becoming Souls in Limbo: Suggestions Toward Dialogizing Difference

As a "lecturer" in writing at UCLA, I once attended a meeting to discuss university budget cuts and their potential impacts on the system's writing programs. As you can imagine, the conversation between university administrators, union representatives, and writing programs lecturers became, at times, quite heated and emotional. At one point, a composition instructor stood up and said, "Writing programs represent the conscience and soul of this institution." While this sentence has emotional resonance to me—I am already convinced that writing programs make the academy a more accessible and humane place to be—I see this kind of statement as politically problematic. For me, it exemplifies the romantic, elitist, moralistic, and nondialogical stance that writing programs faculty sometimes assume toward the academy. Too often, I see writing programs dichotomizing our place in the academy—defining ourselves as good (soulful) entities in ceaseless and righteous battle with institutions that we name and dismiss as deliberately malevolent, sexist, racist, classist—and eminently soulless—others.

That instructor's comment also reminded me of something that I had read about the soul in Andre Breton's *Nadja*, a surrealist novel about a man who is simultaneously in love with, and appalled by, a woman he finds to be fascinating, frustrating, and irreducibly enigmatic. At one point, confused about her identity, he asks her, "Who are you?" Her reply—please think here of Beckett's and Hartzog's questions about self-identity which opened this chapter—comes "without a moment's hesitation": "I am the soul in limbo," Nadja replies, and her answer only intensifies her ambiguity (Breton 71).

It is in validating the ambiguity and tentativeness of Nadja's self-definition that I see a potential strength in writing programs' difference from the academy. I see a potential strength in being "in limbo" and in flux. I believe that there is a parallel between the "limbo" transitional status that Nadja accords herself and the "uneasiness" that Hartzog (71) sees as central to writing programs' strength. That state of limbo—of being in flux and undefined—

frees us from certain restrictions such as narrowly defined hiring criteria and scholarly specialization. It also affords us the time to create, explore, and theorize our field apart from the constraints facing traditional departments. To this end, I suggest that it is beneficial for writing programs to enact the process of self-definition as *différance* in its primary sense—to delay it in time—rather than to rush toward a premature and potentially limiting definition of self.

As we who work in writing programs contemplate a calculated postponement of self-definition in order to retain our plasticity and to mature in our decision-making processes, we may also wish to preserve, rather than diminish, certain aspects of our differend status within the academy. There is a long-range power to the differend, Lyotard writes, since its potential strength remains untapped and unnamed:

> In the differend something 'asks' to be put into phrases, and [yet] suffers from the wrong of not being able to be put into phrases right away. . . . The differend is the unstable state and instant of language wherein something which must be able to be put into phrases cannot yet be. (13)

Like Beckett's narrator, writing programs in all our differences from the academy try to "say I" (3) (I am, I want, I stand for, I deserve, I will not accept), in publications, national conferences, and campus meetings. Yet we still only stammer that which we wish to articulate. We desire those mature proclamations of identity which cannot yet be since our sometimes volatile "field" (Gere) is still growing, still in flux, and still changing.

Yet there is a complexity and dignity to what remains unnamed. For if "naming, . . . the subject of the utterance, . . . presents no particular obscurity" (Lyotard 34) and therefore no interest, intrigue, or supplementary value, perhaps, in the interests of intellectual and pedagogical growth, writing programs ought to remain only partially named in, and a bit unfamiliar to, our institutions. Perhaps we can both contribute to, and benefit from, our interactions with the academy by continuing to present it with some "particular obscurity" and complexity.

If we can be somewhat obscure presences on campus, we can potentially experience some profitable aspects of our differend status. It may well be that a better "reality [for all of us] entails the differend" (Lyotard 55). Differends make intellectual life interesting, and real life challenging, by keeping phrases in dispute and issues unresolved. For as long as there is conversation—not just hierarchial or adversarial exchanges—between different forces, there is openness and the possibility of change. And if Hartzog is right that a writing program's "stability rests on its capacity for change" (54), its ability to successfully capitalize on those changes could depend on a program's willingness to anticipate, negotiate, and help determine its institution's future needs.

If writing programs' nature is to be fluid and transitional—to be in limbo —and to promote change within ourselves and within our institutions, it may also be in our best interests for our programs to advocate, work for, and shape change dialogically with them. It may behoove us to see ourselves as "souls" who work for change with others in the academy, souls whose limbo status gives us a freedom to enact our differences creatively, yet dialogically.

Hartzog underscores the importance of dialogue when she states that successful WPAs use "their own leadership in determining what would work [at their institutions], in knowing when to take risks and when to show restraint" (68). This suggestion that WPAs could promote significant change through acts of calculated deference to, and diplomatic disagreement with, our institutions is, to me, much more viable and attractive than the separatist procedures sometimes practiced by writing programs. Yet, as attractive as it is for everyone to remain respectful and dialogical, I can see two reasons why practices of deference, diplomacy, and conversation have not always worked. The first is the relative lack of ongoing theorization on the part of rhetoric and composition specialists, a lack that undermines our intellectual credibility in the academy. The second reason is the sometimes understandable, yet ultimately detrimental, impatience for change voiced both by writing programs and the academy.

Strategizing Difference and Resisting the Dynamics of Haste

The wise Marlene Dietrich once remarked, "There is a haste and lack of dignity to film making and film stardom." I would suggest that the same qualities can hold true for the field of rhetoric and composition. In filling our scholarship with mostly solutions for writing problems and pedagogical success stories, we may be presenting ourselves as a largely results-oriented activity, rather than as a field of ongoing theoretical complexity and sophistication. To borrow Jasper Neel's phrase, we have remained an "immature discipline" by looking for and presuming the existence of "the magic system . . . that will teach students to write quickly and efficiently" (101).

There is also a haste and rush toward efficiency in literacy instruction present in the academy. In professional journals we see different expectations about literacy instruction negotiated between WPAs and department chairs (Bamberg, Ide, Lindemann & Flora). On campus, we may sometimes hear expressions of impatience from institutions and campus communities, and indignation from writing programs staff, about why "students can't write" and why, "given" the new technologies, "teachers can't teach" faster, better, and cheaper.

There is another aspect to this miscommunication, and it has to do with our field's growing sense of maturity. As I see it, writing programs were more appealing to our parent institutions fifteen years ago when, as infants and toddlers, we largely did, or appeared to be trying to do, what was asked of us without questioning those expectations. Now, as adolescents, we may be heard seeking a voice in establishing curricular policy, asking for increased rewards, or voicing our right to a senate vote. By articulating these stances, we may seem to have outgrown much of our cuteness. To use a biological metaphor, as a field, our voices are changing, our gender identifications and resistances are becoming more clarified, and we are starting to ask questions and make demands of our institutions. Worse yet, sometimes our requests are unreasonable, and sometimes we phrase them insensitively. Complicated by an unpredictable but rarely supportive political, social, and economic milieu, writing programs are going through a particularly troubled and troublesome adolescence. In an attempt to reduce the trouble with difference and mindful of offering easy solutions to our problems, I wish to offer some ideas to the academy and to writing programs for internal and, perhaps mutual, discussion.

Ideas for the Academy

To institutions I offer the following ideas for supporting their writing programs:

- Have patience and consider adjusting your expectations. Consider what your writing program and other academic units might do to collaboratively improve literacy instruction given your institution's financial and curricular constraints.

- Create mentoring programs to support your writing programs rather than just looking to them for support.

- Since you know that composition is a young and emerging field, please be patient with its practitioners' rhetoric and results. Give writing programs a chance to prove our worth over time and realize that time, when measured in academic calendars, is often configured in decades.

- Please try to see and value writing programs for what we are and, if possible, to appreciate us for our difference. We cannot maintain our intellectual and personal integrity and pretend that we do not have sometimes liberal, sometimes subversive, interests at heart.

- Please realize that like any other academic unit inspired by lingering and important social problems—e.g., cultural studies, peace studies, race studies, womens' studies—writing programs cannot make our founding "problem," the ongoing need for equitable and responsible literacy instruction, quickly disappear. Here I quote David Laurence, editor of the *ADE Bulletin* and a friend to both English Departments and writing programs:

> Freshman writing courses will not, and should not, disappear. But freshman writing as a requirement that is expected, all by itself, to solve 'the literacy problem' will and should receive intense scrutiny. (4)

To this insight, Laurence adds several questions. Some discuss our collective expectations: "What do students, departments, institutions, and the public really get from the requirement, viewed in the context of students' experiences over four, and frequently more than four, years of baccalaureate study?" (4). Others mention our potential quality of life: "How can faculty members in the

English department and beyond come to experience firsthand what compositionists have long known about the many and varied ways writing can create
new and mutually beneficial possibilities for students and faculty members to
work together more effectively and more enjoyably?" (4). I hope that we will
keep both questions in mind as we prepare for our shared future.

Ideas for Writing Programs

To writing programs, I offer the following ideas. We might:

- Consider doing more listening—to our staff, our senior colleagues, and
  our central administrators. We may be the "experts" on writing, but they
  are experts on our institutions and its current and potential state.

- Examine our rhetoric for inherent elitism and antagonism. Let's try to resist the danger and lure of ennobling our difference from the academy, and
  positioning ourselves in opposition to our host institutions.

- Become thoughtful rhetoricians and politicians within our institutions
  (see McLeod, Wingate, this volume). Recognize and negotiate chains of
  command carefully. Try to anticipate and strategize the timeliness of, and
  obstacles to, long-term change.

- Guard against a hasty and uncritical push for professional power and prestige within the academy. Such premature attempts toward departmental-
  ization may lead our programs to replicate patterns of oppression, exclu-
  sion, and elitism that are already at work in the academy.

- Develop and explicate criteria for recruiting, evaluating, and tenuring
  composition faculty that are comprehensible to review boards and comparable to those of other faculty members. With regard to promotion and
  tenure processes, writing programs' differences from the academy should
  not always be so stark or apparent. Remember that our being seen as in-
  comparable does not automatically mean that we will be perceived as in-
  valuable to our institutions.

- Continue to theorize and articulate our differences from the academy, so
  that we can help our colleagues and central administrators see that our differences are based on a careful blending of scholarship, experience, philosophy, and epistemology (see Hansen, this volume), rather than an id-
  iosyncratic response to a particular classroom or institutional context.

These suggestions are intended to help writing programs continually reinvent ourselves through dialogue with our students, within our programs, and
with administrators, so that we can avoid taking a self-destructive, adversarial
stance toward our institutions. If we can re-conceptualize "difference" as
something that is ideologically and theoretically informed, yet still supple, dialogic, and negotiable, we can responsibly and more profitably enact our status
as only partially predictable agents of educational reform. We can then become

not just experiential but essential anomalies in the academy, anomalies whose supplementary power resides in our ability to maintain our difference, while being dialogical with our institutions in order to make informed judgement calls about when and how to defer and when to differ.

A Final Note

Any suggestion that writing programs are "woven of differences" (Derrida, *Margins* 21) comes as no surprise to anyone who knows us. Derrida's words about the irreducible difference that imbues writing itself have everything to do with our professional development and future. As people who care intimately about writing—the very space of *différance*—we work in a field "whose *conception, formation, gestation,* and *labor* we are only catching a glimpse of today" (Derrida, *Writing* 293, italics in original). Derrida admits to employing these words

> with a glance toward the operations of childbearing—but also with a glance toward those who . . . turn their eyes away when faced by the as yet unnamable which is proclaiming itself and which can do so, as is necessary whenever a birth is in the offing, only under the species of the nonspecies, in the formless, mute, infant, and terrifying form of monstrosity. (293)

As the academy's unnamable, perhaps initially by circumstance yet increasingly by design, writing programs both enact and complicate Derrida's concept of *différance*. We are neither formless nor completely formed. In "proclaiming" ourselves and saying "I," we are certainly not mute. Yet we are not quite as articulate or compelling as we need to be.

And yet, like any unnamable—Beckett's, Derrida's, or the academy's—we continue to "say I" (Beckett 3). We continue to unleash our unfamiliar voices and unsettling questions on the academy. More than that, we like talking. We like giving witness to what we see, fear, anticipate, desire, and suspect. And we would like to be heard, believed, and "believed-in." As unnamables, we often find the academy's version of limbo to be a vulnerable and uncomfortable, yet familiar and important, place. Still growing, we can only name ourselves tentatively, if immodestly, as a different and dignified "nonspecies" of souls—souls who are sometimes embracing, and sometimes "menacing" in our ambiguity and "monstrosity" (Derrida, *Writing* 293). Yet, we menace with a message, and our message is change. Since we know an important truth about limbo, we are eager to suggest its value.[3]

Notes

1. The irony of my former job title never escapes me. Since lecturing is not an integral part of my (or most composition) teaching, I see this institutional designation (which speaks of rank, rather than pedagogy) as a tacit encapsulation of problems associated with naming new presences in the academy.

2. My Department Chair, Suzanne Gossett, is a distinguished Shakespearean scholar with an irreverent sense of humor. When discussing interdepartmental atomization, she confides that, "In my more negative moods, I guiltily ask myself what keeps an English department from becoming . . . garbage pizza? In Chicago, that's the kind that has everything in the restaurant dumped on the top, with the crust holding all the ingredients present but not blended" (35). Gossett uses the unattractive metaphor of garbage pizza to describe an English department "as a kind of enclosure or base where we co-exist awkwardly and from which we may move outward while retaining our individual entities" (35). Having "supp'd full with horrors" (*Macbeth* V.V.17) of this dish, she poses an essential question: "But does anything unify the individuals in such a department?" (35).

3. I am grateful to Loyola University–Chicago and Dean Kathleen M. McCourt for a Summer Research Stipend, which enabled me to complete this essay. I am also grateful to the following people for their kindness and support in this and many other important contexts: Timothy R. Austin, Thomas E. Conroy, Carmella Fiorelli, Allen J. Frantzen, Suzanne Gossett, Kristine Hansen, Yola C. Janangelo, Christopher Kendrick, Scott R. Krause, Michael A. North, Nancy E. Schaumburger, Chuck Schuster, James Starks Jr., Rita Tessman, Gail Tolstoi, and Farrell J. Webb.

Works Cited

Bakhtin, M.M. *The Dialogic Imagination: Four Essays.* Trans. Caryl Emerson & Michael Holquist. Austin: U of Texas Press, 1981.

Bamberg, Betty. "Autonomy and Accommodation—Striking a Balance: Freshman Writing and English at USC." *ADE Bulletin* 101 (1992):19–22.

Beckett, Samuel. *The Unnamable.* New York: Grove Press, Inc., 1958.

Breton, Andre. *Nadja.* Trans. Richard Howard. New York: Grove Press, Inc., 1960.

"Case Study." *ADE Bulletin* 104 (1993): 56.

Culler, Jonathan. *On Deconstruction: Theory and Criticism After Structuralism.* Ithaca: Cornell UP, 1982.

Derrida, Jacques. *Margins of Philosophy.* Trans. Alan Bass. Chicago: U of Chicago Press, 1982.

———. *Positions.* Trans. Alan Bass. Chicago: U of Chicago Press, 1981.

———. *Writing and Difference.* Trans. Alan Bass. Chicago: U of Chicago Press, 1978.

———. *Of Grammatology.* Trans. Gayatri Chakravorty Spivak. Baltimore: Johns Hopkins UP, 1976.

Ede, Lisa and Andrea Lunsford. *Singular Texts / Plural Authors: Perspectives on Collaborative Writing.* Carbondale: Southern Illinois UP, 1990.

Faigley, Lester. *Fragments of Rationality: Postmodernity and the Subject of Composition.* Pittsburgh: U of Pittsburgh Press, 1992.

Flora, Joseph M. and Erika Lindemann. "English Chairs and Writing Program Administrators: An Antiphonal Reading." *ADE Bulletin* 100 (1991): 35–40.

Gere, Anne Ruggles. Ed. *Into the Field: Sites of Composition Studies.* New York: MLA, 1993.

Gossett, Suzanne. "Reimagining English Departments: What Is Our Future?" *ADE Bulletin* 108 (1994): 34–37.

Hairston, Maxine. "Diversity, Ideology, and Teaching Writing." *College Composition and Communication* 43.2, (1992): 179–193.

Harrington, Henry R. "The Jouissance of English Department Politics: A Tale of Shem and Shaun." *ADE Bulletin* 105 (1993): 23–27.

Hartzog, Carol P. *Composition and the Academy: A Study of Writing Program Administration.* New York: MLA, 1986.

Harris, Charles B. "Mandated Testing and the Postsecondary English Department." *ADE Bulletin* 104 (1993): 4–13.

Hawisher, Gail E. and Cynthia L. Selfe. "Tradition and Change in Computer-Supported Writing Environments: A Call for Action." *Theoretical and Critical Perspectives on Teacher Change.* Eds. Phyllis Kahaney, Linda A.M. Perry, and Joseph Janangelo. Norwood: Ablex, 1993. 155–186.

Ide, Richard. "Issues of Authority and Responsibility: Freshman Writing and English at USC—an Amicable Separation." *ADE Bulletin* 101 (1992): 23–25.

Janangelo, Joseph. "Somewhere Between Disparity and Despair: Writing Program Administrators, Image Problems, and *The MLA Job Information List.*" *WPA: Writing Program Administration* 15 (1991): 60–66.

Laurence, David. "From the Editor." *ADE Bulletin* 102 (1992): 1–5.

Lyotard, Jean-François. *The Differend: Phrases in Dispute.* Trans. Georges Van Den Abbeele. Minneapolis: U of Minnesota Press, 1988.

Mahala, Daniel. "Writing Utopias: Writing across the Curriculum and the Promise of Reform." *College English* 53.7 (1991): 773–89.

Miller, Susan. *Textual Carnivals: The Politics of Composition.* Carbondale: Southern Illinois UP, 1991.

Moulthrop, Stuart and Nancy Kaplan. "Something to Imagine: Literature, Composition and Interactive Fiction." *Computers and Composition* 9.1 (1991): 25–38.

Neel, Jasper. *Plato, Derrida, and Writing.* Carbondale: Southern Illinois UP, 1988.

Owens, Derek. *Resisting Writings (and the Boundaries of Composition).* Dallas: Southern Methodist UP, 1994.

Shakespeare, William. *The Complete Illustrated Shakespeare.* Ed. Howard Staunton. New York: Park Lane, 1979.

Severino, Carol. "The 'Doodles' in Context: Qualifying Claims about Contrastive Rhetoric." *The Writing Center Journal* 14.1 (1993): 44–62.

Terenzini, Patrick T. "Assessment: What It Is and What It Isn't." *ADE Bulletin* 104 (1993): 14–17.

Trimbur, John and Barbara Cambridge. "The Wyoming Conference Resolution: A Beginning." *WPA: Writing Program Administration* 12.1–2 (1988): 13–17.

Tuell, Cynthia. "Composition Teaching as 'Women's Work': Daughters, Handmaids, Whores and Mothers." *Writing Ourselves into the Story: Unheard Voices from Composition Studies.* Eds. Sheryl I. Fontaine and Susan Hunter. Carbondale: Southern Illinois UP, 1993. 123–39.

White, Edward M. *Developing Successful College Writing Programs.* San Francisco: Jossey-Bass, 1989.

Witte, Stephen P. and Lester Faigley. *Evaluating College Writing Programs.* Carbondale: Southern Illinois UP, 1983.

Zeni, Jane. "Literacy, Technology, and Teacher Education." *Literacy and Computers: The Complications of Teaching and Learning with Computers.* Eds. Cynthia L. Selfe and Susan Hilligoss. New York: MLA, 1994. 76–86.

2

Face to Face with Part-Timers
Ethics and the Professionalization of Writing Faculties

Kristine Hansen
Brigham Young University

It's no secret that some thirty years after a resurgence of scholarly interest in composition and rhetorical studies, the teaching of writing still occupies the lowest rung on the ladder of college English departments. Although scholars in recent decades have produced a burgeoning body of research on history, theory, and pedagogy in composition—so much, in fact, that composition studies is now, at many institutions, a legitimate field of academic research—the widespread employment of part-time and temporary teachers in writing programs remains a major indicator that composition studies has not achieved parity with other fields of academic study. Another major indicator of disparity is that composition and rhetoric is generally not a field in which one can get an undergraduate degree.[1] This fact creates an interesting paradox because graduate degrees in composition and rhetoric are becoming increasingly available; Brown et al.'s 1994 survey lists seventy-two graduate programs in rhetoric and composition in the U.S. and Canada, a ninety percent increase in viable programs since 1986.

But for all its success in graduate curricula, the study of writing is still by and large perceived to be a subject in which undergraduates need take only one or two courses. Yet, since generally every student needs those one or two courses to fulfill general education requirements, institutions offer numerous sections of them. The sections by necessity have to be small, since writing cannot be taught in large lecture courses. These multiple sections of a few courses constitute what is called on most campuses "the writing program."

With graduate schools turning out approximately a hundred PhDs in composition and rhetoric each year, universities can now hire someone who could possibly teach only general education courses—or teach others how to teach them—a phenomenon that is virtually unparalleled in the rest of the institution.[2] (Imagine a new assistant professor in chemistry, history, or psychology teaching only introductory general education courses and never students majoring in those disciplines.)

Notwithstanding the increasing production of PhDs in composition and rhetoric, a newly hired assistant professor coming out of one of the various graduate programs is still likely to be one of only two or three professors—sometimes the only professor—on a particular campus whose academic credentials are in composition and rhetoric. Sooner or later (more likely sooner) this new assistant professor will be asked to occupy the position of writing program administrator, directing a staff of teachers that usually has two tiers: At the top will be occasional full-time tenured faculty who by choice, tradition, or necessity teach some composition courses; at the bottom will be graduate students, part-timers and lecturers, or perhaps a combination.[3] Soon enough this new WPA will realize that she is tacitly being asked to participate in the exploitation of a marginalized teaching staff.

I say "exploitation" because the working conditions of the typical TA and part-time composition staff are generally far from commensurate with those enjoyed by the full-time tenure-line professors, even though the second-tier teachers may teach as many or more sections of the same composition courses —and may even teach them better. The litany of disadvantages in the second tier is depressingly familiar to anyone who has taught composition as a graduate student or non-tenure-line teacher: offices, desks, telephones, computers or typewriters—if there are any—are likely to be shared by several people in cramped, undesirable spaces; salary schedules stop after two to four steps based primarily on length of service (merit raises are generally unheard of); benefits are meager or, more likely, nonexistent; course loads, even though they are euphemistically called "part-time," are frequently heavier than the "full-time" loads taught by tenured faculty; notification of employment often comes at the last minute and is likely to be changed or even revoked since employment is contingent on enrollments, budgets, and other unpredictables; freedom to design one's own syllabus and select textbooks is generally restricted; amenities such as a parking permit, a mailbox, access to a photocopier, or a listing in the campus telephone directory are limited or nonexistent; more expensive perks, such as access to funds for travel or professional development, are almost unthinkable. Largely as a consequence of these poor working conditions, the WPA must orient and supervise a partially new teaching staff every year: A fresh bunch of inexperienced teaching assistants will arrive each fall, and some part-time teachers will find better jobs, move away, or simply quit.

The WPA presiding over a writing program thus staffed and provisioned faces an ethical dilemma: How can she in good conscience lead a program that is built on exploitation? If she has already accepted a leadership role, are there ways she can resolve the dilemma so as to engage in her profession without deriving her own income and status from inequitable practices? Another way to put the matter is to ask these questions: What are the implications of creating professional writing program administrators through PhD programs in rhetoric and composition when the majority of teachers in writing programs are, by current definitions, not professionals? Can the status of composition teaching ever rise when only a handful of those teaching it can claim the expertise that comes through formal graduate education? In order to offer some possible answers to these difficult questions, I will first briefly review various explanations for the causes of the two-tiered composition faculty and discuss the pros and cons of CCCC's recommendations for professionalizing writing teachers. Then, I will suggest additional ways to enfranchise those teachers by valuing the knowledge they have created in their classrooms. Finally, drawing on my own experience as a writing program administrator, I will illustrate how a WPA can motivate an institution to treat composition teachers ethically. Throughout this essay I focus particularly on part-time faculty because they constitute probably the biggest percentage of composition teachers in the country and tend to suffer more disadvantages than graduate students or temporary full-time faculty.[4]

Reasons for the Two-Tiered Composition Faculty

The low status of writing instruction and writing teachers results from a combination of historical events, cultural attitudes, and institutional and personal prejudices, as the following summary indicates.

- In the late nineteenth century, American postsecondary education shifted from undergraduate colleges to universities modeled after the German ones, which emphasized separate disciplines, research, and graduate education. This movement was accompanied by a shift in rhetorical education from oral to written discourse. This shift entailed reading and marking written compositions so that the workload for each teacher of rhetoric increased significantly, necessitating the creation of an academic underclass to staff the courses (see Connors).

- The historical development of English departments has institutionalized impoverished ideas of writing and of what is required to teach it, putting composition last in the department hierarchy of values; gender and economic inequities are a result of this hierarchy (see Scholes; Miller; Connors).

- Composition teaching has been feminized, both in the sense that mostly women do it and in the sense that it is perceived as proper work for women. Prevailing cultural attitudes support the employment of women to do what is considered drudge work in part-time and temporary positions with low pay and prestige (see Holbrook; Miller; Tuell).

- Budget stringencies have been claimed by administrators as a reason for hiring part-time and temporary teachers, particularly in academic fields without a strong tradition of research or support for autonomous faculty (see Slevin; Ohmann, "Foreword"). Slevin disputes the truth of these claims on the grounds that college enrollments, and English composition enrollments in particular, actually rose during the period that institutions hired vast numbers of temporary and part-time teachers; nevertheless, it is a fact that when central administrators feel the need to economize, they often look first to the writing program.

- The self-interest of the tenured professoriate in English departments makes them indifferent to the exploitation that makes their own favorable working conditions possible. Newly professionalized writing program administrators may actually contribute to the exploitation by seeking only for themselves the privileges that come from being identified with a tenure-track research faculty (see Sledd).

Taken together, these causes are like morning glory weeds in a vegetable garden: they're perennial, persistent, intertwined, and seemingly impossible to uproot. The new assistant professor who has accepted the WPA position and who has determined to eliminate or reduce the level of exploitation has a long row to hoe. Obviously, no WPA working alone could hope to eradicate the inequities quickly, maybe not even after years of trying. Realizing this, CCCC in 1989 issued the "Statement of Principles and Standards for the Postsecondary Teaching of Writing," a document aimed at starting a national groundswell to help writing programs achieve parity with other entities in the academy.

The Wyoming Resolution and the CCCC "Statement"

The CCCC "Statement" grew out of the Wyoming Resolution, which got its name because it was created at the Wyoming Conference on English in the summer of 1986. Participants at the conference drafted a document noting the deplorable working conditions for composition teachers and asking the Executive Committee of CCCC to carry out three charges: (1) to formulate "professional standards and expectations for salary levels and working conditions of post-secondary teachers of writing"; (2) to establish a grievance procedure teachers could follow when institutions failed to comply with the standards and expectations; and (3) to establish a procedure for censuring institutions for non-compliance (Robertson et al. 278–9).

After the Wyoming Resolution was passed by the members of CCCC at the annual conference in March 1987, the CCCC Executive Committee appointed a Committee on Professional Standards for Quality Education to draft a statement of standards and expectations. The preliminary draft of this statement, published in February 1989, articulated the following as its fundamental premise:

> To provide the highest quality of instruction and research, departments offering composition or writing courses should rely on tenure-line faculty members with a demonstrated commitment to the teaching of writing. Evidence of this commitment can be found in research and publication, participation in professional conferences, and active involvement in curriculum development and design. (CCCC Committee 62)

To actualize this principle, the document recommended that no more than ten percent of a department's writing courses be taught by part-time faculty and that they be used only to meet "*unexpected* increases in enrollment" (63, italics in original); it also urged departments to transform part-time faculty positions to full-time, tenure-track ones. Thus, in carrying out the first mandate of the Wyoming Resolution, the CCCC Committee effectively ruled out part-time teachers as appropriate personnel for staffing most writing courses. As for the second and third parts of the Wyoming Resolution, mandating that CCCC receive grievances from writing teachers and, if necessary, censure practices at some institutions, the committee reported that, after studying the matter carefully, it would not be feasible for the organization to do so. Such procedures would entail additional staff and expenditures beyond what CCCC could support and would probably duplicate existing procedures "available through other agencies, such as accreditation bodies, major education associations, faculty unions, and the AAUP" (65).

The draft statement of February 1989 was discussed further at the annual CCCC meeting held in Seattle the next month. There it was opposed by some who believed it subverted the intentions of the Wyoming Resolution; Gunner says the opponents were denounced as "racists, 'scabs,' and advocates of exploitation" (120). Despite this flare-up, the final draft of the document kept intact its basic principle of professionalizing writing instruction by advocating the hiring of PhDs in rhetoric and composition and the conversion of temporary and part-time appointments to tenure-track. In late 1989 copies were mailed to administrators at 10,000 postsecondary institutions ("Progress" 331), presumably in the hope that on its own the document would begin to spur change.

What it spurred, however, was controversy in the ranks of composition teachers, as most part-time teachers saw in the "Statement" an expression of no confidence in their abilities and a desire to take their jobs away. The committee apparently had not reckoned with the fact that a significant number of part-time teachers actually *wanted* to teach part-time. In October 1991, the major portion of *CCC* was devoted to a discussion of the 1989 "Statement," including a progress report from the committee. They reported that it had been discussed at the summer 1990 ADE meetings, and that participants "generally supported the Statement, although vocal reservations were expressed by a few" ("Progress" 331). Because of the angry reaction of many part-time composition teachers, the committee also attempted to clarify its position "on certain controversial aspects of the Statement" (332). Noting that it might be irrelevant at some institutions which are satisfied with the status quo, the committee wrote that "the Statement aims to give writing teachers who are not satisfied with their conditions of employment clear and forceful principles and policy from which to negotiate for changes at their institution if they choose to do so" ("Progress" 332). They suggested changes that might be much easier to implement in the short run than conversion of part-time and temporary lines to full-time, tenure-track lines—e.g., long-term contracts, smaller class sizes, reduced course loads, and more autonomy in curriculum design and implementation. But the committee held to its position that part-time positions are not in the best interests of the people who hold them, nor of writing programs, nor, indeed, of higher education. However, in an apparent admission that tenuring all composition faculty is unlikely, the committee added this clarification: "While the language of the document emphasizes tenure, we strongly support, as moves toward equality, alternative models of employment and faculty governance that, in different ways, serve the same ends—that grant writing teachers the rights, privileges, and protections traditionally enjoyed by tenure-line faculty" ("Progress" 335). Finally, the committee reiterated the costs of CCCC's getting involved in labor disputes and noted that mediation could be successful only where the standards had already been incorporated in an institution's policies; otherwise, there could be no grounds for requesting mediation, let alone censure.

Pros and Cons of Professionalization

Some (e.g., Gunner; Sledd) see a betrayal of the Wyoming Resolution in the decisions of the Committee on Professional Standards not to establish a grievance and censure procedure and to endorse tenure-line faculty as the most desirable writing teachers. Nevertheless, professionalization, as proposed in the 1989 "Statement," appears to be a better route than legal and job actions, such as strikes and sit-ins, for trying to improve the status of composition teachers. Still it is not without serious difficulties, and I will qualify my support for it later.

Professionalization is the hallmark of the modern university, which was born in the mid- to late-nineteenth century when American society in general began to specialize and "scientize" all knowledge. The emerging professions were shaped by the beliefs that certification not privilege, merit not seniority, competence not sociability or loyalty should be the criteria for admission and advancement (Hariman 214–16; see also Bledstein). These beliefs are now so familiar as to seem commonsensical and completely innocuous, but Ohmann's definition of a profession forces one to notice its monopolistic, exclusive nature. According to Ohmann, a profession is a body of people that "appropriates, shares, and develops a body of knowledge as its own; discredits other practitioners performing similar work; establishes definite routes of admission, including but not limited to academic study; controls access; and gets recognition as the only group allowed to perform that kind of work, ideally with state power backing its monopoly" ("Graduate" 250). Hariman notes that academic professionalism has further elaborated itself by the familiar "academic ranks, academic disciplines, tenure, special languages, [and] the elite forums of the journals, conferences, and conventions" (214). Such trappings can present a barrier to those who want to be party to a profession's knowledge and activities.

Yet considering how the assumptions of professionalism have so permeated the university, it is little wonder that the writers of the CCCC "Statement" would take the path of professionalization in seeking to improve the status of composition programs and teachers: The avenue was already paved and well traveled, having been used by all other fields of study that have achieved disciplinary status. Moreover, the necessary accoutrements of a professional organization (CCCC was established in 1949), journals, and conferences were already in place; and graduate schools were already turning out specialists in the knowledge that defined the profession. Indeed, all that remained was to have fully professional faculties and to begin offering an undergraduate major in writing. To be sure, the last two are giant steps, but the professionalization process had already been launched well before the 1989 "Statement." The authors of the document were simply choosing the route to respectability and equity that the university would understand, since its reward system is already built upon the premises that inform professionalism.

Indeed, it's difficult to imagine how anyone working in composition could not favor professionalizing the field and its teachers. Having become a certified professional compositionist myself, I hate to think that I might still be teaching writing as I was taught to in the 1970s by someone who was taught how to teach it in the 1950s. What I learned in my doctoral program has changed my pedagogy; what I am compelled to continue to learn as a professional enhances my teaching and my scholarship. Would that every part-time and temporary composition teacher could be immersed in the profession, having access to and helping create a body of knowledge that can be criticized, questioned, and reformed through the interactive mechanisms of publications and conferences. The increasingly rapid technological changes in writing effectively mandate more professional training of new teachers and retraining of experienced ones. (See Faigley and Romano's chapter in this volume for examples of how electronic media have changed and will yet change writing instruction.) Yet there are serious difficulties to surmount if all composition teachers are to be professionalized.

A full-scale attempt to professionalize composition faculties would create unique problems not encountered elsewhere in the academy. The first difficulty arises from the unique place of composition instruction in the university curriculum. Improving writing ability is generally considered fundamental to success in college in a way that, say, taking an elementary course in biology or American history is not. First-year students may be required to take Biology 101, American History 101, and English 101 as if each were on a par with the others; but English is much more likely to be a universal requirement, while biology and history may be one of two or three options. The fact that most universities require composition and are willing to support teaching it in small sections is evidence that writing ability is considered vital. Yet, as we've seen, this fact is also responsible for the enormous underclass of teachers who staff it. So the first big problem of professionalizing writing faculties is the sheer numbers of teachers who would have to be certified and admitted to the profession. The graduate schools are not turning them out *that* fast, and while boards of trustees and central administrators might be persuaded to convert some part-time and temporary lines to tenure-track, the CCCC document "effectively calls for at least doubling the tenure-track positions in most [English] departments," writes Robert Merrill, "and those of you who can imagine this occurring in our lifetimes are the last true optimists" (155).

Even imagining this optimistic scenario raises the second big problem: What does one do with the part-time faculty who have been so loyal in spite of poor working conditions—fire them? A more humane answer might be to offer leaves and grants to assist them in becoming certified to keep their jobs, but this cost added to the salary and benefits expenses that come with creating tenure lines (not to mention finding or building more offices to house them) would likely be prohibitive. Still more costs would result from the creation of a fully professional writing faculty, for like other professionals, they might want their own department, with supporting staff, so that they could offer an undergraduate major (which means creating new courses) and more graduate courses in their field of expertise (which would mean even more teachers would be needed to continue teaching the general education courses). They would want released time for research, and they would require funding for their research and travel. So the third problem is obviously cost.

In addition to these logistical and financial problems, professionalization, because of its exclusionary and monopolistic nature, can endanger certain kinds of knowledge and people as the field attempts to meet standards similar to those set by other professions. As Susan Miller explains, this occurred when English literary studies attempted to become a discipline in the modern university capable of competing with the classics and the sciences. Those promoting the professionalization of English literary studies had to overcome its non-serious image by "emphasizing its . . . attachments to philology and to traditional methods of teaching classical language and literature, in order that the subject's work, and its professionals, would be perceived as 'hard'" ("Feminization" 44). Achieving this kind of identity, Miller argues, meant that literary studies had to call composition into identity as a soft, feminine, lower-status partner that would make possible literature's higher position in the superstructure. Miller cautions composition studies not to make the same "intellectual and 'practical' moves toward equality," as such moves will only "reproduce the hegemonic superstructure by implying that bourgeois social climbing and successful competition for intellectual 'clout' are legitimate signs of improvement" (51).

Hariman, however, believes that complete rejection of the university's professional ethic would be foolish, since it has provided a coordinated means of producing knowledge and has enhanced "democratic access to learning within and without the academy" (223). Yet his analysis of professionalism in the university, drawing on Foucault's discussion of knowledge and power, also identifies its self-serving and anti-democratic characteristics. The first is that professionalism depends on a system of social control which Foucault calls the "disciplinary system." In this system, knowledge is "disciplined" to create expertise, from which comes power. This power is used to specify the "effective instruments for the formation and accumulation of knowledge—methods of observation, techniques of registration, procedures for investigation and research, apparatuses of control" (Foucault qtd. in Hariman 216). These instruments are then used to direct people to spend their time and labor in producing and consuming knowledge according to the dictates of expertise. "Expertise is disciplined behavior, behavior marked by strict conformity to procedure rather than by Yankee tinkering" (Hariman 217). In the disciplinary system only professionals possess knowledge: "The learned amateur, the village elder, or the experienced artisan" possesses something lesser, for "anything not capable of formulation into a disciplinary scheme [is] defined as something other than knowledge or reformed (deformed) into a body of knowledge" (Hariman 218).

The second feature of professionalism is that its specialized knowledge derives from a process of spatialization. That is, a discipline establishes itself by marking off boundaries for inquiry, which in turn requires a new administrative unit to coordinate the efforts. The process of spatialization is thus responsible for the fragmentation of the university into separate departments which compete for resources and recognition. Clearly connected to this competition is the third feature of professionalism: Its power "to shape knowledge through the university apparatus is also the power to subjugate knowledge," either by burying it or by declaring it naive, inadequate, or insufficiently elaborated (Hariman 221).

Taken together, these characteristics caution us to think carefully about the way composition studies should proceed to define itself as a profession and to identify who is a professional. Ironically, as Hariman notes, rhetoric was one of the knowledges subjugated at the close of the nineteenth century when modern university and professional culture became established. That the study and teaching of it is now becoming a profession behooves us to ask ourselves what knowledges we might be declaring naive or subjugating in our advance towards full disciplinary status. One of these subjugated knowledges has to be what Stephen North calls "lore."

North argues that the lore of "practitioners" (teachers of writing trained on the job) has been devalued ever since Cold War-inspired federal funding for educational research spurred a demand for expertise. His account describes the past thirty years in composition as an attempt by the new experts of the disciplinary system to supplant the understanding and ways of non-professionals, of non-experts—the temporary, part-time, and ordinary practitioners who did the hard work of teaching writing before there were PhD programs to create and control the instruments for producing knowledge. North's account also helps explain why so many part-time and temporary teachers resisted the basic premise of the CCCC "Statement," that writing instruction should be done only by tenure-line faculty: The value of what the practitioners thought they knew and had been doing in their classrooms was called into question by the experts who came on the scene later. Because discipline is usually associated with punishment, certified composition professionals ought to consider the implications of Foucault's disciplinary system if they want to follow the usual path of professionalism, yet not punish all who labored in the field before it was disciplined.

Professionalizing Part-Time Faculty

Despite the obstacles to professionalization and the dangers inherent in it, I remain convinced that it is the best route to pursue for the WPA who wants to respond ethically to the problem of the two-tiered faculty. Yet I am also convinced that, despite all we might hope and work for, part-time employment is going to be a feature of many writing programs for some time to come, if not permanently. Judith Gappa and David Leslie, in their important study, *The Invisible Faculty*, state as much: "It is time to admit that part-timers are a substantial and permanent part of the academic profession and should be treated as such" (91). That being so, the only ethical solution is to professionalize part-time teachers—but to do so in ways that avoid devaluing lore and the practitioners who worked in the field before the certified professionals arrived. An ethical stance would demand that these experts also learn from the wisdom of the practitioners who preceded them and who still labor beside them. Thus I believe that WPAs must work to alter the prevailing definitions of both "profession" and "professional"; we must find ways to dignify both what part-time faculty know and who they are in the eyes of the rest of the academy. In the remainder of this essay, I would like to offer two suggestions for how to do this. The first consists of some ideas on how to raise the status of teaching so that it qualifies as a form of professional knowledge-making. The second takes the form of a personal case study that I believe illustrates how a WPA can raise the status of part-time faculty by dignifying them as individuals worthy of professional status.

Valuing Teaching as Knowledge-Making

Patricia Harkin and Ruth Ray both provide ways of thinking about how we can avoid the pitfalls of traditional professionalism and enfranchise the masses of composition teachers who are dismissed as mere practitioners in a university culture that exalts expertise, research, and theory, and denigrates teaching.

Harkin's suggestions center directly on understanding and properly valuing lore. She describes practitioners' lore as non-disciplinary and potentially post-disciplinary because its "irregular, ad hoc procedures" are unconstrained by the institutionalized methods that dictate how knowledge must be produced (130–131). Unlike the facts and theories of rigidly demarcated disciplines, the tenets and strategies of lore travel easily and adapt comfortably to other situations, particularly "overdetermined" ones, in which the simple cause-and-effect explanations of disciplinary techniques are not adequate. Because lore "arranges its data serially, spatially, paratactically, like a rhizome, however they work" (134), it can help us see relationships we might not notice because of our ideological blinders. But even more, lore has the potential to become theory, when it attempts to solve a problem by combining various disciplinary projects, languages, and knowledges. Lore "elides without denying the opposition between theory and practice. And the informed intuition that produces that elision may," Harkin asserts, "be called theory—not in the sense of a metadiscourse, a generalized account of a practice to which all instances of that practice can be referred, but rather as a way of coping, contending with the overdetermined words of knowledge production" (134). To harness the power of lore and eventually change the academy's understanding of how knowledge is produced by teaching, Harkin proposes

> a series of conferences that ask us to work up from the practices of lore, not down from a theory of writing, conferences in which experienced, gifted teachers address a problem delineated for the occasion, a problem like students' writing in open-admissions colleges, cultural literacy, or exit exams. (136)

By unobtrusively videotaping various teachers' praxes prior to these conferences, various examples of how to deal with the problem could be collected. These videotapes would then be viewed and analyzed by "a panel of theorists, representatives of disciplinary ways of knowing, experienced in thinking through the implications of a practice" (137). Not only that, but a wider audience would be viewing the tapes and the panel through satellite links; they could then telephone to question or comment on the tapes or the theorists' discussion of the practices. In this way, the usual conference format, in which practitioners take ideas from theorists, would be reversed. "A conference about practitioners working on a problem would create a situation in which that work could be valued. And technology, because it is expensive, is a way of marking that value," Harkin claims (138). Because lore is created out of the urgent necessities of teaching and in the privacy of classrooms, where it can "escape the panoptic gaze of the disciplines," Harkin believes we must do all we can to bring it out of obscurity and into the center of professional dialogue (138).

Harkin's desire to valorize teaching as a different but nevertheless important form of knowledge-making is consonant with the growing movement to recognize teacher research as a kind of theory-making without which composition studies would not be complete. One of the most ardent defenders of teacher research in college composition is Ruth Ray, who believes that "compositionists in the 1990s will have to broaden their concept of 'research' and 'researchers,' opening up the field to practitioners in a multitude of settings, listening to what they say, learning from their observations, and acknowledging the importance and credibility of what they know" (23). (Harkin's vision of a teleconference already suggests an avenue by which this might happen.) Because teacher research questions the assumption that authoritative knowledge must be generated by detached observation, following the rules of a particular disciplined method, it also questions the traditional theory-practice dichotomy, in which theory generates knowledge and practice transmits it. Instead, Ray argues, theory is best thought of as "a lens, a philosophical perspective, or a stance"—obviously something no teacher could teach without (65). Not a method, but an anti-foundationalist epistemology, teacher research creates what Ray calls an "alternative discourse," one that is narrative rather than paradigmatic (54), thus suggesting that the most valuable knowledge practitioners have to share is their stories. Ray also points out the value of collaboration among teacher-researchers in building a stronger political base for having their knowledge accepted. She predicts that "as more and more teachers become involved in teacher research, their impact on composition studies will inevitably grow," because they will "begin to question and challenge the 'overdetermined' research in composition and the ideologies underlying it" (71).

Harkin's and Ray's ideas for giving teaching more prominence as a way of constructing knowledge and theory suggest ways WPAs might work to raise the status of part-time faculty by valuing what they know and creating opportunities for them to publicly share their knowledge. For example, WPAs could find ways to organize their own work so that observing and evaluating teachers in the classroom would be a way of gathering the post-disciplinary bits of knowledge that come from the application of lore. In addition, without needing a lot of money to carry it off, WPAs could imagine ways to organize part-time teachers in collaboratives so that they could conduct and disseminate teacher research—not just through the refereed journal article, but perhaps through colloquia, the expanding medium of e-mail, and regional and national conferences. JoAnne Liebman and Betty Freeland of the University of Arkansas at Little Rock were able to obtain a grant to offer a seminar in teacher research to their part-time teachers. A second grant enabled them and the eight part-timers to present a workshop on how to conduct teacher research at the 1993 CCCC Convention. They report that the seminar not only enhanced community in their faculty but raised the level of professionalism in their writing program.

Gappa and Leslie, who visited and surveyed all kinds of institutions in their study of part-time faculty, observed that "departmental culture" is the one consistent key to "feelings of efficacy and of satisfaction" in part-time faculty. They found that part-time faculty reported positive feelings in "departments that care deeply about education, about teaching and learning" and that "foster an atmosphere in which faculty members [including part-time faculty] talk with each other about these issues." In such departments

> people sense that they can have an effect on what happens—not just in their own isolated classroom but on the entire program of the department. . . . Even where there is universal dissatisfaction with pay, benefits, and other tangible support, part-timers who feel as if they are part of a collaborative faculty seem to have more positive feelings about their work and about their involvement with the institution. (185–6)

WPAs can certainly do a great deal to foster the kind of departmental culture that Gappa and Leslie describe.

Enacting the Ethical Relation: A Case Study

I am—or rather, was—the new assistant-professor-appointed-WPA whom I describe at the beginning of this essay. After earning the PhD in 1987, I took my first faculty job excited about what I had learned and so eager to share it that I naively accepted the post of associate coordinator of composition at the end of my second year and of coordinator at the end of my third (with assurances that administrative work would count toward tenure, of course). I had a twelve-month contract, a good salary, plenty of support from my chair, and ideal secretarial assistance. Only slowly did I realize the ethical implications of presiding rather comfortably from my third-floor office, with its window looking out on a noble mountain peak, over a staff of some sixty graduate students, who were crammed three and four per cubicle in two maze-like rooms in the basement, and twenty-plus part-timers, who were distributed among four or five offices in the same windowless basement.

Most of the part-timers had been hired before my arrival (some as many as twelve years before), and they were then teaching half of the advanced composition courses for the department, owing to a phenomenal increase in the number of English majors over a ten-year period, which meant professors who had formerly also taught composition now had to teach more courses for English majors. Nearly all of the part-time teachers had MAs in literature; some had had a graduate course in "Methods of Teaching College Composition" in distant years, a few more recently, but for virtually all, their real education in teaching composition had come largely on the job. Nonetheless, by our most effective measure of teaching performance, the university course and instructor evaluation form, they met and often surpassed the standard achieved by the full-time faculty who also taught composition. As I began to visit their classes, I was highly impressed by their knowledge and skill. But as I learned more about their situation, I felt it unfair that they should have to labor with so little recognition or reward. When I discovered that the starting pay of an experienced part-timer was less than that offered the newest graduate student, I became angry and began to act.[5]

The CCCC "Statement" had come out shortly before I assumed the post of coordinator. As I studied it, I was simultaneously hopeful, because it provided goals I could tell my chair and dean we should aim for, and disheartened because I knew it would take more clout than I had to get anyone with sufficient power to take notice and make the needed changes. But I began to circulate the "Statement" and to remind my chair at every opportune moment that we needed to do better by our part-time employees and that we needed to plan for a future that would improve the step-child status of composition in the department. Discouraged at times, I considered resigning in a fit of righteous indignation, but decided that it might be more ethical to remain in the position of WPA in order to keep arguing and working for change in the long run, despite my complicity in unjust practices.

At about this same time, I began to read some literature on ethics as part of a faculty development seminar sponsored by the Philosophy Department. The postmodern philosopher Emmanuel Levinas and the feminist educator Nel Noddings gave me a language for thinking about ethical imperatives and for planning how I might motivate administrators to change. Both Levinas and Noddings describe an ethics that is founded not in abstractions or propositions but in the relationship with the other. For Levinas, the other is whoever disturbs the sameness of the self, thus inhibiting the freedom and enjoyment of the self. In fact, "the fundamental experience," he says, "is the experience of the Other" (293). But this is no passive experience, no mere vague awareness of the other, because simply by presenting his gaze to me, the other demands from me a response. To be conscious of the other and of the infinite difference between our two selves is to be conscious of my moral obligation to the other. If I do return his gaze, rather than totalizing him, or reducing the infinite in his face to a representation, I am obligated to respond to him; I am obligated to be less selfish. This is what it means to be in the ethical relation.

Using somewhat different terminology, Noddings focuses on the same concept. She takes relationship with others as the basic fact of existence "and the caring relation as ethically basic" (3). She distinguishes between natural caring and ethical caring, though she claims the second arises from the first. Noddings posits that a person's finest memory of being cared for in natural caring—for example, in a parent-child relationship—inspires one to ethical caring. This memory "sweeps over us as a feeling—as an 'I must'—in response to the plight of the other" (79–80). In language reminiscent of Levinas', Noddings states that the desire for ethical caring is evoked by the proximate other, "the one who addresses me, under whose gaze I fall" (113), the one "whose real eyes look into mine" (39). The proximate other is whoever displaces my interest from my own reality to his, who causes me to apprehend his reality as a possibility for my own.

If Noddings and Levinas are right that ethics is relational rather than propositional, then it may be that using statements of principles and standards to attempt to change unethical treatment of people is inadequate. Although administrators might assent intellectually to the fair treatment standards outlined in such documents as the CCCC "Statement," I believe they seldom will bestir themselves to act *unless* and *until* they also feel the ethical motivation that comes through the face-to-face relation with the other. It is more common and more convenient for administrators to counter statements of principles and standards with other statements of policy and procedure that are meant to explain why the standards cannot be met. Quite simply, it is easy for administrators to dismiss such documents as the CCCC "Statement," because to provosts, vice-presidents, deans, and sometimes even department heads, part-time teachers of composition are usually faceless, nameless individuals, line items on budget and fact sheets. Perhaps the best explanation for the unethical treatment these teachers are subjected to is that they are known personally only to their students and to the WPA who hires them and supervises their work. The institution's ease in exploiting these folk is directly proportionate to their facelessness—an anonymity that is emphasized by the designation "staff" in the course schedule. I am not suggesting that central administrators are heartless; rather, in the absence of face-to-face encounters with the other, the ethical demand is absent. For the WPA who must return the gaze of these teachers, the face-to-face relation with them calls her into question; it calls for an ethical response. If she is to maintain what Noddings calls the ideal of herself as one caring, she must respond to their need. If administrators are to respond ethically, they must encounter—even if only imaginatively—the face of the other. With this understanding of ethics in place, let me now recount what I did to help administrators realize that part-timers are people whose very existence presents them with an ethical demand.

First, I wrote memos. As a new WPA I wrote a twelve-page memo to my department head, spelling out in great detail the teaching burden our part-timers carry—often more than a full-time faculty load—and the way our department treated its part-time faculty. I then proposed short-term solutions to improve the conditions that could be remedied immediately at the department level with little or no cost. I also spelled out long-term solutions that would require time, money, and approval from higher administrators. The chair was impressed enough to authorize such things as inclusion of the part-time faculty's names in the campus phone directory, new desks and filing cabinets for their shared offices, and waiver of the deposits they were required to pay to obtain keys for their offices. He also was willing to come up with money to pay them for extra assignments and attendance at meetings that asked them to commit time beyond the scope of their teaching assignments. These small steps at least recognized some of the basic needs of the teachers and boosted their morale. When this department head stepped down a few months later, I updated and improved my earlier memo for the new chair. He was impressed enough by it to forward it to the new dean, who eventually forwarded it to an associate academic vice-president, who used parts of it later in a report that I shall mention below.

Another memo I wrote sparked a review of parking requirements for the part-time faculty. As a supervisor of university personnel, I was invited by the Assistant Vice-President for Human Resources to attend a seminar on human resource management. The guest speaker from the Organizational Behavior Department pointed out types of unethical organizational abuse of employees. Upon returning to my office after the seminar I learned that this same Assistant Vice-President for Human Resources had just issued a memo to all part-time faculty commending them for their service and then informing them they were about to lose their privilege of parking in faculty lots; thenceforth, they would have to take their chances with students in the lots on the outer limits of campus. I wrote a reasoned memo to this Assistant Vice-President, explaining to her that requiring part-time faculty to park so far from where they taught seemed to me to be an organizational abuse of employees, which I had just been taught in her management seminar was unethical. I informed her that fully fifty percent of our advanced writing courses were now taught by these teachers, and that their work, their classes, and their students were in most respects no different from the work, the classes, and the students of full-time faculty. I described for her the greater needs part-timers have for flexibility in parking, since they are often juggling teaching with child care and other responsibilities. No doubt chagrined by my memo, she replied within two days, saying I could plead a special case with the Traffic Office. The result was that every part-time teacher who wanted one could obtain a special parking sticker allowing them convenient access to two buildings. The morale boost this gave to part-timers was much larger than I ever would have thought. I relate this to point out that when the need is described in human terms, administrators can be persuaded to act fairly. Later, the entire parking policy was reviewed, and all limitations were removed from part-time faculty. I think I was able to cause these administrators to think of part-timers as people with faces and lives rather than merely as drivers whose cars occupied precious parking spaces. So I am convinced that carefully written memos are a powerful way of getting results.

Second, testing Sledd's contention that if things are going to change, it will be because part-timers themselves become their own advocates, I arranged for three of them to meet our new dean face-to-face. One spoke to him about the general situation of the part-timers in our department; another about her research interests and her frustration at receiving no rewards for improving her knowledge and abilities through a regular program of self-initiated research; and the third about the difficulties of parenting a family alone on the meager salary she earned as a part-timer with no health insurance or retirement benefits. The dean was moved most, I'm told, by the third of these, although not to the point of giving a generous cost-of-living increase to part-timers that fall. He did, however, forward to the associate academic vice-president the long memo I had written to my chair.

Third, I created and mailed out a survey to collect data from other institutions in the Rocky Mountain region to see how their treatment of part-timers measured up to my institution's. Sharing the collected data with administrators and the part-time faculty themselves at least raised consciousness of our shortcomings and also pointed out some of our strengths in comparison to other institutions. Some of this data eventually came into the hands of the associate academic vice-president, as I will relate below.

Fourth, I found a way to offer professional development to the part-time teachers, so that they could recharge their stores of knowledge and re-examine their teaching, and so that I could argue that their value to the university had increased. In November 1991 I applied for a campus grant to support general education course development. I proposed a seminar for part-time faculty on the rationale that although they taught half of the 175 sections of the advanced courses each year, most of them had had no education in composition theory, history, and pedagogy beyond on-the-job training. I also pointed out that they had no release time and no institutional incentives or budget (and given their meager salaries, probably no inclination to spend their own money) to pursue professional development. "This state of affairs," I wrote in the grant proposal, "obviously contradicts the university's frequently stated position that good teaching is inextricably connected with an ongoing program of professional development and scholarship. Providing some much needed professional development for these teachers will have a potential impact on thousands of students over the next few years." I asked for over $10,000 to fund the seminar, including $6,000 to pay a $500 stipend to each of the twelve participants planned for. The proposed budget included money to buy each participant three books for the seminar and a two-year membership in NCTE with subscriptions to *College Composition and Communication (CCC)* and *College English*. The proposal was accepted and half the requested funds were granted by the Dean of General Education, with the rest coming equally from the English Department and the College of Humanities.

My colleague Grant Boswell, the Associate Coordinator of Composition, and I planned a seminar which we held for six days in May 1992, three hours each day, with a follow-up symposium the next month, at which each participant read a paper. We ordered three texts: Golden, Berquist, and Coleman's anthology, *A Rhetoric of Western Thought*, to give our teachers some acquaintance with the broad sweep of rhetorical history; Susan Miller's *Textual Carnivals*, to give them a perspective on the history and politics of composition teaching in the U.S.; and Lisa Ede and Andrea Lunsford's *Singular Texts/Plural Authors*, to give them a glimpse of a very useful kind of research that is contributing to significant pedagogical change in the teaching of writing. We also reserved some time in the seminar to discuss selected articles from 1991 and 92 issues of *CCC* and *College English*.

Twelve participants signed up in the first few hours after we announced the seminar. We thought at first we would have to go at a rapid pace to "cover all the material," but from the first day, we realized that "coverage" should not and would not be our goal. We barely had to bring up an issue or ask a question at the beginning of each meeting, and the participants were off and going. Their combined experience and reflective attitudes toward their teaching as well as toward the reading led to some of the most stimulating and engaging discussions I have ever been involved in; teaching the seminar was one of the most satisfying professional experiences I have had. In the evaluations participants filled out after our seminar, all mentioned not only the new ideas they were planning to try in their classrooms but the heightened sense of professionalism and community they felt as well. I realized then that the part-time faculty lacked a face-to-face relationship not only with administrators, but frequently even with each other.

The seminar was topped only by the symposium at which each participant delivered a paper on a topic of her choice prompted by our readings and discussion. In order to enact the philosophy that ethics is founded in the face-to-face relation with the other, and in order to bring administrators face to face with the unknown, unnamed part-time faculty, I invited to the symposium every important administrator who had anything to do with writing instruction from the provost on down. Although previous commitments prevented nearly all of them from attending, the associate dean of my college and the two associate chairs of the department attended, along with several full-time faculty who are involved in the leadership of the advanced writing program. These people afterward expressed sincere admiration for the quality of the presentations, some of which included very gutsy statements about the problems associated with part-time teaching. One participant even presented a resolution on part-time employment for our campus. Her eloquent presentation was, I believe, the most effective plea that could have been made for change. The symposium was followed by occasional gatherings during the 1992–1993 year to discuss selected articles in issues of the journals that the part-timers continued to receive.

These efforts produced a number of results. First, in the early spring of 1992 an associate academic vice-president organized and chaired a committee composed of part-time faculty from across campus. The purpose of this committee was to review part-time employment in all departments and to attempt to standardize university practices. In June 1992 he presented a comprehensive report to the provost and other vice-presidents, outlining uniform nomenclature and professional rank designations for adjunct faculty. Using some of the data I collected in my survey, the report outlines as well as the benefits the university ought to seek to provide for adjuncts: salary schedules that reflect experience, merit, credentials, and worth; medical and dental insurance, life insurance, savings and retirement, and such things as tuition waivers for dependents. It recommends that, in order to show the value it places on the contribution of part-time faculty, the university review its policy of denying cost benefits to part-time faculty. Most significantly, the report recommends creating a professional part-time track with four rank designations, and it provides a way for people to cross from the professional to the professorial track when their credentials, abilities, and engagement in research, as well as the department's need, warrant it. I wish I could say this vice-president's recommendations had been adopted already, but owing to his being replaced shortly thereafter with another vice-president who also was replaced less than a year later, the recommendations have now languished for two years. But I have been reassured by the central administration that they are still viable and that the questions related to providing benefits are still being studied; I am therefore hopeful a genuine willingness remains to create just working conditions for part-time faculty.

One reason I am hopeful is that a month after this report was presented, the Academic Vice-President issued a memo to all deans directing that certain no-cost steps be taken in every college and department to recognize the significant contributions of what he called "important colleagues" and "valued contributors" so that they would know that "we appreciate their work and are concerned with their welfare." The directive asked deans and chairs to invite all part-time faculty to annual faculty meetings and to other academic and social events, and to include their names in telephone and building directories. These directives have been followed even more recently with memos asking chairs and deans to take other steps to improve the recognition and rewards given to part-time faculty.

Finally, at the time I was about to step aside as WPA, in late 1993, my department chair promised me that regardless of the plans and timetable of the university or college to improve salaries of part-time faculty, he was prepared to act unilaterally to improve their salaries from funds at his discretion. This proved to be unnecessary, as the central administration provided money to bring part-time salaries in the English Department in line with those of part-time teachers doing comparable work in other departments and, for the first time, the beginning part-time salary topped the graduate student pay scale.

I offer this case study not as a narrative with myself as hero but as illustrative of the kinds of steps even an untenured WPA can take toward achieving some of the conditions outlined in the CCCC "Statement" when such steps as legal and job actions or hiring all tenure-line faculty are out of the question. Measured materially, the steps taken so far fall short of some of the standards outlined by the CCCC: the per-course compensation still does not equal what full-time faculty with comparable duties, experience, and credentials earn; there are no merit increases nor health and retirement benefits; the contracts are still issued semesterly rather than for longer terms; there is only very limited support for travel and none for research. However, measured in terms of improved understanding by administrators, improved morale for part-timers, and improved human relations, the changes are significant. These changes have come about not because of my shaming or manipulating administrators; instead, I brought those administrators into a relationship with the part-time faculty because relationships are the venue for ethical action. Administrators have so far responded caringly to the demand in the face of the other, and there is no reason to think they won't continue to do so.

Through showing that we value part-time teachers by treating them ethically and by respecting teaching as a legitimate means of knowledge-making, we can move a long way toward dismantling what Miller calls "the hegemonic superstructure" of the university that now keeps composition and its teachers at the bottom. On the other hand, if we "buy into"—and that is the appropriate phrase to use here—the current university hierarchy of values by esteeming only those who have "PhD" next to their names and by creating only the kind of knowledge that comes from marking off a narrow space and following disciplinary rules, we WPAs may improve our own status as professionals, but we won't improve the status of the field nor of its many teachers. If WPAs seek only for ourselves the privileges of professionalism that are purchased with the services of underpaid, overworked part-time faculty, we contribute to the maintenance of the hegemonic superstructure by supporting the ideology that ghettoized composition and its teachers in the first place. "An *actually* improved status" for composition, says Miller, "depends on openly consolidating the field's resistances to the cultural superstructure that first defined it" ("Feminization" 51, italics in original). She suggests that members of the field use the methods employed by the feminist and civil rights movements to expose what is at stake in the maintenance of such an oppressive system. While our field may not have a Susan B. Anthony or a Martin Luther King to lead such a movement, it does have a growing number of writing program administrators who can creatively work on their own campuses to professionalize part-time faculty and to insist on ethical treatment for them.[6]

Notes

1. There are starting to be exceptions, as noted in a recent survey of 264 four-year institutions conducted by Chapman, Hult, and Harris. They found that sixty-nine percent of the institutions surveyed offered an emphasis in writing to English majors, but the majority of these were in creative writing, technical and professional writing, and unspecified kinds of writing. Only seven percent were identified as "rhetoric and composition," suggesting that, nationwide, rhetoric and composition typically remains a general education requirement only.

2. Brown et al.'s survey of doctoral programs in rhetoric and composition estimates that in 1993 there were 1,174 students pursuing degrees, an increase of 123 percent over the 1985–1986 figure of 526. Huber reports that in 1991–1992, 117 PhDs were granted in rhetoric and composition. Of those, 85.5 percent reported finding employment, with 97 percent of that figure taking jobs in postsecondary institutions.

3. I am generalizing here. A number of institutions, such as UCLA, employ full-time (but untenured and untenurable) employees in their writing programs. These institutions have eliminated many of the worst abuses of employees in writing programs by offering long-term renewable contracts, good salaries, benefits, decent working conditions, and much autonomy to their employees. What they generally don't offer, however, is the chance to be tenured. Ellen Strenski's chapter in this volume details the kinds of entrepreneurial activities that to some extent compensate for this lack of status.

4. Recent statistics concerning the whole labor market indicate that 35 million people in the U.S. are temporary and part-time workers; of these, women make up sixty-six percent of the part-time employees (see Kleiman). Part-time composition teachers likely consti-

tute a similar percentage of all composition teachers; Holbrook estimates that two thirds of composition teachers are women. For those reasons I am focusing on the part-time teachers, but I am not insensitive to the injustices that other composition teachers suffer. Graduate students often labor under less than ideal conditions. But they are helped by the fact that they are real faces in the graduate seminars of the professors who are officially invested in the training of future professionals. It is difficult to mistreat people if a department's graduate program depends on offering attractive stipends and fair working conditions to applicants. Besides this, graduate students are sometimes not subject to certain withholding taxes, and they sometimes have health insurance or the option to have it. They are also more prone to organize and work unitedly to improve their working conditions. Finally, their exploitation is more likely to be temporary, as they can improve their status by completing their degrees and seeking tenure-line positions. Temporary full-time faculty, though also exploited, usually have to be given benefits as a result of their full-time status. They are in that respect better off than part-timers.

5. While I was also actively involved in advocating the cause of graduate students, an aggressive graduate coordinator was looking out for their welfare and was able to secure some important financial help for them, principally tuition benefits. For a discussion of how a concerned WPA and English department chair can successfully argue for improved working conditions for TAs, see McLeod and Schwarzbach, who describe an apprenticeship at their university that makes TAs better students and better teachers, thus benefitting the university in every way.

6. I am grateful to Beth Hedengren, Mara Holt, Joe Janangelo, and Chuck Schuster for reading earlier versions or portions of this chapter and for their useful suggestions for revision.

Works Cited

Bledstein, Burton J. *The Culture of Professionalism: The Middle Class and the Development of Higher Education in America*. New York: Norton, 1976.

Brown, Stuart C., Paul R. Meyer, and Theresa Enos. "Doctoral Programs in Rhetoric and Composition: A Catalog of the Profession." *Rhetoric Review* 12 (Spring 1994): 240–389.

Bullock, Richard, and John Trimbur, eds. *The Politics of Writing Instruction: Postsecondary*. Portsmouth, NH: Boynton/Cook, 1991.

CCCC Committee on Professional Standards for Quality Education. "CCCC Initiatives on the Wyoming Conference Resolution: A Draft Report." *CCC* 40 (February 1989): 61–72.

Chapman, David W., Christine Hult, and Jeanette Harris. "Agents for Change: Undergraduate Writing Programs in Departments of English." Forthcoming in *Rhetoric Review*.

Connors, Robert. "Rhetoric in the Modern University: The Creation of an Underclass." Bullock and Trimbur 55–84.

Fontaine, Sheryl I., and Susan Hunter, eds. *Writing Ourselves into the Story: Unheard Voices from Composition Studies*. Carbondale and Edwardsville: Southern Illinois UP, 1993.

Freeland, Betty. Telephone interview. 27 Oct. 1994.

Gappa, Judith, and David W. Leslie. *The Invisible Faculty*. San Francisco: Jossey-Bass, 1993.

Gunner, Jeanne. "The Fate of the Wyoming Resolution: A History of Professional Seduction." Fontaine and Hunter 107–122.

Hariman, Robert. "The Rhetoric of Inquiry and the Professional Scholar." *Rhetoric in the Human Sciences*. Ed. Herbert W. Simons. Newbury Park, CA: Sage, 1989. 211–32.

Harkin, Patricia. "The Postdisciplinary Politics of Lore." *Contending with Words: Composition and Rhetoric in a Postmodern Age*. Ed. Patricia Harkin and John Schilb. New York: MLA, 1991. 124–138.

Holbrook, Sue Ellen. "Women's Work: The Feminizing of Composition." *Rhetoric Review* 9 (Spring 1991): 201–229.

Huber, Bettina J. "The MLA's 1991–92 Survey of PhD Placement: The Latest Findings and Trends Through Time." *ADE Bulletin* 108 (Fall 1994): 42–51.

Kleiman, Carol. "Women Make Up Majority of Temporary Workers Among 35 Million in U.S." *Salt Lake Tribune* 11 Sept. 1994, F3. Reprinted from *Chicago Tribune*.

Levinas, Emmanuel. *Difficult Freedom: Essays on Judaism*. Trans. Sean Hand. Baltimore: Johns Hopkins UP, 1990.

McLeod, Susan H., and Fred S. Schwarzbach. "What About the TAs? Making the Wyoming Resolution a Reality for Graduate Students." *WPA: Writing Program Administration* 17 (Fall/Winter 1993): 83–87.

Merrill, Robert. "Against the 'Statement.'" *CCC* 43 (May 1992): 154–158.

Miller, Susan. "The Feminization of Composition." Bullock and Trimbur 39–53.

———. *Textual Carnivals: The Politics of Composition*. Carbondale and Edwardsville: Southern Illinois UP, 1991.

Noddings, Nel. *Caring: A Feminine Approach to Ethics and Moral Education*. Berkeley: University of California Press, 1984.

North, Stephen. *The Making of Knowledge in Composition: Portrait of an Emerging Field*. Upper Montclair, NJ: Boynton/Cook, 1987.

Ohmann, Richard. Foreword. Bullock and Trimbur ix–xvi.

———. "Graduate Students, Professionals, Intellectuals." *College English* 52 (March 1990): 247–257.

"A Progress Report from the CCCC Committee on Professional Standards." *CCC* 42 (Oct. 1991): 330–344.

Ray, Ruth E. *The Practice of Theory: Teacher Research in Composition*. Urbana: NCTE, 1993.

Robertson, Linda, Sharon Crowley, and Frank Lentricchia. "The Wyoming Conference Resolution Opposing Unfair Salaries and Working Conditions for Post-Secondary Teachers of Writing." *College English* 49 (March 1987): 274–80.

Scholes, Robert. *Textual Power: Literary Theory and the Teaching of English*. New Haven and London: Yale UP, 1985.

Sledd, James. "Why the Wyoming Resolution Had to Be Emasculated." *Journal of Advanced Composition* 11 (Fall 1991): 269–81.

———. "How We Apples Swim." *Composition and Resistance*. Ed. C. Mark Hurlbert and Michael Blitz. Portsmouth, NH: Boynton/Cook, 1991. 145–49.

Slevin, James. "Depoliticizing and Politicizing Composition Studies." Bullock and Trimbur 1–21.

"Statement of Principles and Standards for the Postsecondary Teaching of Writing." *CCC* 40 (October 1989): 329–336.

Tuell, Cynthia. "Composition Teaching as 'Women's Work': Daughters, Handmaids, Whores and Mothers." Fontaine and Hunter 123–39.

3

Going Electronic
Creating Multiple Sites for Innovation in a Writing Program

Lester Faigley and Susan Romano
University of Texas at Austin

Large writing programs at major public universities live in a perpetual state of contradiction. Typically they are charged with offering over a hundred sections of one or two courses. Typically credit for these one or two courses is required of all students, and typically they are perceived as "gateway" courses to other courses in the university. They serve both to initiate students into the literacy expectations of the university and to certify that students possess a requisite level of literary skills. Every large writing program continually negotiates tensions that arise from the institutional need to encourage continuity across numerous sections of the same course and the centrifugal forces of heterogeneity that the teachers and students bring to these courses. No matter how faithfully an instructor believes she is following a common syllabus, her immediate situation with a particular group of students at a particular time and in a particular place, her personal history of schooling and literate experiences, and her unfolding perceptions of her students and interactions with those students lead inevitably to a particular instantiation of the course she is teaching. Consequently, every director of a large writing program shortly realizes that the orderly description of what happens in a large-section writing course is to a great extent a convenient fiction. This fiction of a unified and coherent writing program has nonetheless served to justify both preserving the requirement and allocating a relatively large share of the humanities teaching budget to writing programs at most universities.

The fiction of a coherent writing program has withstood challenges because what it is charged with teaching—essayist literacy—seems so commonsensical as the subject matter of the course. "Essayist literacy" is a term popularized by anthropologists Ron and Suzanne Scollon to characterize the literacy most valued in European and European-influenced cultures over the last three centuries. The Scollons have identified essayist literacy as a historical phenomenon accompanying the rise of science in the seventeenth and eighteenth centuries. Michel Foucault in *The Archaeology of Knowledge* describes essayist literacy in terms of an "episteme" associated with the formation of other modern institutions such as factories, prisons, and schools. Marxist-influenced scholars (e.g., Street) maintain that essayist literacy is part of the ideological machinery of capitalism and through its decontextualizations supports a dominant ideology that conceives of workers as interchangeable parts. More recently, many feminist scholars (e.g., Lloyd) have pointed out that essayist literacy is a thoroughly masculine construct. Essayist literacy assigns to the "feminine" such genres as personal narrative that do not claim to convey universal truth.

The resistance of essayist literacy to theoretical critique comes as no surprise. Essayist literacy is so deeply institutionalized that it is difficult to critique its assumptions from within the academy without using its conventions (as this essay demonstrates). Even though we now understand academic discourse to be a multiple construct, certain assumptions about essayist literacy are shared across the different versions of the form, and these assumptions, which prevail across academic disciplines, are among the principal unifying forces within a university. While lately attention has been given to the differences in ways of arguing across disciplines, the form of the academic essay and its marks of quality have remained remarkably stable in this century.

In essayist literacy "good" writing is defined by those characteristics most prized in an academic essay. In a "good" piece of writing, logical relations are signaled, references to sources carefully documented, and statements of bias either absent or well-controlled. The presence of these features signals to readers that the author is truthful and that what he or she writes may legitimately pass for knowledge. Appeals to pathos as conventionally understood, unless carefully managed, are apt to discount author credibility. Both writer and readers are imagined as rational and informed people not inclined to excessive passion, fragmented reasoning, or posturing. Both author and audience are imagined to reside in a community where sobriety and calm prevail.

Even though critiques of essayist literacy have become familiar in the academy, these critiques have made few changes in how writing is taught in American schools and colleges. The predominance of essayist literacy serves to justify its being taught. Its invulnerability within college writing instruction, however, comes in large part from the classroom practices used to teach writing during the past century. We have come to know some of these practices under the cover term of *current-traditional,* coined by Daniel Fogarty in 1959. Following Richard Young's critique of current-traditional pedagogy in 1978, the term took on strongly negative connotations, representing all that is "bad" about writing instruction. But if the term is to a large degree a valid one for describing teaching practices that dominated writing instruction for over a century, then the longevity of these much criticized practices is truly remarkable, especially considering the magnitude of the changes in higher education from the mid-nineteenth to the mid-twentieth century.

The process movement took certain current-traditional practices (especially error hunting) as a point of departure and transformed writing pedagogy in ways that seemed radical because the point of instructor intervention in student work changed dramatically. It is little wonder that this change, coming in tandem with the revival of classical rhetoric for the teaching of composition, was hailed at the time as a paradigm shift. In light of the changes triggered by technological advances, however, the process movement does not now seem nearly so radical as it did in the late 1970s and early 1980s. Because focusing on process alters neither the form of the product nor the marks of quality, process-influenced literacy only seems at odds with the literacy advanced in current-traditional rhetoric. The evil of current-traditional pedagogy turns out to be its inefficiency in teaching students to produce essays. The durability of the form suggests that we mistook a better mousetrap for a revolution.

It is difficult for writing program administrators and writing teachers to question the utility and value of process pedagogy. Its ubiquitous appearances across the curricula mark the increasing influence and stature of composition studies in the academy. The multiple drafts and peer critiques that now are the staples of nearly every college writing program have been so institutionalized that official descriptions of what fulfills the writing-intensive course requirement at the University of Texas at Austin and at other universities specify these requisite precursors to the final product. Indeed the process approach to writing has come to feel so normal and natural that our most uninterrogated teaching practice is perhaps the emphasis on revision. Multiple drafting is billed unproblematically as a solution to plagiarism, slipshod research, half-baked arguments, want of critical thinking, and poor style. Claims about the relationship of process pedagogy to the production of quality essays are our bread and butter.

In this essay we argue that writing instruction using networked computers has the potential to overturn the privileging of the essay in a writing classroom because teaching practices that we advocate and that have gone largely unquestioned are exposed as unsuited to the task. That electronic media would so destabilize the pedagogies which only recently have been canonized was not evident when the technology was first introduced. On the contrary, placing personal computers in front of students seemed to enhance rather than disrupt process pedagogy. Similarly, putting networked computers in writing classrooms seemed to enforce social constructionist pedagogies. The initial perception of "fit" between good writing pedagogy and electronic environments has proved to be premature and oversimplifies the complex relationships between technology and human and institutional agencies. The unproblematic correspondences between process pedagogy and word processing software, between social constructionism and networked conversations, between poststructuralist theory and hypertext have been questioned (Lanham; Faigley; Tuman), but few have been willing to disturb the marriage between comfortable writing pedagogies that form our disciplinary core and the entire range of new media for writing.

If computer technologies are as intrinsically disruptive of traditional literacy practices as we believe them to be, administrators of writing programs charged with maintaining the fictions of coherency and order will have to create new fictions. At the University of Texas at Austin, The Division of Rhetoric and Composition (DRC) is committed to teaching the great majority of its courses in classrooms equipped with networked computers by 1998. The DRC and the University administration alike believe that students should learn to write using the tool they will most certainly employ for most writing during their lifetime. The new fictions we must invent about coherent writing programs and effective teaching strategies are not just for upper-level administrators; they are for us as scholars of rhetoric and composition and as classroom writing teachers.

When personal computers invaded the academy in large numbers beginning in the early 1980s, they lacked the power and memory to do the big jobs required of mainframes. In the humanities these machines were used largely as memory typewriters, and the motivation for academics to learn to use them was directly related to the absence or decline of secretarial support services. Even teachers of composition, whose vision for computers in the humanities was more far-reaching, dreamed primarily of courseware that would enable teachers to substitute the computer for the human instructor and thus produce manageable workloads. In the early days, computers were imagined as simple labor-saving devices, even though they rarely made life easier for teachers.

Several technological developments quickly altered that vision. Personal computers became enormously more powerful in memory and speed. They became capable of reproducing and generating images and sounds in addition to storing text and calculating numbers. The development of hypertext software made possible the connection among a variety of media in nonsequential arrangements. Personal computers became linked to other computers, large and small, through local and wide-area networks. In tandem these developments have leapfrogged existing communications and information storage technologies. With the introduction of World-Wide Web, integrated text, graphics, sound, and video can be transmitted over the Internet and accessed by twenty-five million users. Not only do the resources of the world's libraries become available to individuals, individuals can also become producers of sounds, images, and texts.

Given the development of the "information highway" and the promise of access to people of all economic and social strata, pronouncements that we are entering a new age of literacy have become commonplace. Jay David Bolter's *Writing Space* is one of the more prominent manifestos announcing our present encampment in the "late age of print" (1). The much lamented fragmentation of the humanities, according to Bolter, "is only a problem when judged by the standards of print technology, which expects the humanities . . . to be relatively stable and hierarchically organized" (234). In the world of electronic writing, however, "nothing is more natural than the centrifugal disorder of our present cultural life. There is no conceptual problem (although many technical ones) in feeding all these conflicting tasks into the computer and generating one vastly reticulated, self-contradictory hypertext" (235).

Celebrants like Bolter link the electronic revolution to recent poststructuralist and postmodern discourses, which leads them (problematically) to claims for the democratic potential of electronic technologies. Bolter views hypertext as the fulfillment of the American dream of freedom of choice: "That freedom of choice includes everything: profession, family, religion, sexual preference, and above all the ability to change any of the options (in effect to rewrite one's life story) at almost any time" (233). The Global Village has arrived, not as McLuhan's broadcast media but rather as a vast network of linked computers.

Of course no panegyric to the progress of Western civilization will parade down the main street of the academy nowadays without challenge, and encomiums to electricity are no exception. Stanley Aronowitz is representative of left critics of computers and electronic media in general. Aronowitz grants computer-mediated communication has subversive potential, but as now used in schools and in the workplace, he finds computer technology "integrated into the prevailing scheme of management-directed production of goods and services" and part of the self-policing mechanism that controls professionals (122). He allows that the widespread use of computers has promoted entrepreneurialism in software development, but once that development has taken place, he sees it used to constrict rather than enhance the authority of professionals. Aronowitz cites examples of how computer-aided design (CAD) software has reduced the knowledge and skills required of engineers and the range of their decision making. He accuses the capitalist state of making "herculean efforts to quarantine technoculture in trivial pursuits and to confine its applications to entirely conventional areas" (137).

Both Bolter and Aronowitz foreground their interests in promoting democracy, but neither allows much space for human or institutional agency. Bolter predicts greater democracy as the outcome of a new stage in the history of literacy; all we have to do is surf the electronic wave. Aronowitz sees electronic technologies as new forms of control in postindustrial capitalism and links them to the demise of participation in electoral politics. In both visions of technological domination, people are caught up in the sweep of history.

The sweep of history and evolutionary change looks very different from located perspectives, and our locations are as director and assistant director of the Division of Rhetoric and Composition at the University of Texas at Austin. The schedule of implementation to teach the great majority of writing courses in classrooms equipped with networked computers by 1998 is made immediately possible by an information technology fee of six dollars per credit hour levied on all students. This institutional commitment is preceded by a history of human commitment. Briefly, a faculty member in the Department of English, Jerome Bump, obtained in 1986 a grant from IBM that allowed the establishment of a classroom equipped with networked computers. A team of then graduate students (Valerie Balester, Wayne Butler, Locke Carter, Fred Kemp, Nancy Peterson, and Paul Taylor) became interested in new ways of teaching writing using networked computers, which eventually led to the formation of a company and the development of the Daedalus Integrated Writing Environment software. Subsequently John Slatin, an English professor drawn to computers by his interest in voice synthesis, took over leadership of the computer lab and facilitated the launching of additional computer-assisted classrooms in two platforms, the development of hypertext courseware, and the installation of Internet access from these classroom (for accounts see Bump; Butler; Kemp; Slatin; Taylor). Because the facility was so closely involved in writing instruction, it was incorporated into the new Division of Rhetoric and Composition in 1993. The point of this brief history is that the local story of the coming of computers to writing instruction at Texas or anyplace else is a story with human and institutional agency. If certain people had not been present in a particular institutional structure, it would have all turned out quite differently.

In the remainder of this essay, we focus on the agencies of both students and teachers in the computer writing classrooms at the University of Texas. We have chosen the following examples not because they are representative, but rather because disparate episodes illustrate the sorts of agility and ingenuity required of teachers in computer classrooms. We argue that the significant pressures placed on writing instruction by computer technologies result not so much from new tools and altered metaphors, malleability of text, or flattening of hierarchies as from the extracurricular literacies of today's university students.

Because it is a commonplace of our discipline that students bring multiple literacies to the classroom, writing teachers may be puzzled by a call to attend to the literacies of their students, when in fact most teachers give careful consideration to their students' personal, local, ethnic or national literacies and to the ways these various literacies both complicate and enrich student writing. When informed writing teachers take alternate literacies into account, they tend now to do so not in terms of deficiencies but in terms of differences to be accounted for, examined, and often valued. However, these literacies have never before disrupted the two major assumptions that undergird the teaching of writing—first, that the essay form is important, and, more to the point, that students have little practice replicating it. Writing teachers have embraced the assumption that most students seldom write on their own in any significant way. While it is certainly the case that few students do much essay writing, a significant percentage of middle-class students at universities like Texas arrive in the composition classroom with years of experience writing and reading on computer networks.

In the course of addressing a University of Texas graduate student conference this past year, Vincent Fabello remarked that a "generation is growing up now that knows the electronic landscape as well as it knows the bars." When they come to college, many students become or remain active in various electronic forums, from private bulletin boards to the Internet. First-year composition students of the 1990s may well have operated bulletin boards on Fidonet, a non-academic parallel to the Internet; they may be knowledgeable in the online arts of flaming, arguing, and monitoring; they may have seen action in LambdaMOO's "Metaphysical Boxing Ring" or constructed objects using the programming languages readily available to MOO inhabitants. (MOO is an acronym for Multi-user, Object Oriented.) These students counter the conventional disciplinary wisdom that students have no reason to write, that they have never written before, that they have to be instructed in the value of writing, and that they need to be taught the form. In fact, increasing numbers of university students are more knowledgeable about writing in virtual spaces than their instructors, and the online abilities of these students far surpass those of most writing program administrators. The term *literacy*, historically native to writing instruction, has never before represented a range of skills that students possess in greater measure than their instructors, a recognition that is increasingly troubling to writing instructors (e.g., Hawisher and Selfe). The teachers who field the challenges posed by these literate students by no means concede authority. They reassert professional expertise by inventing situated pedagogies in response to the multiple literacies of the students registered in their classes and of the nonstudents who enter the classroom via the Internet.

The message quoted below offers an example of what happens when the extracurricular literacy of a student meets the pedagogical and technological expertise of an experienced instructor. The example is from a literature course designed specifically for student use of electronic forms; it could as easily have come from one of the DRC's elective writing courses on electronic discourse. The message was posted on Megabyte University, an electronic discussion list for teachers of writing in computer environments. The list has several hundred subscribers and is a major arena for discussion of electronic writing pedagogies. The author, Susan Warshauer, is an experienced teacher of writing and literature courses, and she is one of the most technologically knowledgeable members of the DRC teaching staff:

```
>From owner-mbu-l@TTUVM1.TTU.EDU Thu Jan 27 20:13:40
1994
Date:  Thu, 27 Jan 1994 17:48:42 -0600
Reply-To: "Megabyte University (Computers & Writ-
ing)" <MBU- L@TTUVM1.TTU.EDU>
Sender: "Megabyte University (Computers & Writing)"
<MBU- L@TTUVM1.TTU.EDU>
From: Susan Warshauer <swan>
Subject: hypertext v. mud n lit class
```

```
To: Multiple  recipients  of  list  MBU-L  <MBU-
L@TTUVM1.TTU.EDU>
I'm teaching an American lit survey course and as-
signing a final project in Storyspace, Hypercard, or
MacroMind  Director  (the  default  program  is
Storyspace, but some students already know Hypercard
and MacroMind). The assignment is to trace a par-
ticular theme or issue through the course of Ameri-
can literature, using a certain # of works from the
class, and a few of their own choosing that they
find relevant. I'll give them a list of 15-20
themes. They also have the option to develop their
own themes.
The rub: one student is interested in designing part
of a MUD for his project, and at first I was encour-
aging of this. But now I'm considering not having
that as an option.
```

Although calls for assistance on this list are common, Warshauer's dilemma is remarkable. Warshauer reports that a student wishes to substitute for the new literacy project she has assigned yet another new literacy project—a MUD. MUD is an acronym for Multiple-User Dungeon, which, as its name suggests, has direct lineage to the fantasy game Dungeons and Dragons. In MUDs participants create characters who explore, pose, emote, speak, and create and manipulate objects in a virtual environment. What this particular student is proposing, however, goes beyond participation on a MUD; this student wants to define in text the virtual landscape in which characters will interact.

Unlike some university administrators who have banned MUDs on their campuses, Warshauer is enthusiastic about MUD construction and interaction, but in the course of working out her response, she must cobble together a pedagogical underpinning for such a project that is in keeping with her course goals. In this case process pedagogy does not come to mind. Rather she reaches into a personal repertoire of English studies activities and pulls out "creative," "realism," and "fiction," simultaneously employing vocabulary more closely aligned with the visual arts and architecture than with rhetoric. The student, writes Warshauer, will "draw," "depict," "construct," and "design":

```
I think designing mudspace is creative and good for
bringing alive a fictional vision or environment, or
for reproducing a set of ideas in (usually) a real-
istic mode, but the kind of construction done there
may be less conducive—in contrast to the type of
work done in hypertext—to drawing and depicting re-
lationship [sic] between a set of literary works—es-
pecially if the person has little experience doing
mud design & literary analysis. . . . I'm thinking
```

that non-mud hypertext may be more valuable pedagogically at this point, though I don't like the
idea of taking away a creative option for a student,
and one that *might* be constructive, depending on
what he/she does with it. There are interesting
things happening with MOSAIC too, and hypertextual
MOO environments, but it may be expecting a lot to
have the student work in design in those areas. Any
ideas?

In the final part of her message, she imagines how indeed these two
literacies—electronic and essayist—might meet satisfactorily were she to allow the project, adding to it two pedagogical staples common to literary and
rhetorical studies—"critical analysis" and "context":

For example, if a student wants to design a Puritan
society, town square, church with characters et al,
I'd say (to ensure that the work wouldn't just reproduce a version of a Puritan society without a
kind of critical analysis of it, or context for understanding religious or other themes in relation to
other works in the course)—I'd say just be sure to
incorporate other works, or an attitude toward other
works/ways of interacting. There could be a dead end
street, and the reason someone might not be able to
go further would be because that was the way Roger
Williams went, or the writer could have alternative
texts appear as actual books on a table, with the
writer expressing an attitude toward them—or better
yet, the mud writer could play with time and make
associative shifts in who populates the Puritan village based on an ahistorical commonality with char-
acters/themes in works from another period.

Because reading and writing in all forums made available by electronic phenomena are seen as central to the development of computer-based writing instruction at Texas, MUD construction is deferred, not denied. This project is
shelved until a pedagogical control or justification can be put in place.
(Warshauer further develops her analysis of MUDs in "Aesthetic Approaches
to the Design and Study of MUDs [Multi-User Domains] in English and Performance Studies: Interface, Realism, and the Dialectic of Interacting.")

Our next example features composition courses taught by electronically
savvy University of Texas graduate students Bret Benjamin, Chris Busiel, and
Noel Stahle. These instructors spent Spring Semester 1994 working with students and other instructors in computer-mediated classrooms to create pedagogical units using TurboGopher and other tools to connect students with the
Internet. They wanted their students to observe and practice public discourse in

the electronic age and in a global arena, heeding one of the currently popular justifications for rhetorical studies and the DRC's own justification for a course syllabus directed toward public issues. A major thread of historical scholarship in rhetoric is to identify circumstances when rhetorical education was considered important for responsible citizenship. Historians of rhetoric are particularly interested in the conditions that have given rise to civic rhetoric at various times from classical Athens and republican Rome to the colonial and early national periods in America. All of these historical instances evoke nostalgia for the conditions under which academic and public rhetoric come together as "real-world" discourse (e.g., Halloran, Miller). Aware that the Internet produces discourse unlike that of the polis of Athens or the Old South Meeting House of colonial Boston, Benjamin, Busiel, and Stahle nevertheless test the viability of the Internet as a means for involving students in issues of global concern.

All three instructors consistently represent the Internet as a source of information for research purposes that is superior to conventional libraries. For Benjamin and Busiel, the advantage lies in the availability of texts that will never come to light through conventional publishing conduits, particularly those texts generated in Third World hot spots such as South Africa and, more recently, Haiti and Chiapas. These instructors are not naive about the ironies of imposing evaluative systems on texts they themselves champion as liberated from the shackles of capitalist publishing practices. Nevertheless, because the main difficulty with online research is the vast and unwieldy amount of material, Benjamin and Busiel introduce to students a vocabulary of descriptors designed to sort strong rhetorical performances from weak ones and well-documented arguments from poorly documented ones. Remarkably, Benjamin and Busiel were careful to value all messages, even those not conforming to academic standards, as important contributions to complex issues. Benjamin and Busiel's analysis is peppered with comfortable composition terminology such as "collaboration," "audience," "discourse community," and "critical analysis," and, by their account, a reasonably happy if somewhat chaotic marriage between the old and new literacies is do-able; it is a matter of stamping the new behaviors with traditional nomenclature.

In a more controlled model of Internet research, Noel Stahle uses various Internet conduits as lenses through which students may re-envision both research procedures and research topics. Like Warshauer, Stahle rigorously specifies pedagogical justification for his procedures before the fact: Newsgroups enable identification of major issues and provide a sense of immediacy; Lexis-Nexis serves as a rich source of documents; Turbogopher provides the images for applications in visual literacy. Relying more heavily than Benjamin and Busiel on conventional classroom procedures, Stahle's students dilute their Internet research with conventional, off-line sources that flesh out, frame, and tame the spectacle of online information.

Despite the careful integration of new forum and traditional pedagogy, the hegemony of essayist literacy that ultimately prevails in these courses suffers

certain hairline fractures. On the Internet appeals to pathos are far more powerful than in the essays of conventional anthologies. Benjamin and Busiel's
strong bias in favor of global hotspots was evident in their presentation at the
DRC Spring Colloquium, where they featured student reactions to emotional
messages from the South African political front. Stahle's colloquium presentation foregrounded the research procedures of students who used the net to
solicit on-the-spot updates regarding the violence surrounding the elections in
South Africa. Apparently, the immediacy of the net compels instructors and
students alike to give great authority to eyewitness accounts and subverts the
model of reasoned public discourse offered not only in course syllabi and textbooks, but throughout the academy. Although the success of these units in the
eyes of our discipline follows upon a careful introduction of Western scholarly
procedures to a global Internet, and although the freedom of choice so her-
alded by network theorists becomes a highly directed and culturally condi-
tioned one, the academic essay is forced to share the limelight with less
entrenched forms of discourse.

As composition teachers and administrators who might be described as
only partially literate (although we do not create spaces or objects on MOOs,
we do occasionally inhabit them and are active Internet users), we cannot help
but observe that the terse chunks of writing common to computer spaces resist
the benefits of typical process pedagogy interventions: peer critiques, drafts,
and revisions. Much Internet writing is single draft. Much sustained writing on
the Internet, such as MOO or realtime writing, consists of one-liners, rapidly
fired. Peer review is a function of response/no response. Unsuccessful pieces
of writing are as frequently abandoned as revised. Although Internet exchanges provide opportunities for rhetorical analyses based on the classical
appeals, such analyses become enormously complex given that Internet communities are in a continual state of flux. "Discourse community" and "audience" lose explanatory power for students and teachers alike when identities
are masked, multiple, and unstable. Building a credible ethos on the net entails
rhetorical moves unsanctioned for the traditional essay. The appeal to pathos
and humor is strong in electronic exchanges, and frequently students whose
rhetorical strategies resemble those of Beavis and Butthead or Comedy Central performers garner positive peer feedback. Yet this success is unwelcome
in classes geared to essayist literacy.

There are other complications in going electronic. It is commonly noted that
gender, age, ethnicity, and sexual orientation are effaced during electronic communication, and University of Texas writing teachers often complain that this
freedom from location and embodiment makes for hurt feelings and community
disruptions that impede their teaching. The common response to such incidents
is to take time away from the machines to re-integrate student bodies and student
words, and University of Texas teachers currently are working out pedagogies
that serve this purpose. Pedagogies designed for electronic literacy must necessarily confront the uncomfortable paradox that by creating unreliable personas

and by refusing responsibility for words, our most literate students demonstrate their substantial control over the writing form we purport to teach and their understanding of discursive power. They practice well a literacy whose most prominent feature is the ambiguous relationship between body and text.

Our examples illustrate the remarkable abilities of graduate-student instructors to make sense of new literacies that meddle with the core pedagogy that the Division of Rhetoric and Composition at the University of Texas at Austin publicly endorses. These instructors and their students are exploring what teachers mean when they claim to "empower" students, especially students from economically secure backgrounds. Their pioneering work calls into question why many writing teachers believe their students to be disempowered. If teachers believe that students are disempowered only because they cannot write proficient academic essays, then essayist literacy serves as a Berlin Wall between teacher and student literacies. When we use this metaphor, we do not imply that the wall has been crumbling or torn down, but rather that many routes now exist around it and that some students have traveled these routes before us. We expect to be traveling new roads with our students not because we have entered a new era of literacy but because students now demand an education they perceive as relevant to the twenty-first century and not the nineteenth. We writing program administrators depend upon innovators like Susan Warshauer, Bret Benjamin, Chris Busiel, and Noel Stahle to negotiate between the new and the old and to invent the new fictions by which writing instruction will continue to form an important part of the liberal arts curriculum.

Works Cited

Aronowitz, Stanley. "Looking Out: The Impact of Computers on the Lives of Professionals." *Literacy Online: The Promise (and Peril) of Reading and Writing with Computers.* Ed. Myron C. Tuman. Pittsburgh: U of Pittsburgh P, 1992. 119–137.

Benjamin, Bret, and Chris Busiel. "Have I Got Some News for You: Incorporating Macintosh Internet Research Tools into the Rhetoric and Composition Classroom." *CWRL: Computers, Writing, Rhetorics and Literature: Electronic Journal of the Computer Writing and Research Labs.* University of Texas at Austin. November, 1994.

Bolter, Jay David. *Writing Space: The Computer, Hypertext, and the History of Writing.* Hillsdale, NJ: Lawrence Erlbaum, 1991.

Bump, Jerome. "Radical Changes in Class Discussion Using Networked Computers." *Computers and the Humanities* 24 (1990): 49–65.

Butler, Wayne. *The Social Construction of Knowledge in an Electronic Discourse Community.* Diss. U of Texas at Austin, 1992.

Fabello, Vincent. Message posted to the Fourth National Graduate Student Conference on Lesbian, Transgender, Bisexual and Gay Studies. University of Texas at Austin, March 1994.

Faigley, Lester. *Fragments of Rationality: Postmodernity and the Subject of Composition.* Pittsburgh: U of Pittsburgh P, 1992.

Foucault, Michel. *The Archaeology of Knowledge.* Trans. A. M. Sheridan Smith. New York: Harper, 1976.

Halloran, Michael. "Rhetoric in the American College Curriculum: The Decline of Public Discourse." *Pre/Text* 3 (1982): 245–69.

Hawisher, Gail E. and Cynthia L. Selfe. "Tradition and Change in Computer-Supported Writing Environments: A Call for Action." *Theoretical and Critical Perspectives on Teacher Change.* Eds. Phyllis Kahaney, Linda A. M. Perry, and Joseph Janangelo. Norwood, NJ: Ablex, 1993. 155–186.

Kemp, Fred. "The Origins of ENFI, Network Theory, and Computer-Based Collaborative Writing Instruction at the University of Texas." *Network-based Classrooms.* Eds. Bertram Bruce and Joy Petyon. Cambridge: Cambridge UP, 1993. 161–180.

Lanham, Richard. *The Electronic Word: Democracy, Technology, and the Arts.* Chicago: U of Chicago Press, 1993.

Lloyd, Genevieve. *The Man of Reason: "Male" and "Female" in Western Philosophy.* Minneapolis: U of Minnesota P, 1984.

Miller, Thomas. "Introduction." *The Selected Writings of John Witherspoon.* Ed. Thomas Miller. Carbondale: Southern Illinois UP, 1990. 1–56.

Scollon, Ron, and Suzanne B. K. Scollon. *Narrative, Literacy and Face in Interethnic Communication.* Norwood, NJ: Ablex, 1981.

Slatin, John. "A Brief History of the Computer Writing and Research Lab." Unpublished essay.

Stahle, Noel. "Postcolonial Sights/Sites: Vision in Coetzee's *Waiting for the Barbarians* and the Eyes of the Electronic Classroom." *CWRL: Computers, Writing, Rhetorics and Literature: Electronic Journal of the Computer Writing and Research Labs.* University of Texas at Austin. November, 1994.

Street, Brian V. *Literacy in Theory and Practice.* Cambridge: Cambridge UP, 1984.

Taylor, Paul Harlan. *Computer Conferencing and Chaos: A Study in Fractal Discourse.* Diss. U of Texas at Austin, 1993.

Tuman, Myron C. *Word Perfect: Literacy in the Computer Age.* Pittsburgh: U of Pittsburgh P, 1992.

Warshauer, Susan. "hypertext v mud n lit class." MegaByte University Electronic Discussion Group. Texas Tech U, Lubbock. 27 Jan. 1994.

———. "Aesthetic Approaches to the Design and Study of MUDs (Multi-User Domains) in English and Performance Studies: Interface, Realism, and the Dialectic of Interacting." *CWRL: Computers, Writing, Rhetorics and Literature: Electronic Journal of the Computer Writing and Research Labs.* University of Texas at Austin. November, 1994.

Young, Richard E. "Paradigms and Problems: Needed Research in Rhetorical Invention." *Research on Composing: Points of Departure.* Ed. Charles R. Cooper and Lee Odell. Urbana: NCTE, 1978. 29–47.

4

Two-Year Colleges
Explaining and Claiming Our Majority

Elizabeth A. Nist
Anoka-Ramsey Community College
Helon H. Raines
Armstrong State College

In two-year colleges composition is a core requirement for all degrees, most diplomas, and many vocational/technical certificates. Consequently, English departments in community colleges generate the largest numbers of student FTE, sections of courses, and faculty. As composition specialists in these colleges we therefore see our work as central to the mission of our institutions. A non-elitist, non-hierarchical philosophy of education drives the mission of two-year colleges, which is to serve our diverse population. The majority of the disenfranchised student population that compositionists say they want to empower, and indeed need to reach, take writing courses at two-year colleges (see Fearing; Griffith and Connor; "Facts"). Given this fact, we believe our work *should* be central to research and scholarship in composition studies and in writing program administration. In this essay we will explain the centrality of composition in two-year college English Departments and point out ways in which these programs challenge the field of composition to demonstrate its often proclaimed commitment to empower students.

By fostering a shared understanding of two-year college writing programs between two- and four-year writing faculties, we hope to underline the necessity for finding the resources and opportunities to work together for stronger composition programs across the spectrum of higher education. In order for this shared understanding to occur, however, our four-year colleagues must learn something of the history, the students, the faculty, and the writing curriculum at two-year colleges. Therefore, we will briefly profile these areas; then we will consider some important differences between two- and four-year institutions. We will conclude by proposing projects for collaboration that the Council of Writing Program Administrators can support and additional projects in which our four-year colleagues can be partners with us.

Historical Overview

A brief historical overview demonstrates that the two-year college is a uniquely American creation. The first institution was established in Joliet, Illinois, in 1901 (Doucette and Roueche). After World War I the two-year college movement gained impetus because of the need for skilled workers, the drive for social equality and upward mobility, and the persistent belief that education could solve the nation's problems (Cohen and Brawer). A number of "vocational centers" were established in the 1940s with a primary function of providing war production training, and by the 1950s these became permanent state institutions for vocational training. Nationwide, by the end of the 1960s, most two-year programs embraced the present comprehensive functions of career programs, transfer programs, compensatory education, and community outreach.

According to Goldenberg and Stout, the phenomenon of mass education, largely attributed to the GI Bill and the establishment of a national network of community colleges, "markedly expanded the student population not only by number but, more importantly, by social demographics. Working class and minority veterans . . . enrolled in colleges and universities and changed the curriculum by their experiences and insights" (95). These authors also attribute two-year college growth to the 1960s and 1970s desegregation and sex equity policies which led to special studies. The expanding postwar economy, the return of Vietnam veterans throughout the 1970s, and regular incoming waves of immigrants and refugees with educational needs maintained steady growth among two-year institutions.

By the 1960s and 1970s a majority of two-year institutions were established as "community colleges" with the authority to award the Associate of Arts (general education transfer programs) and Associate of Science degrees (technical or semi-professional transfer programs). Vocational centers also began to award the Associate of Applied Science and the Associate of Science degrees as well as vocational certificates and diplomas. By the 1970s many of these vocational colleges also were accredited as open-door community colleges providing curricula and related training in vocational, technical, business, health, general education, and paraprofessional subjects. The Associate of Arts degree is now widely offered and articulation with baccalaureate programs is a high priority.

Among two-year colleges, governance and funding vary widely because so many kinds of institutions exist: private two-year colleges, parochial colleges, business schools, flight schools, health occupations training centers, public vocational centers, technical colleges, liberal arts colleges, and comprehensive community colleges. In some states public two-year colleges are administered and funded by local school districts; in others they are funded as a statewide system; in still others these campuses are part of the state's higher education network governed by a Board of Regents or Higher Education Board. The numbers of students enrolled also range from several hundred to over 65,000 (Raines, "Is There").

Thus, making generalizations about two-year college writing programs is problematic because each institution has a unique history, mission, philosophy, and administrative structure. In spite of these differences, we will generalize to some degree about two-year college writing program students, faculty, and curricula.

Students

Most two-year colleges serve only lower division students. Nevertheless, because of open-door policies and a wide array of vocational, technical, and transfer programs, students enter our institutions with extremely diverse writing needs and abilities. Many are first-generation college students from families that do not use standard English. Some lack high school diplomas; others cannot write or read English at all. Adult basic education and ESL programs address some of their needs. Into this mix, add honors students, who select a community college because of location, affordability, special programs, professional lower division faculty, and smaller class size.

Not only are our students' language experiences and entry level competencies widely diverse, their learning styles, learning rates, cultures, and educational goals also vary. The two most common goals are preparation to enter the work force and preparation to transfer to a baccalaureate program; however, many come to our campuses for retraining in a constantly changing labor market. Others are high school "stopouts," now adults, returning to earn high school diplomas. Some hold bachelors and graduate degrees and come to the community college to update their knowledge in computer software and other technical areas. They also come to enrich their lives with the humanities and fine arts courses they never had time to take as undergraduates.

Also, because of the need for lifelong learning in our rapidly changing techno-culture, the student population is older. In fact, the average age is twenty-nine (Cohen and Brawer 32). The majority are financially independent; many are parents themselves. These "nontraditional" students usually are less naive, more responsible, more "street smart," and more committed to education than "traditional" eighteen-year-old students at any college or university.

Increasing numbers of students flood our campuses every year. One of the greatest challenges most two-year colleges have faced over the past ten years is a large, sustained growth in enrollment with little or no increase in legislative appropriations and even budget cuts in some states. Projections indicate continued growth, especially in the outer suburban rings of metropolitan areas. Some states anticipate population doubling over the next twenty years, with minorities comprising much of the anticipated growth. According to demographer Harold Hodgkinson, "of the 20 million new workers who will enter the work force between now and the year 2000, 82 percent will be female, nonwhite or immigrant" (qtd. in Griffith and Connor 112). Given Hodgkinson's findings, the community college's proven track record of successfully educating diverse populations is certain to influence the direction of higher education in the next century.

English Faculty

Two-year college faculty are veteran teachers who are committed to thirty- or forty-year careers teaching lower division English. Annual salaries for full-time faculty (nine-month academic year) start around $25,000 and, over a career, can increase to upward of $50,000. Medical and retirement benefits are substantial and usually offer the teacher a variety of career options such as phased-in retirement. Many contracts also include some provisions and funding for professional development, conference travel, and sabbatical and academic leaves. Hiring practices, salary schedules, and seniority policies discourage job change after four or five years at one institution, so we don't move around very much.

About half of today's full-time faculty at two-year colleges were hired during the 1960s boom. On many campuses this group has become an entrenched political entity with philosophies and methods brought from graduate school experiences in the late 1950s and early 60s. The other half of the permanent faculty may be newcomers hired recently through national searches. If predictions hold, we will see more change in the full-time faculty makeup in the next ten years as nearly half of the present community college faculty retires. Many sources predict a forty percent retirement by the year 2000 (e.g., Gabert, cited in Fearing).

In most two-year colleges the faculty teaching load is fifteen credits per term. Research or publication is rarely considered part of the faculty member's assignment. A teacher typically has two or three writing sections and one literature section—about 100 to 150 students per term. Some faculty hours also may be scheduled in the writing center or computer lab in place of classroom hours.

The amount of freedom the individual faculty member has in course design and text selection depends on departmental makeup. Where the number of full-time permanent faculty is small and consensus is possible, the department may adopt a common syllabus and text for each core course. However, in larger departments with diverse faculty and teaching philosophies, common adoptions are impractical if not impossible. Here the department establishes guidelines within which each faculty member has considerable autonomy.

This academic freedom is valued highly by teachers who enjoy it and fought for adamantly by those denied it.

The Composition Curriculum

With this description of students and faculty in place, we now attempt the more problematic task of generalizing about the two-year college writing curriculum. The English faculty is charged with the design of a carefully articulated developmental and college-level curriculum that addresses the needs of the diverse student body—even as financial resources become increasingly limited. Added to this is the concern to help students make connections between their technical classes and those in the humanities. Many voc-tech students avoid non-vocational courses and even those technical courses with academic prerequisites. Often, in Applied Science degree programs, the required first-year writing course may be designed to introduce the specific kinds of writing encountered in the student's vocational or technical field.

Our challenge then is to create an integrated curriculum that uses the collaborative, hands-on, problem-solving approaches of technology preparation and invites cooperative instruction among faculty in English and areas such as engineering, computer science, nursing, math, and auto mechanics. For instance, some teachers have experimented with linked courses. This focus means that two-year college English teachers often emphasize classroom practice and applied learning over theorizing about writing.

The "core" first-year composition requirement is at the center of the English curriculum—a two- or three-course sequence preceded by several levels of developmental writing and, often, an ESL sequence. Most colleges now administer some kind of entrance assessment of students' language competencies, and many have implemented mandatory placement policies as well as exit exams.

Two-year college English departments may also have responsibility for any combination of the following: developmental reading, technical writing, creative writing, literature courses, the WAC program, a writing center, and computer labs. These programs may be offered in evening and extension programs, for credit and non-credit, as well as in traditional day school programs.

Departmental course outlines as well as policies for all courses are usually reviewed by the English faculty at least every five years. Often the course design in current use at the state college or university influences curriculum decisions since transferability is always a major concern. It is important, however, to remember that the students served by the community college have different needs and educational goals from the "traditional" university student. Furthermore, the faculty directing their learning experience also bring different professional preparation and expertise to the classroom. For many reasons, two-year college writing courses should not be clones of university courses. Yet many composition textbooks, rhetorics especially, reflect the assumption that the two are identical. Pedagogical practices that a teacher working with a single section of university freshmen finds interesting and effective often are neither for the experienced community college teacher working with three sections of Composition I.[1] The lack of suitable rhetorics for two-year college writing courses is likely due to a lack of research using two-year student populations. Despite the paucity of research on the needs of two-year college writers, faculty must still do their best to design a curriculum that meets the needs of the two-year students and that addresses articulation requirements.

Two-Year College Teachers in the National Profession

In "Arguments with Which to Combat Elitism and Ignorance about Community Colleges," Doucette and Roueche claim that community colleges have entered the 1990s as mature and sophisticated institutions that are making important contributions to an economy and an educational system struggling to cope with changes brought about by the dawning of the information age. Yet, they write, "the potential of community colleges remains largely untapped, in no small part due to persistent elitism among leaders in the media, business, and government" (*Leadership Abstracts* 4.13). Other educators predict that two-year colleges are the institutions best suited to lead academia in the twenty-first century. Griffith and Connor caution, however, that measuring the success of community colleges by the criteria used for universities is inappropriate and leads to misperceptions about the quality of education. For example, measuring institutional effectiveness by the percentage of entering students who stay to complete a two-year degree program ignores the thousands (even millions) of students who achieve their educational goals by "dropping in" for a smaller block of course work. Such inappropriate measurements are one source of budget cuts that pose serious threats to the comprehensive and democratic missions of two-year colleges. Without recognition of our past achievements and knowledge of the country's future educational needs, the public, even the educational community, very likely will overlook the two-year colleges as a valuable resource for leadership in the next century.

In terms of writing programs specifically, we believe that lack of knowledge, even among writing program administrators, is perhaps our most serious impediment. The impression of university elitism and a sense of being misunderstood is further heightened for two-year college faculty by differences between two-year college and university titles. To university faculty the names commonly used in two-year colleges for all faculty, such as "instructor," often convey meanings that underrate our positions and our professional expertise. Without program and personnel titles recognized by our four-year colleagues, what we do in two-year colleges and those who do that work frequently are unidentified and unacknowledged as WPAs or even as composition specialists. Yet, as long as composition is a core course of the two-year college curriculum for associate and baccalaureate degree programs, and literature courses are part of a smorgasbord of distributive requirements for "general education," the ratio of writing sections to literature sections in two-year colleges will continue to be about five to one. In that sense, a better name for the English department might be "General Education Department" rather than the more limited term "writing program."

In addition, because of small sizes, limited budgets, philosophies that promote more full-time teaching and less administering, and a long history of anti-elitist, pro-democratic attitudes, our institutions do not and probably never will designate a title, a position, or a salary for someone to "direct composition." Often a few faculty who have time and interest, or faculty who serve under a rotation system, carry out the duties of the composition "director" after consultation with others at department meetings. Decisions on curriculum planning, class scheduling, and managing of department resources are generally made by committee or department consensus. Sometimes a department chair or a coordinator of several disciplines assumes these responsibilities, and occasionally a faculty member may have release time to coordinate the composition courses or the writing center.

This absence of WPAs in two-year colleges reflects the overall absence of faculty titles. Just as the term "WPA" is alien to most of us, so is "professor." Two-year college faculties infrequently enjoy (or suffer) academic ranking. Because our role is necessarily primarily teaching, research and publication are not criteria for promotion in permanent status or salary. Regardless of highest graduate degree held or length and quality of professional service, the job title on most of our employment documents is "instructor." Reasons exist for the predominance of two-year colleges naming all faculty "instructor," none of which has to do with value, ability, or education. Yet, "instructor" in university language designates the bottom of the academic hierarchy and connotes fewer degrees, less experience and/or ability, and minimal, if any, scholarship or publication.

As a final example, consider the status designated in the name "junior" college, as American two-year colleges were originally called. Dropping the "junior" from the name of the national organization which now is American Association of Community Colleges (instead of *Junior and* Community Colleges), indicates recognition among the leadership that "junior" is a misnomer (Griffith and Connor 137). All of these linguistic issues do little to help universities and colleges identify us accurately, much less find areas in which to identify *with* us.

In spite of some significant differences, we do face a number of shared challenges and common problems. These include the following: (1) supporting, promoting, and strengthening writing instruction throughout American public education at all levels; (2) responding to the national demand for standards and fair assessment; (3) improving articulation of curriculum and students to facilitate transfer; (4) researching and developing personal, professional, and institutional strategies for coping with burnout among writing program faculty and administrators; and (5) resolving conflicts that result from tensions among various groups. For these reasons we propose some actions that the Council of Writing Program Administrators can take and some additional steps that four-year college faculty can take to create joint solutions to the problems we all face as writing instructors in postsecondary education.

Actions the WPA Council Could Take

Following are some suggested steps that the Council of Writing Program Administrators could take to foster a greater role for two-year colleges in the organization and to promote collaborative problem-solving:

- The Council should regularly invite two-year college faculty to serve as advisors for WPA national and regional conferences. Beyond introducing four-year panels or speaking at two-year sessions, two-year college faculty should serve in more than a perfunctory capacity; we should participate in significant and visible aspects of the conference, from its planning (choice of topics, speakers, location) through its production.

- The Council should appoint at least two community-college representatives to its board. We applaud the Council's reserving a position for one two-year representative on its board, admitting that this percentage of "representation" is generous, considering the number of two-year college faculty who are members of WPA. However, one board position remains relatively conservative, given the number of students we serve. Having only one two-year college member on the board, no matter how knowledgeable, professional, and articulate this person may be, in fact means that she or he must operate from a minority position.

- In planning future conferences, particularly joint WPA/ADE conferences, the Council should consistently seek a number of two-year college faculty for the program. The Council should regularly invite two-year college faculty as keynote speakers, conference leaders, and panel participants, recognizing that the composition community represented in WPA needs to hear what we have to say. The Council should also be sure to invite speakers with various specializations and viewpoints, demonstrating its understanding that no one person represents the whole, seeking the dissenting views that exist among two-year college writing faculty as much as they do elsewhere.

- The Council should promote, even more vigorously than in the past, two-year college memberships, both in the national organization and in the regional affiliates. Encouraging participation among two-year faculty who do not see themselves as WPAs could take many forms. One way would be to announce in promotional materials that, while many two-year colleges do not have WPAs, the organization invites all interested two-year college faculty to bring their knowledge and expertise in the work of administering writing programs to the conferences. Regional affiliates should recognize the potential for growth because two-year college faculty are more likely to be able to attend regional meetings than national conferences. Each region could commit to mailing a special invitation to two-year college English departments to join the organization and to engage in conference planning and execution, as well as to serve in leadership positions.

- The Council should use its influence with publishers to get them to offer scholarships or other awards to sponsor the attendance of both full-time and part-time two-year college faculty at national professional conferences. Two-year, four-year, and research university authors with successful publishing records and books from the same publishing house also could speak in a unified voice to emphasize to their publisher the need to expand the knowledge base about composition by having more two-year college presence in the professional organizations. These companies surely are aware of the community college market for their books, as evidenced by the number of texts by two-year college teachers.

- Two-year faculty must be invited to serve on the Council's Consultant-Evaluator board. Beyond issues of equity, this move would make the consultant-evaluator service as credible and effective for two-year institutions as it currently is for four-year institutions. Two-year colleges frequently are not receptive to bringing in consultants from universities, having too long suffered from "articulation" meetings where faculty from the state flagship university come "down" to instruct the English faculty in the most recent changes at the university. Indeed, two-year college English Departments will more likely hire and heed consultants who know the community college from the inside, who are cognizant of our strengths, and aware of our constraints. Consultant-Evaluators from community colleges would also be able to talk to our faculty and administration clearly—apart from the often obscure terminology of composition theory.

- The Council should revisit the Portland Resolution. In discussing "Articulation," the writers of the Portland Resolution argue that a WPA should be responsible for "coordinating with high school (AP/CLEP, concurrent enrollment) programs" (94). Yet the resolution says nothing about working with two-year institutions. Two-year college faculty cannot be omitted from the important resolutions and statements of our professional organizations. We would like to have our students, our work, and our contributions recognized and represented in a published revision of this section of the Resolution.

- The most profound and far-reaching action the Council should take is to commit to organizing and funding a major pilot project to model collaborative research between two-year and four-year faculty. This model project would unfold in three phases:

  - First, the Council could sponsor a focus group at any of the national professional conferences, such as NCTE or CCCC. Some members of this focus group would be invited by the Council both to assure representation from both two-year colleges and research universities and to initiate a commitment from those who accept the invitation to continue, if chosen, in the pilot project. The focus groups would brainstorm and decide on possible projects.

- Second, the Council would select one project and commit to seeking funding for it, mentoring its progress, and finding publishing outlets for its results.

- Third, the Council would sponsor inter-institutional teams created to draft grant proposals. It is important that university faculty with experience in writing grant proposals, who have access to release time and administrative support, serve as coordinators of these projects, training two-year faculty in research methods.

In this way, the Council could pursue through a structured format the realization of a project that could become a prototype for future research. Of the many issues such research could test, we believe the most important is to learn whether the work in composition for the last fifteen to twenty years has reached the six to ten million students in two-year colleges. If so, the researchers could investigate whether these new methods work, which ones work where and on what populations, how well they work, and why they do or do not work. In the process, of course, we would identify other areas where more knowledge should be developed.

Actions Faculties at Universities Could Take

Many of our colleagues from four-year colleges and research universities have demonstrated that they recognize the value of including us in professional discussions about literacy instruction. Evidence of that value appears in various forms: One is that increasingly leaders in the profession request more two-year college faculty to serve in organizations, give presentations, contribute articles to journals and books, and participate in ongoing professional conversations about English studies (Raines, "Reseeing" 100). However, considerable work remains to be done. Here are some steps that our colleagues in four-year institutions can take to foster a greater collaboration with two-year institutions:

- Universities should incorporate texts that study the culture and work of community colleges into the teacher preparation curriculum. Two essential books published in 1994 are Mark Reynolds' *Two-Year College English: Essays for a New Century* and Marlene Griffith and Ann Connor's *Democracy's Open Door: The Community College in America's Future.* Both provide provocative and significant insights into our institutions and should be required reading for anyone who wants to know more about two-year colleges.

- We seek *more* than textual representation in university courses. We suggest that you consider inviting two-year college faculty to work on curriculum planning committees for undergraduate and graduate teacher preparation courses. You also might invite us to speak to or teach your composition methods and theory students. It is well known that many MAs, ABDs, and PhDs make their careers at two-year colleges. Educating graduate students about two-year college programs could improve the university placement records and establish universities as important *faculty* feeder institutions.

- Universities should encourage students to write senior and masters' theses and dissertations about literacy and literature instruction at community colleges. To support this activity, universities could also create internships in which graduate students teach one semester at the two-year college, under the supervision of an experienced community college instructor, and then bring that knowledge of our student body to their home institutions. This pioneering work could test the validity of theories generated at research institutions against the literacy activities experienced by our students, who are, and probably will remain, the majority of college students in the United States.

In proposing all of the above steps, we do not mean to imply that we have been left out of the Council's activities completely. Two-year college composition specialists who have actively participated in WPA reap significant benefits. We certainly are welcomed as colleagues. Individual members give us valuable collegial support and work with us to raise consciousness about two-year college programs. We are included in some conversations about conference planning, as well as in discussions of many of the issues we have raised here. *WPA* is an important source of information on writing program administration, and we are invited to submit our work for publication. By sponsoring joint conferences with ADE, the Council also helps us reach colleagues who more readily identify themselves as English department chairs than as writing program administrators.

But now it is time to move from communication and accommodation to cooperation and collaboration. If the Council's board and membership want more participation of two-year college writing program faculty, then the organization has to serve institutionally as well as individually. Because the two-year college is finally different from the four-year institution, we English faculty and administrators must forge our own identity. Being unnamed WPAs should not be viewed by us or by our university colleagues as being uninformed and inexperienced in WPA work or in teaching composition. Through this publication and others, we are addressing issues of difference: resolving or effacing those differences which serve merely to stigmatize or marginalize us, yet naming and claiming those differences that preserve unique advantages for the students and teachers who interact on our campuses.

Notes

1. For example, consider texts that present the "controlled" research paper assignment with a given set of readings which all students are expected to use as sources to support their theses on the assigned topic. A TA might appreciate the control and structure that such an assignment provides. It may also be easier for the inexperienced teacher to make evaluative judgments about student papers that are all responding to a common prompt. However, for the community college teacher, who has multiple sections of the same course—as many as nine sections in a year—reading seventy-five or 100 research papers a term on the same topic is torture. Even shorter papers, e.g., an assignment asking students to summarize three different readings on the same topic, challenge the most patient and attentive readers.

Works Cited

Cohen, Arthur M., and Florence B. Brawer. *The American Community College*. 2nd ed. San Francisco: Jossey-Bass, 1989.

Doucette, Don, and John Roueche. "Arguments with Which to Combat Elitism and Ignorance about Community Colleges." *Leadership Abstracts* 4.13. Austin: League for Innovation in the Community College and the Community College Leadership Program, 1991.

"Facts in Brief." *Higher Education and National Affairs*. 6 Oct. 1986: 3.

Fearing, Bertie. "Renewed Vitality in the 21st Century: The Partnership Between Two-Year College and University English Departments." Reynolds 185–195.

Goldenberg, Myrna, and Barbara Stout. "Writing Everybody In." Reynolds 94–107.

Griffith, Marlene, and Ann Connor. *Democracy's Open Door: The Community College in America's Future*. Portsmouth, NH: Boynton/Cook, 1994.

Hult, Christine et al. "The Portland Resolution." *WPA: Writing Program Administration* 16:1–2 (1992): 88–94.

Raines, Helon. "Reseeing the Past, Recounting the Present, Envisioning the Future: The Teaching of English in the Two-Year College." *TETYC* 20.2 (1993): 100–108.

———. "Is There a Writing Program in This College?" *College Composition and Communication* 41.2 (1990): 151–165.

Reynolds, Mark, ed. *Two Year College English: Essays for a New Century*. Urbana: NCTE, 1994.

Part II

The WPA Within
and Across Departments

5

Making a Difference
Writing Program Administration as a Creative Process

Lynn Z. Bloom
University of Connecticut

A classic Steinberg cartoon shows a small girl speaking in arabesques of fanciful, gloriously-colored butterflies, to which a gray father-figure responds with slashes of dark straight lines. This visual dialogue emblematically depicts the difference between creative and literal approaches to, among other things, life, liberty, and the pursuit of writing program administration.

For administration of writing programs, as of any other complicated system, represents a balance between the straight lines and the butterflies—bureaucracy and creativity, the preordained, the pragmatic, and the precedent-setting. Some aspects of administration are boring—endless forms to fill out, memos to circulate, meetings to call, details to follow up on and follow up on and follow up on. Other aspects are downright unpleasant, dealing with malcontents, malevolence, and—because WPAs are among the chronically fiscally challenged—budgets and the priorities and hard choices these impose. Together these constitute program administration's dark straight slashes, necessary but not fun. The administrator needs always to envision the butterflies beneath and beyond these confining boundaries if writing program administration is to make a significant difference to the people and programs it affects.

Consequently, this essay will concentrate on the butterflies, the creative potential of writing program administration, which can transform a routine endeavor into a creative enterprise with enormous benefits for students, faculty, institutions—even the entire profession. I will focus on four areas of writing program administration in which I have firsthand experience that a WPA's

73

efforts, individually and collaboratively, can make a particular difference, and in a relatively short time: training teachers, influencing graduate education, influencing undergraduate education, and establishing or enhancing the institution's reputation in writing. Creativity, it should be noted, is a relative term; what is innovative on one's home ground may be well-established (or even passe) in other settings. Yet no one person can or should work in isolation; to make a difference in the long term, the WPA must initiate, encourage, and reinforce collegial endeavor within not only one's home department and university, but throughout the profession.

I am drawing here on my varied administrative experience as Freshman English director (University of New Mexico), Writing Director (College of William and Mary), English department chair (Virginia Commonwealth University), and currently, endowed chair of writing (University of Connecticut), as well as vice-president and president of Writing Program Administrators. The contexts of my work have probably been fairly typical for WPAs trained in literature or literature/language/rhetoric programs, for everyplace I've taught has hired me, as a specialist in both writing and literature, to bridge that gap and to infuse professional knowledge of writing into a fairly conventional, traditional literary curriculum. One other personal note: a wise administrator once told me that he thought five years was long enough for most administrative positions. "It takes a year to learn the new job," he said, "two years to invent changes, and two more years to get them into place. After that you get wedded to the status quo and are much less willing to shake things up." Except for my current position, which is infinitely varied by day, week, and month, my own experience has proven him right. I offer this philosophy well aware that a number of career WPAs are brilliant, innovative exceptions to this rule; they are not only among my best friends, but the profession's.

Training Teachers

A writing director can and should take charge of training those who teach in the writing program. In every place where this has been my responsibility it has meant making a major difference in changing the departmental expectations, and hence the institution's, of what a writing program is and what it can be expected to do. If the department's practice has been to dragoon a literary specialist into serving as writing director for a limited period of indenture, it is not surprising that the job would be treated as, at best, routine paper-pushing, student-sorting, teacher-assigning; at worst, the site of the scenarios from hell sketched with dramatic economy by Anson and colleagues. With more people trained in composition and rhetoric now taking WPA jobs, either alternative may become as rare as a Model T Ford. Here's why.

A knowledgeable WPA can make a significant change in the tradition of amateurism in teaching writing that has prevailed in English departments ever since the Harvard Committees of the 1890s "shaped the nature of composition studies" by concentrating on "the most obvious mechanical features of writing" which it was assumed that anyone could teach without specialized training (Gere in Bloom et al. forthcoming). Put simply, to teach writing in ways that draw on current research and pedagogical theory requires teachers themselves to have a passing familiarity with the following:

- rhetorical theory and history, classical through contemporary
- literary theory, including deconstruction, post-structuralism, feminism, Marxism, reader-response, postmodernism—and various subsets of each
- characteristic research methods in composition studies, ranging from criticism to case studies, "classical" experimental models, teacher-research, and assessment models (from holistic scoring to portfolio evaluation)
- the genres of creative nonfiction
- other disciplines, their assumptions, perspectives, and characteristic research methodologies, including stylistics, criticism, linguistics, philosophy, ethnography, computer science, and pedagogy

By "familiarity" I mean not just a casual flirtation with a few "names," but sufficient acquaintance to be able to read with comprehension and comfort the major journals and other publications in the field. The section titles of the newest publication on my desk, *Composition Theory for the Postmodern Classroom*, Olson and Dobrin's compilation of articles from the past decade of *Journal of Advanced Composition*, illustrate this point: "The Process of Writing," "Theory and the Teaching of Writing," "The Essay and Composition Theory," "Gender, Culture, and Radical Pedagogy," and "Rhetoric, Philosophy, and Discourse." "Gender, Culture, and Radical Pedagogy" includes such chapters as "Sexism in Academic Styles of Learning," "Paolo Freire and the Politics of Postcolonialism," "The Dialectic Suppression of Feminist Thought in Radical Pedagogy," and "Peer Response in the Multicultural Classroom." Pedagogy still modeled on handbook rules and the glories of the five paragraph theme will simply not prepare students to function in this postmodern universe of discourse.

If the teachers of composition ground what they do on a basis of theoretical and research knowledge, can the rest of the faculty be far behind? A cutting-edge contingent of composition teachers over time can and does make a major impact on even the most traditional of English departments. In a rational world, at least, their colleagues would have to cease regarding the teaching of writing with indifference or contempt and begin regarding it as a respectable and appropriate professional endeavor—particularly if the composition faculty engages in the common scholarly activities of their peers, such as research, publication, and presentations at professional meetings. The presence of this critical mass of composition faculty in turn affects the outlook and morale of the entire faculty, for whether or not a given individual teaches composition, he or she is working in a climate that respects that teaching.

Some signals of this change of climate for composition are clear:

- hiring a specialist in composition and rhetoric as the Writing Program Administrator, who in turn hires, trains, and monitors a knowledgeable staff
- awarding that person tenure—which means validating the WPA's scholarly research, and validating as well the WPA's administrative efforts—not only as "service," but as aspects of teaching and of research (see Boyer, Gere, Cambridge)
- hiring more than one specialist in composition and rhetoric to diversify curricular offerings as well as teacher training, reasoning that such faculty are no more identical than are specialists in literature and that a single generalist shouldn't be expected to do it all (cf. Trimbur in Bloom et al.)
- involving other regular full-time faculty either in teaching composition in the English department or across the curriculum, or training those who do, or both

The latter point is especially important; a WPA can't and shouldn't be expected to be the only full-time faculty member with responsibility for the way the institution teaches composition. Other faculty must be involved. The WPA can initiate or sustain a mentoring system for new composition teachers, and can make sure that colleagues participate in the mentoring process itself. Likewise, the WPA can promote awards honoring the efforts of composition teachers, and can engage faculty in determining both the criteria and the awards. The WPA can also organize faculty discussion of grading criteria, problem papers, writing curriculum and course content, and research articles on teaching writing. The dialogue that ensues in such meetings educates everyone who attends. Efforts such as these also enhance the university's demonstration of concern for undergraduate teaching, an area of neglect in many contemporary multiversities.

Influencing Graduate Education

Graduate education in composition and rhetoric can encompass much more than the training of TAs, even in a small program with limited resources. The WPA can often make a major difference in graduate education, through introducing rhetorical theory and composition research into the graduate curriculum and preliminary exam system. Beyond the requisite composition/rhetoric/writing pedagogy course for new TAs, which in itself can be quite varied, there are a host of possibilities that can accommodate a wide range of scholarly interests:

- composition and/or rhetorical theory
- history—of an aspect of rhetoric or composition
- stylistics

- pedagogy (theory, history, practice, administration)
- genre studies (including analyzing writing in other disciplines—the sciences, law, business; or textbooks)
- writing various forms of creative nonfiction, or autobiography
- empirical research
- testing and measurement
- basic or developmental writing
- ESL
- connections between reading and writing
- linguistics
- philosophy
- writing across the disciplines (or in a particular discipline)
- social constructionism; political activism

How extensively any of the areas identified above or in the previous section can be covered, and how often, depends not only on faculty resources within a given department, but on collaboration throughout the university, among individual faculty and departments. Given the fact that few campuses employ more than one or two WPAs/composition specialists, the course offerings and research possibilities of a given school can be greatly expanded through cooperation among area institutions—of higher learning, or secondary and college, or of universities with community centers etc. (see Gere, Flower, Heath re sites of learning/research in Bloom et al.). For example, the four land-grant New England universities granting doctorates in English (Connecticut, Massachusetts–Amherst, New Hampshire, Rhode Island) collaborate to make it possible for students enrolled in one institution to take courses at the others which are unavailable on their own campuses.

The presence of faculty with expertise in composition and rhetoric makes it possible for students to present work at professional meetings, publish articles, and write dissertations either in these areas, or in areas that combine rhetorical and literary studies. In addition to presentations at CCCC, NCTE, MLA, and specialized conferences on computer pedagogy and peer tutoring, student dissertation research in my own department, for example, has included the following: a theoretical analysis of "the hermeneutic and dialogic nature of rhetoric"; an exploration of "voice" in personal essays; creative nonfiction family history; historical biographical fiction; rhetorical studies of Thoreau's metaphorical use of geography, and of Hawthorne's sketches, prefaces, and essays; and an analysis of the rhetoric of physical disability in contemporary nonfiction. Interdisciplinary projects include a music thesis analyzing Renaissance music according to the form and terminology of Aristotelian rhetoric, and an English/Education dissertation on *Coaching and Judging: The Writing Teacher's Dilemma.*

An expanded scope of graduate courses and research embeds the potential benefits of broader graduate admissions criteria (to include people wanting to work in the "new" areas) and increased opportunities for graduate students to attend and present papers at professional meetings related to composition studies. The two greatest benefits are interrelated: A rise in the level of knowledgeable discussion of teaching writing, formal and informal, is parallelled by the graduates' own prospects for postgraduate employment. Gone are the days when seat-of-the-pants classroom experience was a sufficient credential for teaching writing. Without some sophistication in rhetoric and composition, most PhDs in English simply aren't competitive for those jobs with either primary or secondary emphasis on teaching writing which have comprised fifty to seventy-five percent of the MLA job listings in recent years.

Influencing Undergraduate Education

All colleges, all curricula, all courses have a pervasive complex of agendas—not only pedagogical, but social, political, institutional. Some are overt, others are so implicit or covert that teachers rarely think of them, let alone tell their students. Budgets are allocated; courses, testing programs, and writing centers are designed and staffed; textbooks are chosen and writing assignments are made to reinforce these agendas, implicit or explicit. WPAs need to understand what these agendas are, and to imagine how the multiple and perhaps conflicting perspectives of a diverse clientele will regard them. For not only is composition taught to enable students to write in particular ways at particular levels of proficiency, it is taught to serve the sponsoring institution, and in turn, the sponsors, which may be private organizations or taxpayers and boards of education. Thus individual WPAs may conceive of the curriculum as a negotiated space among varied and competing constituencies, with themselves as chief negotiators.

What do we want students to know and be able to do at what stage of their academic careers? In what ways do we want them to learn and how do we want that learning to be reinforced? Although cynics have said that it's easier to move a graveyard than to change a curriculum, the WPA can be enormously influential in determining what is taught and how, both within the English Department and across the university or university system, either through writing majors or minors or a WAC program, or both. An up-to-date WPA can ensure a state-of-the-art curriculum.

Although, contrary to popular perception, writing programs do not necessarily begin nor end with freshman composition, the WPA may need to remind administrators, who fund campus writing programs, and curriculum committees who design them, of the potential breadth and depth of a composition program and its constituent courses. Memos, meetings, and collaborative grant proposals all play a part in this generic consciousness raising. Because courses and programs are so thoroughly embedded in their own institutional contexts, I will not discuss specific curricula here, but will focus on creative ways to conceive of composition courses, basic writing through advanced composition.

The following agendas that have particular influence on students may be seen as forms of *socialization, initiation,* and *indoctrination.* Introductory writing courses in particular *socialize* new students into their new college by making them aware of their community of peers (as in peer response and peer editing groups); by showing them how to use and manage resources (such as computers and libraries as sources of holdings and of information retrieval) and time (by establishing study and writing schedules); and—usually—by insisting on writing that reproduces the surface features that society regards as the marks of an educated writer—conventional spelling, grammar, and mechanics.

Introductory or more advanced, disciplinary-based writing courses also *initiate* students into the language and values of one or more specific discourse communities—of the local student and college community, and as writers and potential workers in a particular field and in a particular format (see Cambridge). Advanced composition courses initiate their students into the profession of writing, as well. Initiation also implies *indoctrination* in the college's prevailing values and beliefs (such as the desirability of political correctness) and those of the discipline on which the course focuses (such as the virtues of collaborative writing, or networked computers, or critical—read argumentative—thinking) (cf. Trimbur, Spellmeyer). More specific aspects of indoctrination in particular disciplines include *intellectual content*—what's classic, what's passe, and what's hot in a particular field; and *aesthetic (or political) sensitivity* to the culture's prevailing standards—what books should students read? avoid? what films should they like? dislike? Under what conditions should the students' styles be short or sweet or stuffy?

Establishing or Enhancing the Institution's Reputation in Composition and Rhetoric

Professionally visible WPAs can enhance their institutions' reputation and public commitment to composition studies through the customary faculty avenues of research, participation in professional meetings, competition for grants and other funding, and encouragement of publication by faculty colleagues, graduate students—and sometimes undergraduates, as well. Recently, writing program administrators have begun to study various aspects of writing program administration—a sure sign that the profession has come of age. Research grants awarded by the Council of Writing Program Administrators in 1993 and 1994 include Wendy Bishop and Gay Lynn Crossley's ethnography of "the intellectual formation and development of WPAs within English departments"; Sheryl Fontaine's study of "how different models of administration affect the training of graduate TAs and their initiation as apprentice WPAs"; Barbara Walvoord's analysis of the impact of "departmental pressures on faculty [seeking change] after attending Writing-Across-the-Curriculum workshops"; Nedra Reynolds's examination of "how teachers are constructed through the discourses of instructors' manuals and instructors' versions of college writing textbooks"; a survey by Julia Ferganchick-Neufang, Joan Jung, and Tilly Warnock of "gender-based problems of women writing teachers and administrators"; Pat Belanoff's survey of how recent PhDs in literature "make career choices" to teach writing and concentrate professionally on composition; William Smith and Richard Bullock's "national survey of first year writing programs"; and a study of "external validation of portfolio assessment" by Michael Allen, Jeff Sommers, and Kathleen Yancey (Bizzell).

As the range of these projects indicates, research has the potential in both theory and application for pinpointing administrative and instructional needs, problems, and solutions. Articulating these can enable institutions and administrators (including WPAs) to set priorities for funding, and for implementing programs and staff. The knowledge gained from research can improve the WPA's ability to do good work, in administration, textbook selection, teacher instruction, and assessment, among other areas. Such research efforts and programmatic improvements—disseminated through professional meetings and publications as well as through the institution's public relations media—enhance the reputation of both the program and the institution.

Professionally active WPAs can also make a difference in the field through leadership in national professional organizations, participation in national or regional seminars and workshops, and establishment of relations, formal and informal, with other universities and community enterprises. WPAs, organization mavens all, even love to organize each other; areas where they congregate are populated with state and regional WPA conferences (in addition to the national annual WPA Workshop and Conference); and a host of meetings devoted to composition, rhetoric, and teaching writing, such as the conferences at Penn State, Wyoming, San Diego, and the University of New Hampshire.

Yet no WPA can do it all, or do it all alone. Butterflies are not free from constraints. For creativity to flourish, WPAs need the time and energy to focus on research and ideas for imaginative teaching, rather than on being chronically bogged down in the energy-depleting intricacies of administrative minutiae, such as the intricacies of scheduling or whether the locks on the adjuncts' office doors will work. That way be monsters! WPAs can help to ensure the survival of their creativity by reinforcing the importance of writing in their institutions' priorities—an activity that in itself may require considerable creativity. High priority for writing programs translates into continuous, guaranteed year-round funding for personnel (including year-round administrative and secretarial assistance), space, equipment, and supplies. This level of support should do much to avoid the traumas of last-minute hiring and curricular change, and the climate that transforms otherwise creative people into drudges-of-all-work (see Bloom, 1992; Holbrook).

Creative WPAs might be called, in T.E. Lawrence's terms, "the dreamers of the day," "dangerous people, for they may act their dream with open eyes to make it possible." It is appropriate, realistic, and necessary to conceive of writing program administrators as initiators of change, rather than merely as reactors to the dark straight slashes of either the status quo or retrogression. The creative, soaring butterfly aspects of writing program administration are expressed through the dynamic, inextricably interwoven activities of training teachers, influencing graduate and undergraduate education, and contributing to the research and other ongoing dialogue of the profession—in the university, the community, the world.

Works Cited

Anson, Chris M., Joan Graham, David A. Jolliffe, Nancy S. Shapiro, Carolyn H. Smith. *Scenarios for Teaching Writing: Contexts for Discussion and Reflective Practice.* Urbana, IL: NCTE, 1993.

Bizzell, Patricia. Letter to Lynn Z. Bloom, 22 March 1994.

Bloom, Lynn Z. "I Want a Writing Director." *College Composition and Communication* 43.2 (1992): 176–78.

Boyer, Ernest L. *Scholarship Reconsidered: Priorities of the Professoriate.* Princeton: Carnegie Foundation, 1990.

Cambridge, Barbara. "Identifying the Impact of a Writing Program on an Institution." CCCC Convention. Nashville, 17 March, 1994.

Flower, Linda. "Literate Action." *Composition in the 21st Century: Crisis and Change.* Ed. Lynn Z. Bloom, Donald A. Daiker, and Edward M. White. Carbondale, IL: Southern Illinois UP, forthcoming 1995.

Gere, Anne Ruggles. "The Long Revolution in Composition." *Composition in the 21st Century: Crisis and Change.* Ed. Lynn Z. Bloom, Donald A. Daiker, and Edward M. White. Carbondale, IL: Southern Illinois UP, forthcoming 1995.

Heath, Shirley Brice. "Work, Class, and Categories: Dilemmas of Identity." *Composition in the 21st Century: Crisis and Change.* Ed. Lynn Z. Bloom, Donald A. Daiker, and Edward M. White. Carbondale, IL: Southern Illinois UP, forthcoming 1995.

Holbrook, Sue Ellen. "Women's Work: The Feminizing of Composition." *Rhetoric Review* 9.2 (1991): 201–29.

Olson, Gary A. and Sidney I. Dobrin, Eds. *Composition Theory for the Postmodern Classroom.* Albany, NY: State University of New York P, 1994.

Spellmeyer, Kurt. *Common Ground: Dialogue, Understanding, and the Teaching of Composition.* Englewood Cliffs, NJ: Prentice Hall, 1993.

Trimbur, John. "Writing Instruction and the Politics of Professionalization." *Composition in the 21st Century: Crisis and Change.* Ed. Lynn Z. Bloom, Donald A. Daiker, and Edward M. White. Carbondale, IL: Southern Illinois UP, forthcoming 1995.

6

Recruiting and Retraining Experienced Teachers
Balancing Game Plans in an Entrepreneurial Force-Field

Ellen Strenski
University of California–Irvine

The notion of field presupposes that one break away from the real-
ist representation which leads one to reduce the effect of the milieu
to the effect of the direct action that takes place in any interaction.
It is the structure of the constitutive relations of the space of the
field which determines the forms that can be assumed by the visible
relations of interaction and the very content of the experience that
agents may have of them.

Pierre Bourdieu (192)

A WPA need not turn to French social theorist Pierre Bourdieu to sense the
complexities of the force-field generated in any writing program. But writing
programs do illustrate perfectly his analysis of institutional arrangements where
"the practical or theoretical relation that agents have with the game is part of the
game and may be at the root of its transformation" (194). Entrusted with ad-
vancing its institution's mission for general education, constrained by less iner-
tia than are traditional academic departments with their permanent faculties and
standing committees throughout the institution, marginalized by its anomalous
quasi-service, quasi-disciplinary status, and endowed with minimal FTE and
other resources, any writing program is an unstable, dynamic force-field full of

conflict and opportunity whose agents are working out very different game plans. Recognizing these differences is the first step towards, if not reconciling, then at least calculating their impact and thereby managing them.

Game plans of individual teachers may differ from each other's, from the WPA's, and from the institution's that the WPA represents. Differ, and clash. For example, some writing instructors are waiting for a literature job to open up in their fields. Others want the on-the-job-training in composition that will make them more marketable. Others want to be in that particular location in order to make contacts with local journalists or creative writers, or to seek consulting jobs in industry. And still others, with little mobility, are simply grateful for a pay check. These and other, different personal goals thereby shape different perceptions of the interaction between the teaching cadre and its administrators and also the interaction among instructors. Hence the relevance of the opening quotation from Bourdieu. Managing the resulting clash, intensified by conflicting—if not incompatible—pedagogical beliefs and practices, is the WPA's challenge and responsibility.

Beyond the clash of individuals within the writing program force-field, the writing program itself often clashes with the institution's sense of itself, its mission and priorities. Although evolving, writing programs are notoriously impermanent (with such notable exceptions as Syracuse University), often materializing as a response to a "writing crisis" which, it is believed, will go away, as should the writing program, when the public schools "get the message" and improve the undergraduates-to-be in their charge, or when their own "real" faculty assume more responsibility for students' general education and literacy. Facing ambiguous standards of quality and unusual markers of achievement (for instance, the possible claim to research originality by co-authors of writing textbooks), universities and their promotion and tenure committees would rather not deal with the anomalies represented by writing instructors who seem to be providing a "service" by teaching "skills," not professing a legitimate discipline.

No one will dispute that writing programs are uneasy places. "Marginal," usually pejorative, is a common description. Yet this very marginality is the major source of the energy in the writing program force-field. Although it can be a convenient excuse for neglect, this marginality—this different, anomalous status—can also render a writing program a very valuable resource for its institution as a change agent. Edges can be cutting; they can be dangerous, exciting places.

Cultural anthropologists have remarked on this kind of liminal phenomenon, for instance, Victor Turner's well-known analysis of the potency of liminality, or Mary Douglas's explanation of institutional threat responses to polluting presences perceived as dangerous. Writing instructors are exactly such presences. They deal with uncleanness, that is, students' incompetence, not just ignorance. Ignorance is respectable; incompetence is shameful. Undergraduates' incompetence, their difficulties with writing, tend to be perceived as unfortunate problems that need to be fixed somehow by writing instructors. Other faculty address students' ignorance, which is a different problem, less polluting because it calls, not for repair, but for the information "professed" by these other instructors. As a result, universities are necessarily caught in an uneasy if not unwelcome death embrace with the large cadres of instructors required to provide even minimal, labor-intensive composition courses.

The WPA is caught in the middle of all this, more so than the chair of any department, necessarily mediating instructors' clashing career and other personal goals and needs on the one hand, and campus administrators' sense of wider programmatic need and institutional obligation on the other hand. The potentials of the resulting force-field—for self-destruction as well as for innovative reform—are exacerbated in high prestige, usually urban, research universities. These institutions often recruit ABDs and PhDs for full-time positions teaching writing in order to relieve the "real" faculty of that obligation and thereby provide them with more time for their research and graduate instruction. Many of the courses taught by these writing instructors are aligned with the professional schools, such as business, engineering, law, and medicine, that help define the modern research university. These instructors are decidedly non-tenurable, and, once hired, they must often compete with each other for available continuing positions. Writing programs with a critical mass of such instructors will be the subject of this chapter.

The problem is this: Writing programs are institutional units continually undergoing change. They *must* change. In addition to being new academic units still searching for compelling theoretical justifications and disciplinary models, writing programs are designated outriders for their institutions that in turn must respond to changing circumstances—everything from new funding sources to new technology to new populations of students to the changing visions of new chief administrators. How can a WPA best manage these changes, first of all by enticing the best instructors to join his or her writing program, bringing the best intelligence, energy, and willingness to invest in this often temporary job? Then what kind of professional development can a WPA foster that can begin to compensate for the lack of job security and traditional markers of professional achievement? The simple but not easy answer to these questions is an entrepreneurial model that explains this marginal situation as one involving risk yet also offering the possibility of valuable returns on agents' investment of their time, imagination, and creativity.

This entrepreneurial model may displease some WPAs and writing instructors who entertain different models of the academy. Some others, for instance, perceive the university as a haven of scholarly enquiry and aspire to departmental organization and tenurable rank for composition studies comparable to that legitimizing traditional disciplines. Others would like to see rank and security of employment for writing instructors conferred as a reward for valued service to undergraduates. Given the present division of labor in research universities, however, these other models are fanciful. Meanwhile, an entrepreneurial model offers explanatory power and hope. It interprets the anomalous, liminal nature of a writing program as essentially dynamic, and uniquely valuable for that very energy. Such a perception of a writing program automatically reveals emerging opportunities that can be exploited by resourceful instructors, encouraged and supported by shrewd WPAs.

A cynic might consider all this futile, if not offensive, observing that two current, if not worsening conditions ensure a large pool of applicants for writing jobs: a national oversupply of new PhDs and a high concentration of competent faculty spouses who hold themselves hostage in one labor market. According to this cynic, to expect such cannon fodder, once hired, to respond to and exploit opportunities for professional development while at the same time devoting time and attention to such activities outside the classroom constitutes insult added to injury. Yet, without being a Pollyanna, a WPA can in some ways manage this force-field, determined by institutional impulses towards change, and defined by its service (as opposed to research) culture, in order to reconcile and even advance individual, programmatic, and institutional game plans. To describe such is the purpose of this chapter.

Consider these two very different writing instructors who share an office in a large, urban, public research university: Adam and Eve.

Scenario

Adam is twenty-eight, a new PhD from a respectable midwestern university. This is his first job. His degree is in literature, but he did take some graduate courses in rhetoric and composition beyond his recent preparation to be a teaching assistant, which was in itself good solid training. He is interested in composition and has published one article in composition that grew out of a graduate paper. Thanks to some good advice from that seminar's professor, Adam sees tangible career benefits from working up a demonstrable competence in teaching composition.

Eve is forty-eight, married to a faculty member in the Economics Department, and has one young child. She has a PhD in literature from a prestigious Ivy League university, and almost twenty years ago published several New Critical articles on Victorian novels that reworked parts of her dissertation. Eve has had several similar writing jobs at various other universities as she accompanied her husband from place to place, and she cannot avoid comparing her present position to her husband's lighter teaching load, higher salary, job security, and other perks. Eve makes more money than does Adam because she has been in the program longer and has thereby accumulated more merit increases over these years.

Eve resents Adam for his mobility (partially predicated on his youth and gender), his credentials in composition, for his familiarity with recent trends in literary and composition theory, and for his energy. She feels threatened by him and sees him as an ambitious prima donna. Meanwhile Adam, overhearing Eve on the telephone speaking Spanish to her child's nanny, envies Eve's standard of living. Adam spends weekends in the library, while Eve is enjoying her beach house. He also resents having to take the scheduling leftovers— Eve cannot teach before 10 a.m. because she has to drive her child to school. Traditionally presumed to be unencumbered, Adam is expected to teach the 8 o'clock classes. Because in his writing program there are more instructors like Eve, Adam also feels outnumbered, as if the Eves had ganged up on him.

Given their personal and professional situations, these two instructors are already disposed to dislike each other. Another notable ingredient fueling their antagonism, and additionally charging the force-field of their writing program in a special way, is their contempt for each other's pedagogical allegiances. Adam and Eve embody two of the six profiles of writing instructors analyzed by Edward M. White in *Developing Successful College Writing Programs* (38–55): literature, peer workshop, individualized writing lab, text-based rhetoric, basic skills, and service course. White's exhaustive study of over 400 composition teachers in the California State University system revealed that their beliefs and practices tended to cluster automatically into six different "patterns of instruction" (41).

Briefly, Adam subscribes to the peer workshop approach. When he was a TA he had been impressed by some of Peter Elbow's ideas about collaboration, and on the basis of a persuasive seminar paper he wrote was given permission to use an Elbow textbook in his own writing classes. Encouraged by his success with this textbook, Adam has continued to involve his writing students in a great deal of peer and group editing and other collaborative activities. He is concerned that students learn to use the writing process for self-discovery and understanding, and to further this aim he assigns personal journals and he stresses invention skills such as prewriting, clustering, brainstorming, using matrices, and other heuristics to enhance the creative process. Students in Adam's class generate material to write about from their own experiences; their writing is considered effective when its authenticity compels attention from other members of the class through various stylistic devices; and the classroom is deliberately student-centered. Adam uses this approach no matter what the specific level of student or course description. For example, his upper division technical writing students work in teams to generate proposals addressing problems on campus such as inadequate parking, just as his moonlit community college freshman composition course students work in groups to investigate gender bias in advertisements that together they determine to be offensive.

Eve is equally loyal to a particular pedagogy, but in White's terms, hers is the literature approach. Eve believes equally passionately that students should learn to read great literature and emulate it in their own prose. She is proud of her own expertise, and feels a strong professional obligation both to share its refined and subtle classifications with her students and to encourage students to develop their own analytical appreciation and hence to love literature, too. She dismisses her students' interest in popular culture, for example, ruling out their parallels between "Dr. Quinn, Medicine Woman" and heroines in the nineteenth century novels she sometimes assigns. Eve tries always to include literary readings in her writing courses and reserves for herself the professional right to grade rigorously students' writing about these literary texts. For example, due to a colleague's sudden resignation, Eve found herself assigned to teach an upper division course for pre-med majors. Undaunted by one of the syllabus' announced assignments of a personal statement, of the kind submitted to graduate admission committees, Eve has stipulated for this unit that her students read and discuss not only William Carlos Williams' *Autobiography*, but some of his poetry as well. Eve's students do not work in groups. They write traditional essays that include considerable *explication de texte*. And Eve is often heard complaining proudly about the stacks of student papers that she has been "correcting."

So, Eve believes that Adam is a lazy faddist, an opportunist who has betrayed his dubious professional training. Adam believes Eve is a tyrant, abusing her authority to maintain a hegemonic and discredited set of values. Moreover, Adam and Eve have colleagues that embody the other four, equally incompatible, approaches identified by White. When these instructors all find themselves competing for scarce continuing positions, the conflict is exacerbated. This academic conflict is so conspicuously acerbic and baffling to outsiders that it has even caught the public's eye. For example, writing about freshman composition in a *New York Times* special education report, "In-Your-Faceism vs. Light," journalist Joshua Mills recently remarked on "this abundance of ire" (19), "this surprising spleen" (19), exhibited by college writing teachers.

Faculty in other departments also disagree with each other, of course. However, it is worth acknowledging how the faculty in writing programs differ systematically in this respect from faculty in other academic departments. In writing programs, theoretical approach and pedagogical practice do not co-vary with course taught. Although they bring to their teaching very different values, expectations, and pedagogical practices, Adam, Eve, and their colleagues, no matter which of these six pedagogical approaches they may prefer, all teach courses with the same catalog descriptions, at all levels (basic to advanced). They are all expected to be able to teach all kinds of writing courses (from academically or personally esoteric to applied vocational) in classes both large and small. What goes on in one section—kinds of assignments, possible topics, grading practices, for example—may be very different from what happens in another section of the same course taught by a colleague with different assumptions about the teaching task. Although very different one from another, these approaches are not necessarily incoherent given the six different sets of bedrock beliefs that inform them, but they surface randomly in the courses taught by the writing instructors who espouse them.

However, in other departments, say sociology, although the ethnomethodologists are far removed in theoretical affiliation and method from the statisticians or the historians, it is the ethnomethodologists who *always* teach, or at least prefer to teach, the courses in conversational analysis, and the historians who *always* teach the courses in Marx and Durkheim, not the other way around. So, too, the pedagogical approaches of the ethnomethodologists and the historians or statisticians differ appropriately from each other. The ethnomethodologists may assign their own kind of classroom activities, say, requiring students to conduct structured observations; the historians, too, assign specifically suitable textual analyses of classics in sociological theory; the statisticians require students to generate and manipulate numerical data. In other words, in sociology, instructors' pedagogical practices complement the methodological principles informing their particular disciplinary specialties. They bring different pedagogical approaches to the teaching of their own specialties, for which they were hired, and they don't teach each other's courses. The authority, credentials, and pedagogical choices conferred on these other faculty are certified by their specific academic preparation, graduate courses on their transcripts, theses, dissertations, and subsequent publications.

On the other hand, the six kinds of writing instructors can be found teaching all kinds of courses using any number of pedagogical techniques and curriculum materials. Adam and Eve, for instance, often teach different sections of the same course, yet teach them very differently. Although writing instructors' tastes and preferences may be shaped, as were Adam's, by a haphazard acquaintance with specific academic readings or mentors, their *expertise* is derived from various other grounds besides the rather rudimentary instruction in composition theory that most writing teachers have received as TAs. For example, their expertise may be informed by experience in technical or medical editing, creative writing, journalism, public school teaching, or simple on-the-job experience and professional development activities once they begin teaching composition. Clearly, a traditional English degree in literary study prepares instructors for only one approach (literature) of White's six categories. Yet, once they begin teaching, writing instructors evolve for whatever reasons into passionate, often splenetic, adherents of five additional, different approaches. Managing these differences begins with recruiting the instructors who embody them.

Entrepreneurial Opportunities

From an applicant's point of view, what could possibly attract an instructor to teach in this inevitably contentious writing program in the first place? A variety of real institutional incentives do capitalize on the writing program's anomalous, marginalized nature and its impulse towards change. They include heightened attention to classroom teaching performance; textbook publishing; the development of other curriculum materials including videotapes and computer software; participating in campus seminars, colloquia, and institutes; access to technology such as the Internet; collaboration on interinstitutional projects with community college and high school colleagues; and administrative experience. The impermanence, so resented by non-tenurable teachers, and the program's hybrid status in the institution, can also offer opportunities to the entrepreneurial teacher who will associate with this dynamic of mobility and take deliberate advantage of it.

Large, usually urban research universities with sizable writing programs can offer the equivalent of a post-doctoral apprenticeship, or breathing space, which appeals to two distinct groups: new PhDs and writing instructors, often older, with applied experience in high school teaching; journalism; editing; desktop publishing; or technical, medical, or business writing. The prestige of affiliating with such an institution works for any department or program to attract applicants on the "I'd rather be a citizen of Rome than emperor of a dunghill" principle. The *MLA Job Information List* continues to advertise more composition teaching jobs than jobs teaching literature, and more people are eligible for these composition positions.

Unlike most highly competitive searches in literature to select the tenurable assistant professor who will be the least expensive, most promising investment within traditionally defined fields such as Victorian novel or Romantic poetry, writing programs' continually changing curricula require continually renewed expertise. For example, although new critical tools may illuminate Trollope, few methodological innovations affecting the criticism and teaching of the Victorian novel have had the dramatic technological impact of, say, word processing on revision, Internet access on conducting research, or computers on the emerging genre of e-mail. These latter changes are the special province of writing instructors who teach research paper courses or who use networked classrooms. So, too, although literary scholars of genre may modify their understandings of the novel, the impulse to do so is not nearly so urgent as the pressure on composition instructors to help students understand and master a repertoire of emerging genres in professional writing, for example, patient case histories in medicine or proposals in business and engineering—common kinds of upper division writing courses in research universities.

Correspondingly, composition instructors' new expertise can be demonstrated in additional and different ways from those offered by the more conventional applicants for literature positions, all of which results in a wider variety of age, degrees, and experience in a typical writing program's faculty profile. Not only is this job market more open, but the very diversity of the results can be an added appeal for an applicant seeking professional stimulus. The different faculty profile within an urban research university's writing program is reflected in its different student body. America's cities are increasingly diverse—linguistically, ethnically, racially. The richness of the one as a working environment mirrors the richness of the other.

Even in those institutions that require instructors to teach from a common set of textbooks, the pressures to accommodate students from diverse and changing constituencies can impel imaginative and creative teaching. Given the division of labor at research universities, WPAs can authoritatively claim exemplary teaching as the special province of the writing program that, in turn, deserves to be institutionally appreciated and rewarded. The service of teaching undergraduates to become better writers is not ignoble, even if not tenurable. Research universities, responding to public criticism, need to be able to demonstrate good teaching. Writing programs provide such an illustration, real, even if unfortunately by default as other faculty abdicate this obligation, responding to the other, different pressures on them to pursue research and scholarly publication. A major opportunity, then, exists for writing instructors and their WPAs to seize this moral high ground about teaching.

Writing instruction is increasingly being scrutinized for several reasons (Strenski). Such scrutiny is, first of all, part of a broad institutional response to the national reform movement to improve college teaching. Second, the levelling effect of a lack of rank—remember that Adam and Eve and all their colleagues are lecturers—results in a common, collectively marginal identity. All such lecturers have the same self-interest in maintaining a corporate campus identity of excellent teaching in the writing program, and are thereby willing to invest effort in formative review of their peers' teaching. Third, not so benignly, with the increasingly adversarial relationship induced by collective bargaining and budget stringencies, non-tenurable faculty, like writing program lecturers, are increasingly subject to summative assessment. In any case, the culture of a writing program is informed primarily by the central activity of teaching (as opposed to expertise in professing a disciplinary subject), and as a result writing program instructors must be perceived by undergraduates as good teachers who care about teaching.

This preoccupation with teaching shapes such writing programs into institutional seedbeds of textbook development, another form of entrepreneurial activity. For example, in 1990, more than half the forty lecturers in the UCLA Writing Programs had contracts with major publishing companies to write or revise composition textbooks. Such imaginative and creative teaching can also be codified into other publications, such as local *Instructor's Guides*, and into conference papers. Without the pressures to publish their "research," non-tenurable writing instructors can give their full attention to writing textbooks and pedagogical articles based on their classroom experiences and the opportunities in these classrooms to experiment and pre-test instructional materials.

This very advantage can also, of course, contribute to program conflict. Reconsider Adam and Eve. Each has worked up well-received courses. Each invests much time and thought during the summer in refining well-received, imaginative, and effective sequences of readings and assignments for their versions of these courses, however different their pedagogical practices may be. Not surprisingly, each has a book contract. Each feels he or she "owns" that course or version of it, and expects to be assigned to teach it as often as possible. Given their radically different pedagogical beliefs, neither wants to teach the other's course or version of it. But Adam and Eve have colleagues, some new hires, who do want to get involved in whatever it may be—scientific or business writing, teacher training, basic writing pedagogy, etc. Balkanization of the writing program—a proliferation of "special topics" courses representing the different interests and strengths of its faculty—is possible only to a certain extent. Teaching requests justified by who got there first and staked a claim to the course can be perceived by newcomers as an unjust claim to entitlement.

Another major attraction of teaching in such a writing program is the opportunity to acquire administrative experience. Given a writing program's hybrid character and anomalous but tentacular relationship with the rest of the university, numerous opportunities exist to serve on committees and work groups that address the needs of transfer students, minority and underrepresented students, faculty in other departments engaged in writing across the curriculum, graduate student instructors in other departments, relations with high schools, etc. These committees may not be the officially sanctioned ones comprised of university senate members, but they can still offer the writing instructor early and valuable administrative experience that his or her literature counterpart, struggling to publish enough scholarly articles to get tenure, may see only as a burden.

A miscellaneous collection of perquisites is in principle available readily to writing teachers. Once hired, then, writing instructors can take advantage of a range of professional opportunities. But given the instability of writing programs that inevitably renders them change agents, how can a WPA hire appropriate instructors in the first place, that is, instructors who will seize these opportunities, deriving a positive return to themselves and benefiting their institutions?

Recruitment: Matching Instructor's Approach, Institutional Mission, and Programmatic Need

From a WPA's point of view, which applicants are the most attractive candidates? As White convincingly demonstrates, "There is no single best approach to the teaching of writing under all circumstances and with all students" (*Developing* 54). A program or institution that expects to get a generic best composition instructor, either through initial recruitment or through retraining later, is chasing a will-o'-the-wisp. Each of the six approaches White identifies is better at some aspects of teaching composition than others. The problem, then, is how to create and support the best cadre of individual writing teachers who professionally are very different from one another—a difference much more marked and problematic than with an otherwise comparable group of instructors in an academic department. Addressing this problem involves calculating optimal arrangements for first finding, and then developing, the most appropriate instructors in order to advance the program's or the institution's mission. In the absence of timeless articulated goals, the challenge then becomes getting the most comprehensibly responsive set of instructors who can best meet the widest range of students' needs, given the institution's current writing curriculum.

These calculations in turn involve first recognizing the strengths represented by instructors' differences and then institutionalizing ways to protect and enhance these strengths—good administrative stewardship.

The approaches embodied in Adam and Eve (like the other four approaches identified by White) clearly further the aims of different constituencies and institutional arrangements. For example, Eve's literature approach is most easily accommodated in the belletristic tradition of an English department; Adam's peer workshop, in a writing program or a writing center. So, too, the other four approaches, for instance, the basic skills approach in a vocational context, or the service course approach with writing across the curriculum. The point is that these six approaches identified by White complement different missions, and it is the WPA's responsibility in recruitment to try to match up approach and mission, given that different constituencies on and off the same campus express decided preferences for different approaches.[1]

How can a WPA calculate ways to match up the recruitment of different kinds of writing instructors with different institutional needs? Consider the advertisements for composition jobs, which differ significantly from ads for literature jobs. Ads for literature positions are much more specific and detailed, reflecting a refined disciplinary classification system, whereas ads for composition jobs tend to be vague. Compare, for example, these ads from various recent issues of the *Chronicle of Higher Education*:

1. Generic literature

   "Assistant Professor, tenure-track, in seventeenth century English literature, with Ph.D. in hand and dissertation or significant publications preferably on poetry or prose of the period."

2. Generic Composition
   "Rhetoric/Composition Specialist, to teach writing courses beginning fall. Ph.D. in rhetoric/composition or related area, experience teaching writing and involvement in scholarly activities required."

3. Hybrid
   "Primary responsibilities: freshman composition and sophomore-level humanities courses (Homer, Virgil, Dante, Shakespeare, Pope, Wordsworth)."

Note the parenthesis in the last example: "(Homer et al.)." What if the committee members had wanted to buy a longer ad? What information might they have put into a comparable descriptive parenthesis to balance the composition responsibilities? The point is that there is no easy answer, an observation which is reflected in the current debate about whether or not composition studies is a discrete discipline, and, if so, what exactly it is. In the absence of any resolution of this larger debate, the default position in composition is to appeal to experience, even as in one ad, "two years of full-time, paid teaching experience." But the "experience" option is an untheorized blur, a regress back before the experience to formative influences in graduate school, from office mates, readings, or other sources.

Just in this haphazard way, Adam and Eve were hired as lecturers to teach composition in the same department, responding, indeed, to the same generic ad. They now share the same office, but they are dramatically different teachers. Unlike the new recruit in seventeenth century, whose expertise in poetry or prose complements his seventeenth century colleague's expertise in drama and whose expertise is acknowledged and respected, Adam and Eve, beneath their surface cordiality over such matters as whose desk the telephone stands on, see each other respectively as dilettante and traitor. And remember, Adam and Eve have colleagues in the same office who embody the other four approaches identified by White. No wonder that the seeming incoherence of instructional practice within a Writing Program is often baffling. But these differences are not necessarily disastrous. These dangers can be minimized, in the first place, through careful recruitment. This is not to say that Adam and Eve should not have been hired, but only that this potentially fruitful and potentially painful conjunction could have been better managed at the time of their recruitment.

It is worth repeating that the key concept in the careful recruitment of composition instructors is a match—the best match possible of applicant predilection and potential with institutional mission—not the usual, simpler prestige contest. Indeed, the recruitment process in composition, like a department review, can be an opportunity to prompt just this kind of reflection about the aims of the writing program, and like a department review it is enhanced by the presence of a member from outside the writing program. Such an outsider on the hiring committee requires a public translation and practical elaboration of otherwise potentially arcane shorthand ("He's assigning *Revising Prose*," "She teaches proofreading," "He conferences with the edit groups," "She doesn't assign any textbooks"). "So what?" the outside member can ask, soliciting answers that necessarily reveal the beliefs held by those presently responsible for writing instruction. And it is these beliefs, in light of whatever can be established of the institution's hope for its writing program (to further the liberal aims of general education, preparation for jobs or graduate school or general good citizenship or self-discovery, preparation for the English major, etc.), that operate best to select a short list of candidates to interview.

Interviewing candidates to teach writing is different from interviewing candidates to teach in other academic departments. In other departments, for example Sociology, the hiring committee is concerned to judge the solidity and appropriateness of the candidates' academic preparation—what courses they took and from whom and where, as well as what courses they have developed and taught that could be imported as new or replacement components in the hiring institution's course offerings. Whether the candidate will end up teaching sociology courses like "Durkheim and Other Major Sociological Theorists," for instance, or "Occupations and Professions" or whatever other specialties are advertised, or whether the candidate will assign reading journals, peer groups, content analyses, field work, library research, fiction, or statistical compilation and analysis matters much less than the institution's confidence in the minimum requirement that the candidate knows enough about these aspects of sociology—the counterparts in sociology of seventeenth century poetry in English—to teach them well. The same concern obviously does not apply to composition, given that TAs, as Adam and Eve had been, are often entrusted in their first year of graduate school with teaching freshman composition.

What information about candidates that can be established in an interview is most useful to a hiring committee? Information that will identify their affiliation with one of the six categories posited by White. Why? Because this affiliation will determine their pedagogical practice over which they have any choice—textbooks, assignments, grading. Once his or her position has been identified, any candidate can be questioned about how he or she would both exploit this position's strengths and compensate for its weaknesses. For instance, Adam could be challenged about his reliance on personal journal writing given Cooper and MacDonald's research findings that students so prepared do worse on their other college assignments; Eve could be asked how she expects students to transfer the skills of literary analysis to the analysis of other texts and to kinds of analytical academic papers that she requires of students in her own composition courses. Interviews are not only opportunities for the hiring committee to ask questions; they are occasions that set a tone, a climate for subsequent professional behavior, and that ought not to be squandered. A hiring committee that centers its questions around the situating of candidates within these six categories cuts to the quick. So much for the principle of interviewing. How can it be accomplished in practice?

Several means enable this exchange of valuable information, especially candidates' responses to a sample student paper and candidates' syllabi. Beforehand, candidates should be sent a typical student paper with its accompanying assignment. The paper should be not too good, not too bad, and candidates should be asked to read and think about it as a draft and to bring it to the interview. Once in the interview they can then be asked how they would help the student writer improve this draft—surely a central responsibility for any writing instructor. This task elicits a range of telling responses, from the candidates who are ready to do a New Critical or deconstructive analysis of the student text, to the candidates who arrive with a grade and many copy editing marks on the student paper, to the candidates who role-play an imaginary conference with the student writer about his or her paper. Like a kind of ink blot, the sample student paper reveals a great deal about the candidate's pedagogical values and practices.

So, too, candidates' syllabi are revealing, and candidates can be asked to bring them to the interview and then to gloss them. Many graduate student candidates have no control over readings and assignments in the course syllabi they have been hired to teach. But they can be asked what they would change if they had the opportunity, and why they would want to do so. Every aspect of a syllabus can be reviewed for its effectiveness in helping students become better writers—the common goal of any composition course. Moreover, a syllabus created by any candidate, as opposed to a departmental syllabus from which everyone teaches, can indicate organizational and rhetorical skills or lack thereof that bode well or ill in someone who may be hired to teach these skills.

The extent to which writing instructors themselves can be expected to be good writers, just as a professor of neurosurgery is expected to be an able physician, a professor of architecture a good designer, or a professor of mathematics a good mathematician, is unresolved (Strenski). A good professor of kinesiology, after all, may be a poor athlete; or a professor of art history, a poor artist. This issue, beyond the scope of this essay, is nonetheless worth the hiring committee's time to tease out, because discussion about it quickly reveals members' fundamental beliefs about the place of a writing program in its institution and therefore the most appropriate kinds of new hires. How the committee defines "good writing" and "good writer," and the presumed or demonstrated relationship of candidates' writing ability to their pedagogical promise, will color the program's developing sense of its purposes and its subsequent achievements.

Once hired, a new writing instructor joins a pedagogical melee, adding an additional, potentially divisive ingredient simply by behaving according to the principles informing his or her preferred approach to teaching. How can a WPA subsequently help instructors accommodate, and even respect, each other's differences? The answer, again simple but not easy, is to arrange practical occasions for such meetings of minds.

Retraining: Incentives, Motives, and Means

Incentives (and disincentives) to change the practices of writing instruction on a campus are to some extent part and parcel of a wider institutional imperative (or failure to try) to improve teaching in general, and differ only, as analyzed above, in that the beliefs underpinning writing instructors' practices may be more intractably incommensurable than those of faculty in other disciplines. How then can different colleagues in a writing program learn effectively from each other and thereby enlarge their ideological affiliations in order to accommodate alternatives? How can these different pedagogical beliefs be exploited for mutual enrichment and reinvention? The administrative problem is one of arranging opportunities for these beliefs to materialize for inspection and assessment outside of class, and thereby to import knowledge into the writing program without recycling the faculty.

One means, of course, is the WPA's review of individuals' teaching performance (Hult). A second means is focused group reading and discussion of key theoretical texts in a faculty reading group. The most important ingredient here is a carefully selected reading list—material expressing the potential for common ground and an ecumenical vision rather than an individual, deliberately divisive agenda—for example, not Susan Miller's *Textual Carnivals* (which might be read very usefully in some other context) but Richard Beach's recent *A Teacher's Introduction to Reader-Response Theories*. All writers must read and all writing instructors must necessarily contend with reading in their courses to some degree, since at the least students must read their own drafts, so Beach's book is relevant for such faculty development. His book acknowledges a number of different models of reading (the psychological, historical, etc.) and presents them as essentially complementary, not competing, thereby inviting individual instructors to supplement the author's account with information from their own experience—a precondition for sharing it.

Of course, some instructors, perhaps Eve, may simply be unwilling to attend regular meetings of such a reading group. She already believes that she knows how to read texts, and that others, like Adam, are simply wrong. However, Eve recognizes the value of a teaching portfolio when she is being scrutinized for reappointment. Such a portfolio needs to include concrete examples of her teaching effectiveness, and Eve will want to present and gloss these examples in the most attractively compelling way possible to impress her audience of peers and WPA. Her own self-interest will therefore recommend that she attend such events as the reading group in order to get information on the basis of which she will be able to make this kind of effective presentation.

Hence, even more productive for professional development are occasions when faculty meet, not just to discuss their different pedagogical approaches in some specific context, for example relating them to reader response theories, but to *do* something—make decisions and perhaps produce some document codifying these practices. Participating as a member of a personnel peer review committee or a hiring committee is just such an activity. For example, Adam and Eve and the WPA of their writing program, at the MLA Convention to interview candidates for the one opening in their program, would have had to discuss these beliefs in some detail in order to place the most efficient and informative ad in the first place and then to agree on a ranked list of candidates to invite for an interview. Writing instructors who serve as judges for campus essay contests experience the same give and take. So, too, group grading of student papers presents instructors with student work embodying different values. Assessing this student work often involves appealing to first principles which are evoked to arbitrate disagreements. Edward M. White, for instance, comments on this powerful effect of group-graded exams: "Bringing a staff of writing faculty together to develop and score a test is the single most effective way to organize a faculty development program" (*Teaching* 48). Faculty who come together to grade students' written exams, inevitably discuss the place of writing in the curriculum, its kinds, values, and ways to enhance it—faculty development of the first order.

Opportunities to codify curriculum materials can have a similar beneficial effect on faculty development. These documents can be locally published *Instructor's Guides* to specific courses, updated with new sample syllabi and assignments as the instructors responsible for these courses change. The experience of the UCLA Writing Programs has demonstrated that these *Instructor's Guides* not only help the novice instructor about to teach such a course for the first time, but they also provide a concrete occasion for the old hands to work on making coherent what could otherwise be a potentially very chaotic and conflicting set of course objectives, readings, and assignments. As a further example, at UC Irvine comparable information is provided electronically on a gopher server and is thereby amenable to instant revision and access on the Internet. At least one publishing company, Burgess, specializes in producing comprehensive textbooks tailored to the writing instruction on particular campuses, for example, the University of Arizona or the University of California at Irvine. *A Student Guide to Writing at UC Irvine* (Hollowell and Russell) includes syllabi, detailed information about course objectives and relationships to other kinds of campus instruction, grading practices, and sample student work. The value of this publication, quite apart from its convenience for undergraduates, certainly includes a great deal of serious and intense faculty development as the various players (administrators, lecturers, graduate student TAs, undergraduate writers) discussed and finally agreed on what the *Guide* should contain. Moreover, these guides embody concrete evidence of distinctive accomplishment and provide useful products for entrepreneurs concerned with marketing themselves.

Conclusion

Any writing program is really nothing but the people we hire, retrain, and retain. The writing program force-field at research universities is not merely one of conflicting interests within a static arena, for example, the institution's search for quality vs. the instructors' longing for security and the traditional reward of faculty rank (although that is usually the case, too). In addition, many different, but predictable perceptions of personal, professional, and programmatic need shape a distinctive force-field. This force-field is best understood and managed as a source of entrepreneurial energy which the WPA can tap and channel. The alternative attempt to constrain this dynamic and shape it into an approximation of traditional departments' advancement through scholarly publications works less well for all concerned, particularly for the undergraduates whose welfare the writing program is essentially dedicated to serve. Instructors are well advised to exploit this momentum and channel it into professional, pedagogical development that will allow them to turn their unique marginality to special advantage by becoming simultaneously more valuable to their institution and more marketable elsewhere. The WPA's challenge is to promote such a characterization of this entrepreneurial activity.

Undoubtedly some will not welcome this characterization and defense of the research university's writing program as an anomalous, marginalized institutional arrangement that may seem to present its writing instructors as glorified, semi-permanent post docs. True, this vision does not fit writing programs in other universities and colleges where teaching responsibilities are shared, and the common academic culture is defined less by scholarly research and publications that pull instructors' attention away from the classroom. However, writing programs at research universities currently fill a special niche and meet special needs. They are service-oriented change agents, best when most responsive. Their anomalous, liminal character is often best suited for this mission.

A non-tenurable cadre of writing teachers can therefore be very appropriate for the fundamental task of helping undergraduates at research universities become better writers, better able to control their ideas on paper. This is not a cozy picture. Edges can cut many ways; risky endeavors may fail. However, not given tenure or other security of employment, writing teachers can still be well treated and supported in other ways, for example, with release time from teaching, travel funds, access to information about extramural funding and help in seeking it. Indeed they should be so supported in order for the institution to protect its investment in them and benefit, too, from the return on their entrepreneurial professional, teaching-related activity. WPAs and instructors alike should be clear-eyed and hopeful about these unique opportunities. Again, Bourdieu puts this point well:

> But a lucid perception of the truth of all vocations and acclamations condemns us neither to abdication nor to desertion. One can always join the game without illusions, by making a conscious and deliberate resolution. (197)

Notes

1. For example, with sponsorship from its Career Placement and Planning Center, its Office of Instructional Development, and its Writing Programs, UCLA recently conducted a survey of the hundred largest companies and institutions that regularly recruit UCLA students, inquiring about writing abilities that make UCLA graduates especially attractive as entry-level employees. Although many of the employer respondents flagged such attributes as "ability to think objectively and clearly," "strong organizational skills," many also stressed "proper grammar and correct spelling," even in this day of computerized spellcheckers and style checkers. Typical is this comment: "Our biggest complaint is lack of attention to detail. In school, students aren't penalized for 'typo's' [sic] or spelling mistakes. These items are *crucial* in our business." Or, another example: "We would like to see students who can . . . write a simple declarative sentence. Knowledge of grammar. Ability to spell." The basic skills approach, to use White's label for yet another category, is evidently what many employers would like writing programs to endorse. However, this approach is now unfashionable, to say the least, among some writing instructors who sneer at an emphasis on mechanical correctness as inhibiting.

Works Cited

Beach, Richard. *A Teacher's Introduction to Reader-Response Theories*. Urbana, IL: NCTE, 1993.

Bourdieu, Pierre. "A Lecture on the Lecture." *In Other Words: Essays Towards a Reflexive Sociology*. Stanford, CA: Stanford UP, 1990.

Douglas, Mary. *Purity and Danger: An Analysis of Concepts of Pollution and Taboo*. London: Routledge & Kegan Paul, 1970.

Hollowell, John, and Vicki Russell, eds. *A Student Guide to Writing at UCI*. Edina, MN: Burgess, 1993.

Hult, Christine, ed. *Evaluating Teachers of Writing*. Urbana, IL: NCTE, 1994.

MacDonald, Susan Peck, and Charles R. Cooper. "Contributions of Academic and Dialogic Journals to Writing about Literature." *Writing, Teaching, and Learning in the Disciplines*. Eds. Anne Herrington and Charles Moran. New York: MLA, 1992. 137–55.

Mills, Joshua. "In-Your-Faceism vs. Light." *New York Times* 9 Jan. 1994, Education Life: 19–20.

Strenski, Ellen. "Peer Review of Writing Faculty." Hult 55–72.

Turner, Victor. *The Ritual Process: Structure and Anti-Structure*. Chicago: Aldine Publishing Co., 1969.

White, Edward M. *Developing Successful College Writing Programs*. San Francisco, CA: Jossey-Bass, 1989.

———. *Teaching and Assessing Writing: Recent Advances in Understanding, Evaluating, and Improving Student Performance*. San Francisco, CA: Jossey-Bass, 1985.

7

The Politics of Collaboration
Writing Centers Within Their Institutions

Molly Wingate
Colorado College

> If we do not change our direction, we are likely to end up where we
> are headed.
>
> —Chinese Proverb

As if we needed more proof that we are on the margins, directors of writing programs and writing centers sometimes receive news about major changes in our programs through memos from offices we have not heard from for months. Frustrated and angry, we wonder why we were not part of the planning. A few years ago, my institution initiated a whole-campus process to define its priorities. When completed, the list of short-term priorities included developing an academic resource center that would begin with the already successful writing center. To my surprise and ire, the writing center I direct was about to be significantly affected by a plan I had had no hand in proposing.

How had this happened? I knew that a plan was being developed, but in the face of what looked like endless meetings, I decided to take an observer role. Instead of actively participating in the process to define the college's priorities, I focused on the rapidly increasing demand for the services of the writing center. Nor did I do much observing, since my days were full of tutoring and training new tutors. As a result, I lost touch with the whole process.

In truth, I had some good ideas for an academic resource center, but I did not know exactly what those who wrote the priorities report intended when they said the proposed center would "begin with the writing center." Was I still going to have a job? Was I exerting myself so strenuously to direct a program that was about to be obsolete, or did the writing center dovetail with this new center? One thing was certain: By focusing only on what was near at hand in the writing center, I had isolated it; by choosing not to collaborate with others, I had ensured that the writing center was powerless to shape its own future at a time when futures were being shaped.

I suspect that many beleaguered writing center and program professionals fall into this stance easily. In our zeal to design and create programs with pedagogies that sometimes oppose the prevailing paradigms, we may intentionally stay a bit outside of the institution. Busy bringing programs into existence, we often shun conversation about politics. We are a little confused about our relationship with our larger institutions, a confusion that abates only a bit when we accept our paychecks. I propose to clear up some of this confusion by carefully analyzing the nature of collaboration between writing centers and their hosting institutions, a subject most composition scholars rarely consider.

How a writing center collaborates with its host institution differs from place to place, depending on such variables as funding, the status of the director, and the history of the center. But one constant is that this collaboration is intrinsically political. Although the word suffers from many bad connotations, *politics* can be defined as the art of getting things done inside institutions— finding allies, networking, and working together to achieve goals.

For instance, my college's institutional goals include graduating people who know how to think critically and speak and write effectively. To help achieve this goal, the writing center collaborates with the writing program, the faculty, the dean of the college, the admissions office, the library, the financial aid office, and so on. The institutional goals and the power of the entities involved direct the collaboration. To work effectively and harmoniously, all of us must take into consideration each other's interests. If I do not see that a change in how I hire student tutors affects how the financial aid office awards work-study grants to those students, I will fail to honor the interests of another collaborator. As a result, my collaboration with that office will become less effective: I will have lost their trust in my judgment, and the writing center will lose some power.

Power plays a different role when the collaborating offices have different amounts of control in the institution. In the previous example, the financial aid office and the writing center are neither above nor below each other in an institutional organizational chart. They can affect each other, but neither can threaten the other's existence. This kind of collaboration between equals is usually positive because the collaborators can be honest and trusting as they combine their networks to find creative, workable solutions. If such a collaboration ceases to speak to the interests of an office, it can pull out without risking much power. However, honest and trusting collaboration becomes more difficult when one collaborator has significantly more power. This kind of collaboration can become negative if the less powerful collaborator feels she must compromise her own interests or beliefs to survive. Ede and Lunsford might call the first kind of collaboration dialogic and the latter hierarchical (131).

John Schilb provides other tools for understanding institutional collaborations. Schilb reminds us that collaborations can have a wide range of ethical contexts. He cites the example of Paul de Man who worked for Nazi-controlled newspapers in Belgium and even wrote in favor of Nazi policies. Schilb suggests that our students should get in the habit of scrutinizing their writing collaborations as a way of preparing them to consider carefully the ones they will face in their working lives (107). He uses questions raised by the sociologist C. Wright Mills to show students the wider implications of collaboration. These same questions can be fruitful when asked of the collaboration between writing centers and their hosting institution.

Mills was concerned with defining and cultivating the "sociological imagination." Such an imagination allows one to use information and reason to figure out what is going on in the world and what is happening within oneself. "The sociological imagination enables its possessor to understand the larger historical scene in terms of its meaning for the inner life and the external career of a variety of individuals" (Mills 5). A sociological imagination helps writing center directors understand their host institution in terms of how its parts work and how the institution influences the writing center in particular. Mills suggests three types of questions to stimulate this kind of imagination: questions about the structure of society, questions about the society's position in history, and questions about the people who do and do not succeed in the society. Here are Mills' questions:

1. What is the structure of this particular society as a whole? What are its essential components, and how are they related to one another? How does it differ from other varieties of social order? Within it, what is the meaning of any particular feature for its continuance and for its change?

2. Where does this society stand in human history? What are the mechanics by which it is changing? What is its place within and its meaning for the development of humanity as a whole? How does any particular feature we are examining affect, and how is it affected by, the historical period in which it moves? And this period—what are its essential features? How does it differ from other periods? What are its characteristic ways of history-making?

3. What varieties of men and women now prevail in this society and in this period? And what varieties are coming to prevail? In what ways are they selected and formed, liberated and repressed, made sensitive and blunted? What kinds of "human nature" are revealed in the conduct and character we observe in this society in this period? And what is the meaning for "human nature" of each and every feature of the society we are examining? (Mills 6, 7)

In applying these questions to collaborations between writing centers and their host institutions, we can ask what these collaborations reveal about the structure of our institutions. What kinds of changes are going on? How are these changes taking place? Who are the people causing the changes? Who is being liberated and who is being repressed by these changes? Answering these questions will show how the institution functions and how the writing center fits in. This understanding, in turn, reveals why the writing center does or does not have political power.

With reference to my own case of being surprised by the priorities report, Mills' first cluster of questions requires that I evaluate the structure of the college and where the writing center locates itself in that structure. I see that, at the time, the writing center was neither considered essential to the college nor was it integrated into the institution. It had little meaning for the institution's continuance or change. If I wanted the center to be considered an active part of the planning process, then I needed to establish it in the structure of the institution.

Answering Mills' second set of questions, I see that the college was in a critical period of its history; it was preparing for change and I was not. Since I failed to consider carefully the methods and agents of change, I was unaware of what this change represented in the institution's history. I did not know that the college was preparing for strategic planning as well as a major fund-raising effort because I had not become associated with the committees and offices proposing changes.

Responding to the third cluster of questions tells me that I was unaware of the people who were leading the change and how they worked. I needed to understand what kinds of collaborations were succeeding and which were not. I did not know the people chairing the planning committees, and I was unaware of their considerations. In retrospect, I see that those of us who assumed that the grapevine would keep us informed about goings-on in the college were uniformly left out. Those who followed the process and volunteered for committee work felt appreciated by the institution and knew what kinds of changes were being considered. This analysis underscores the fact that, in order to have a voice in the future of the writing center and the institution, I needed to become more engaged in collaborative activities.

By not engaging in the process of directing change in the college, by isolating myself and not networking, I had cut the writing center off from the power created in positive collaborations. In fact, I was collaborating in a negative way. By staying on the margins, I was helping to create my own powerlessness. But to what degree was my lack of collaboration negative? At what point would treason to the writing center become an issue?

To provide a framework to interpret negative collaborations, I will borrow from the work of German historian Werner Rings, who discusses political collaborations during Hitler's Third Reich. To be sure, collaborations between writing centers and their hosting institutions are not on the same scale as the ones Rings describes; colleges and universities are not Nazis. Still, it is possible for some kinds of collaboration to be unhealthy. Although the literature on tutoring in writing centers has concerned itself with possible negative effects of collaboration—e.g., questioned whether writers level down to the lowest common denominator, voiced concerns about the veiled control tutors can exert over writers, and wondered whether collaborations honor difference—our field does not have a model for describing the kinds and effects of negative collaborations. Rings provides some precision for analyzing the types and the intents of political collaboration.

Rings describes four kinds of collaboration: neutral, unconditional, conditional, and tactical. *Neutral collaborators* believe that they must survive the best way that they can. In the face of the insurmountable circumstance (bankruptcy, unemployment, chaos, or destruction), these collaborators directly and indirectly work for the occupying power without professing any political principles (Rings 73). The most obvious of these collaborators in the Nazi era were the government officials and railway operators who saw to it that occupied countries continued to function. Other neutral collaborators include the many workers who traveled to work in Germany to support their families.

Unconditional collaborators admire and accept the ideas of the occupying power. They are "prepared to do anything and make any sacrifice for the occupying power as long as [they] can thereby serve [the] common cause" (Rings 88). Under the Nazi regime, these willing collaborators strove for their own authority and recognition, which they never received. No matter what position they held, "they were always in the minority and always on the sidelines" (Rings 105), and they never had much support from their fellow citizens.

Conditional collaborators had the attitude that they would cooperate even though they only agreed with some Nazi doctrines. They collaborated because they "wish[ed] to change the circumstances that dictate[d] [their] attitude" (Rings 106). The Vichy government in occupied France was the most open about being conditionally collaborationist, believing that "France should remain France—albeit the sort of France envisaged by authoritarian conservatives and traditionalists" (Rings 113). This policy led to a great deal of confusion and proved dangerous for those trying to operate within it.

Tactical collaborators disguised their resistance; they collaborated to regain freedom, to save innocent lives, or to reach a political ideal (Rings 128). Although some of their acts of collaboration seem quite horrible, the tactical collaborators felt sure that they lessened the pain of others.

Rings ends his discussion of the types of collaboration by pointing out that they are neither discrete nor static. As the pressures of war brought on a great deal of erratic behavior, and as the occupations grew more brutal, collaborations changed notably. Some countries moved from conditional to unconditional collaboration; others moved from tactical collaboration to outright resistance (Rings 148–149).

Applying Rings' categories to institutional collaborations, we must remember that colleges and universities are not cruel forces occupying sovereign writing centers. Nonetheless, the history of the writing center where I work illustrates each type of collaboration. At its inception the creators of the writing center unconditionally collaborated with the hosting institution. All parties involved agreed on the purpose and goal of the center, so it was an easy, positive relationship. The writing center willingly supported the institution by taking on a directive tone meant to help students. In large part, the faculty's wishes directed the writing center's activities.

Upon taking the position of writing center director, I began to change the collaboration to a conditional one. The writing center moved toward a more student-centered approach. I agreed to take direction from the faculty as long as I did not have to drill students in grammar, as I believed such drill represented an unreflective activity that did little to improve student writing.

After a few years, the collaboration became more tactical. The writing center began to provide an antidote to the traditional way writing was being taught by sharing authority during tutorial sessions. We invited professors to our staff meetings. Some were invited to learn more about the writing center; other invitations were a ruse for impressing upon the professor the need to write clearer assignments. All the while, we helped students produce better papers. The writing center thus worked inside and a little against the institutional hierarchy.

But then as I started a family and as the student tutors grew accustomed to the collaborative style of tutoring, our center became less worried about resisting the hierarchical power of the institution and began a neutral collaboration. I found it easier to retreat than engage in changes on campus, especially since the power structure of the college became confused as the president took a sabbatical and shortly thereafter stepped down. My job continued to interest and challenge me, but I was not engaged in the continual process of change in the institution. The tutors got the training, experience, and prestige that comes from being tutors, and while they were concerned with tutoring, they became equally concerned about getting experiences to put on their resumes. We had a nice situation in a smoothly operating writing center. It was too nice; I lost touch with what was happening in the larger institution, and I did not cultivate the network that would ensure the center's ability to thrive in and influence the college.

When the institution began a strategic plan based on the priorities report that had proposed an academic resource center as an outgrowth of the writing center, I was still not part of the conversation. When I complained to colleagues about this grievous injustice, they gave me a puzzled look. It had never crossed their mind to talk to the writing center director. My unexamined policy of quiet, neutral collaboration had led me unwittingly to create a powerless writing center. My actions were not exactly treasonous, but they certainly were not good for the writing center.

In an era of tight budgets, quiet, neutral collaborations are attractive. By not drawing a great deal of attention, a writing center can go about its work without much interference. But such a practice may raise ethical concerns. What if, by maintaining a service attitude, a writing center supports the institutional perception that only deficient students benefit from writing tutors? What if, by actively attracting minority students, the writing center affirms a campus-wide perception that striving for diversity means lowering the institution's standards? These writing center policies might make good, pragmatic sense, but if they are misunderstood throughout the institution, they hinder the center's ability to function. However, with a strong network, the director can make these same policies work to establish and publicize the center's integrity. If it is known that the writing center is a central part of the institution, if it figures in discussions about things the institution does well, then these same policies can be understood as ethically sound contributions to the institution.

To be part of a positive collaboration, I had to change the politics of the writing center's collaboration with the college. I became involved in the ongoing planning discussions. I took every opportunity to explain the writing center's policies and how they related to the goals of the college. I sought out offices with similar interests, entered into more collaborations, and paid attention to how those collaborations worked. By forming liaisons, making proposals, serving on committees, and offering workshops for administrators, I created a politically strong network that gained the writing center more power. As I reasserted myself in the college's planning processes, the writing center's ability to get things done increased.

My job title has not changed, I did not get a big raise, and my work load has not changed. However, I can get more done, and I am less frustrated and less regularly surprised by institutional decisions. As its network has grown and as power has accrued, the writing center draws on the talents and resources of many other parts of the institution to adjust to changing circumstances. With ease, the academic computing office and the writing center introduced an electronic writing center similar to on-line writing labs (OWLS). I was also able to get computers I had been seeking for several years as the budgeting process began to recognize, rather than ignore, the writing center. As the college strives for ethnic and international diversity, the writing center is invited to meetings to discuss proposed projects rather than to pose as the scapegoat for failed programs. When the rumor mill circulates plans to move the writing center from the beautiful historic building which houses it, I know enough to find out who on the committee has interests in common with mine, to diplomatically ask how the renovation plans are going, and thus to determine the accuracy of the rumor. I'm now strategizing how to pay student tutors more and ways to continue to hire professional ESL tutors to complement the peer tutors.

Analyzing the collaboration between the writing center and the institution awakened me from a little nap. The Chinese proverb at the beginning of this essay makes a lot of sense: "If we do not change our direction, we are likely to end up where we are headed." Even if Rings' model does not account for all dynamics affecting the writing center, I now understand that a writing center, like a writing program, cannot isolate itself and expect to flourish. Nor does it have to be imbued with power from higher administrators to affect its fate. A writing center may never sustain all of the multiple levels of collaboration necessary to make it what Andrea Lunsford calls a "Burkean Parlor Center"— one that, because it locates power and control in the negotiating group, actually threatens the hierarchical status quo in higher education and has the potential to "lead the way in changing the face of higher education" (9). But by entering into positive and proactive forms of collaboration with its host institution, a writing center can find, and even make, opportunities for change.

Works Cited

Ede, Lisa, and Andrea Lunsford. *Singular Texts/Plural Authors: Perspectives on Collaborative Writing*. Carbondale, IL: Southern Illinois UP, 1990.

Lunsford, Andrea. "Collaboration, Control and the Idea of a Writing Center." *Writing Center Journal* 12 (1991), 3–10.

Mills, C. Wright. *The Sociological Imagination*. New York: Oxford University Press, 1959.

Rings, Werner. *Life with the Enemy: Collaboration and Resistance in Hitler's Europe 1939–1945*. Trans. J. Maxwell Brownjohn. Garden City, NY: Doubleday & Co., 1982.

Schilb, John. "The Sociological Imagination and the Ethics of Collaboration." *New Visions of Collaborative Writing*. Ed. Janis Forman. Portsmouth, NH: Heinemann-Boynton/Cook, 1992. 105–119.

8

The Foreigner
WAC Directors
as Agents of Change

Susan H. McLeod
Washington State University

In Larry Shue's comedy *The Foreigner* (1985), the main character is, through a series of misunderstandings, taken to be not just a newcomer in town but also a foreigner who speaks no English. Other characters in the play then betray their deepest secrets within his hearing, thinking that he can't understand what they are saying. All the characters, including the "foreigner" himself, learn a good deal from their subsequent interaction, and the world of the play changes considerably as a result.

WPAs who are directors of writing across the curriculum (WAC) programs are a little like Shue's foreigner—they are different, outsiders visiting the territory of other disciplines, and their interaction with the local residents helps to bring about change. But what kind of foreigners are they, and what kind of change do they help bring about? There are many metaphorical models for foreign visits to new lands, models which can be metaphors for WAC directors' roles and their behavior; as Lakoff and Johnson point out, metaphors affect how we see the world, and unacknowledged metaphors can shape reality for us in ways we may not intend. I would like to make some of the metaphorical models for the WAC director's role explicit, arguing that WAC directors are a new breed of foreigner, a change agent; they need to invent their role with care as they venture into new territory. I hope that this examination of roles will help readers understand how WAC directors can make their difference—their foreignness—work for rather than against them as they bring about change in the university.

The Conqueror

One possible role for the WAC director as foreigner, especially in the eyes of some administrators, is that of conqueror. The university power structure is hierarchical; in such a structure it is sometimes the case that administrators think of their roles as analogous to those in other hierarchies, especially the military: the president as the commander-in-chief, the deans as majors, the chairs as captains. Such administrators find it natural to think of program development as something done *to* rather than *with* faculty, established by fiat with an order from the higher ranks to the foot soldiers of the academy; they will often couch program development in terms of winning a fight against an enemy. Sometimes the enemy is illiteracy; a WAC director I know was told that in his "fight for literacy" he would find a "small army" of support for WAC in one particular department. Sometimes the faculty themselves are seen as the enemy. One dean told a WAC director that her job was to "ram WAC down the faculty's throats." A department chair once talked to me about planning "frontal attacks" on particular departments, running workshops that were "right on target," and "shooting down" opponents in meetings. And sometimes students are the enemy; I recently was told of a meeting in which a proposed writing proficiency examination was referred to as a "search and destroy mission" to rid the university of students unfit to graduate.

The dangers of this role are readily apparent. If the WAC director is cast as conqueror, he or she will be seen as the tool of an insensitive, even hostile administration; difference will identify the director with the forces of the opposition, with *them* rather than with *us*. Nothing stirs faculty to defensiveness and active resistance so much as having a program imposed on them from above. Administrative support and enthusiasm are certainly necessary for a WAC program, but they are not sufficient; faculty must own the program as well—there must be grassroots support. WAC directors who come in like conquerors might succeed in establishing something that looks like a program, but it will be a program in name only; compliance will be sullen or nonexistent. In the privacy of their classroom, faculty reign.

WAC directors need to communicate with their administrators about the difficulties of imposing WAC, helping them understand the collaborative and cooperative nature of successful WAC ventures. One excellent way is to invite in an outside consultant, who because of his or her expert status will usually have more credibility than someone on-campus.[1] If there is no money for consultants, WAC directors should contact directors of nearby programs for help and support (see the list of WAC programs in the appendix to McLeod *Strengthening*). Administrators who still believe WAC can be imposed from above should read Milton Glick's perceptive piece, "Writing Across the Curriculum: A Dean's Perspective"; Glick describes a successful program that had his support (in terms of budget and clerical staff) but that was faculty-driven in terms of leadership. Glick concludes that the program has not only addressed the issue of student writing, it has also increased morale by empowering faculty and validating their interest in good teaching.

The Diplomat

In WAC programs run out of or connected with an English Department, the WAC director is sometimes cast in the role of diplomat, the emissary from one department to another. At first glance this role doesn't seem one that could cause harm. Diplomats are supposed to respect the culture they are sent to live in, and they have by virtue of their appointment a certain amount of seniority and influence, not to mention diplomatic immunity in the face of local tensions. Certainly WAC directors need to be diplomatic in their dealings with other departments. But there are also serious difficulties with this role.

A diplomat is one who represents the power and influence of his or her home territory. Diplomats have no real power of their own; they merely represent their government. A WAC director who is an emissary from the English department helps perpetuate the notion that writing is the property of that department. Such a role could easily backfire—Why should other departments be doing the English department's job of teaching writing? If the English department is viewed with some suspicion on campus (because of its relative size and presumed power), the reaction to a diplomat from that department could—like that of some developing nations toward the industrial powers—be downright hostile. The WAC director is then cast in the role of CIA agent, a language spook who will ferret out and expose for retaliation those who are not assigning and responding to student writing in acceptable ways.

While there is some debate about whether or not WAC programs belong in English departments (Blair; Smith), the advice of most seasoned WAC directors is that such a program belongs to the entire university and therefore should be housed appropriately—in a writing center, in the office of the chief academic officer, in a campus writing program office (Walvoord). In this way, the wise WAC director can avoid the role of diplomat who represents the interests of one department, changing it to the role of one whose constituency is the entire university.

The Peace Corps Volunteer

Some administrators think that program development is simply service. Funding isn't necessary—all one needs is an enthusiastic volunteer, someone who will see the need for change and work for the sheer love of it. WAC directors cast in the role of Peace Corps volunteers are expected to do their job with no released time, no funding for workshops, no administrative support. They are supposed to cobble together a program, making do and doing without, working on less than a shoestring.

But the work of program development is such that WAC directors who work on a volunteer basis are headed for early burn-out—even the Peace Corps expects its volunteers to work for only two years. WAC directors should simply refuse to be cast in the role of Peace Corps volunteer; they should negotiate with administrators for an appropriate budget, making it clear that they will not take the job without funding. The budget need not be princely, but it must include some basics for program development: released time for the director, some clerical support, some funding for student support (usually in the form of peer tutoring) and for faculty workshops (including some reward for participating faculty), and some resources for follow-up activities after the workshops (McLeod and Soven). Bringing in an outside consultant, as mentioned earlier, can do wonders to help obtain appropriate support for a program.

The Missionary

Describing their collaborative work with a colleague from the Biology Department in their institution, David Kaufer and Richard Young admit that although they are a bit embarrassed by the fact now, they began their project "rather like missionaries bringing the Word to unbelievers" (75). Their assumption about their role is not unique; it is often rooted in the affective experience that almost always accompanies faculty workshops—an excitement about WAC ideas and techniques that is part of the group experience, a genuine and well-documented enthusiasm (Weiss and Peich). It is tempting to see this affective phenomenon as a "conversion"—indeed, many have used that term to describe it, myself included.

But the role of missionary is an especially dangerous one, not because conversions don't take place (they do), but because the role does not lend itself to the productive faculty dialogue that is part of all successful WAC programs. Missionaries, after all, go forth to convert because they think their particular beliefs and practices are superior to all others. They wish to enlighten the unenlightened, convert the heathen, save the damned. They certainly do not wish to have a dialogue with or to learn from the foreign culture—only to teach their own views as the correct ones. Such cultural imperialism and accompanying sense of moral superiority can make them blind to the worth of these cultures; at worst, it can make them contemptuous of all who are unlike them. In spite of how some directors (or administrators) may feel, WAC is a pedagogical rather than a moral issue; as such, it has no need of missionaries.

WAC directors who preach will be met with indifference, even hostility. Instead, they must listen, be alert to the worth of the local culture, and be aware of how much they themselves have to learn about teaching writing across the curriculum. They will find that many faculty in other disciplines are not unenlightened about teaching writing. When I visit colleges and universities to hold WAC workshops, I find teachers in various corners of the institution doing amazing and wonderful things without benefit of WAC—in marketing, in forestry, in French, in architecture. The wise WAC administrator will use his or her special status as foreigner in other disciplines to seek out these people, validate and celebrate their practice, and work to make such practice not just an isolated phenomenon but part of a well-conceived program.

The Change Agent

What then is the most productive role for WAC directors to play as they work to build a program? I should like to propose that such directors need to invent a new role for themselves—that of change agent.[2] Like the foreigner in Shue's play, WAC directors are change agents largely by virtue of their difference, their other-ness: they are not part of the local departmental power structure, they have no stake in disciplinary arguments, they do not represent any identifiable constituency and are therefore not seen as a threat. They have the same license as a foreigner: seeing things with a visitor's eyes, they can ask questions no one else can ask, do things that no one else can do. Their unfamiliarity with and respect for the local culture combined with a willingness to listen and learn from that culture makes them appealing visitors, makes their knowledge about teaching writing not something to be imposed but something to be discussed, perhaps broadened through dialogue with disciplinary experts.

If WAC directors are change agents, what kind of change are they after? Universities instituting WAC programs usually do so because there is a perceived problem with student writing, one they hope the program will "fix." This is not a bad reason to start a WAC program, but directors and administrators alike should understand that improvement in student writing as a result of a particular program, while it certainly occurs, is almost impossible to measure with our present evaluation tools. As Witte and Faigley point out, there are just too many variables coming to bear on student writing skills to allow us to separate out and test for the results of one particular program. WAC directors aim at helping students improve their writing, but they do so by working to change university curricula and faculty pedagogy, which in turn have an effect on student writing.

Changing Curricula

Because universities examine curriculum periodically, curricular changes are perhaps the easiest to bring about. One of the most visible changes on the university landscape in the last decade has been the appearance of "writing-intensive" courses in the disciplines. These courses differ from institution to institution, but usually have these common features: they are usually upper-division (often for majors), have limited class enrollments, are taught by full-time faculty, and have specifications about papers (length, type) and how these are to be assigned and evaluated (Farris and Smith). The principle underlying such courses is that faculty in the disciplines are those most qualified to teach the discourse of that discipline—history teachers, for example, know the most about writing history, and are best equipped to teach apprentices in the discipline (history majors) how to understand and use that discourse.[3]

WAC directors can help bring about curricular changes like these through the usual university committee structures and review procedures, but it is also important to have a campus-wide body of some sort focusing on writing. Such a body will ensure that all groups who will be affected by curricular change will have some say in (and therefore some stake in) that change; participation by all stakeholders is an important characteristic of innovative programs (O.E.C.D. Report 19). An all-university writing committee, a composition board, a WAC advisory board—all are possible mechanisms for bringing about discussion and revision of curricula to include specific writing-intensive courses. Whatever the mechanism, it is imperative that the WAC director be involved and active; those who write about educational innovation emphasize the primacy of personal contact and of personal contact networks in bringing about change (House).

Changing Pedagogy and Teachers' Theories

The more radical but less visible change WAC directors try to bring about is in pedagogy. Almost all WAC programs have, at one time or another, workshops which bring faculty from all disciplines together. The ostensible aim of these workshops is to help teachers with the practical matters of incorporating student writing into their classes: assigning and responding to writing, handling the paper load, using writing-to-learn assignments. But there is another aim as well—to help teachers become more reflective about their teaching by giving them techniques that will lead to discussion of and change in classroom practice. WAC workshops model the values of WAC programs—they are not presentational but interactive; faculty not only read and listen, they also write and discuss their writing in a supportive atmosphere, working together in small groups (Fulwiler; Magnotto and Stout). Because the process of reflection and subsequent pedagogical change is a slow one, an on-going series of workshops rather than a one-shot effort is far more effective in bringing about permanent change (Fullan, Ch. 15). Faculty try out a few WAC techniques in their classrooms, come back to discuss their use in follow-up seminars, try a few more techniques, and gradually change from a completely presentational model of teaching to one where students are more active learners.

In changing pedagogical practice, teachers change their theories about teaching and writing. This may seem like a paradox, so let me elaborate further. The WAC movement has recently been criticized for not challenging the view of knowledge as a "readily divisible transmitted substance" (Mahala 778). In fact, WAC directors challenge this view all the time, but not in a missionary role, by preaching to faculty about the evils of viewing education only as the transmission of knowledge. Instead they do what all good writing teachers do: They model processes, show strategies, and allow learners to discover things. Faculty seminars start where the faculty are—wanting something they can apply immediately to their classes—and encourage reflective teaching so that faculty can evaluate the changes taking place as a result of the new practice. WAC directors running follow-up seminars soon find more interest in discussing theories of learning and critical thinking; faculty who have tried various techniques with success are now curious to know why the techniques work. They try other techniques, read more about thinking and learning, and want more follow-up seminars for discussion. Their theories of teaching and learning change as a result. Thus, as others have pointed out, changes in theory *follow* rather than *precede* changes in teaching practice (Brooke 2).

Of course, teacher change is a highly personal and individual thing, taking place at many levels. In order to understand this change more fully, it is useful to look at the phenomenon for a moment through the lens of schema theory. Cognitive scientists propose that we store and retrieve knowledge mentally through cognitive structures called schemas (Mandler; Schank and Abelson). A schema is a unit of thought, a generic knowledge structure with particular variables as defining features; for example, most people have a schema for birthday parties that involves refreshments (which vary from party to party). A schema, in other words, is an abstraction based on experience with a number of related experiences that is used to interpret or shape new ones. Based on their own experience as students, the schema that most post-secondary educators have for "teaching" has the teacher standing in front of the room and lecturing while the students sit quietly taking notes. One way to change a schema is to add variables, to add a new set of instances that consistently have some feature that is not in the old schema (Crocker, Fiske, and Taylor 200). WAC seminars do this by involving faculty first-hand in techniques that center not on the teacher but on the student—peer critiquing, writing-to-learn activities, collaborative learning. When teachers try the techniques in their own classrooms, further change takes place. For example, it is difficult for teachers who try using small groups in the classroom to continue to lecture in the same way afterwards; once the energy of the group process is unleashed, students feel freer to speak up and to ask questions. The center of authority has shifted and the dynamics of the class change. Teachers add to their teaching schema not only the variables of the techniques they have learned, but theories about why the techniques work as they do.

What the WAC director as change agent is after, then, is an educational revolution at the university level, one which would move the focal point of the classroom from the teacher in front lecturing to the students actively involved in their own learning through writing. WAC directors, like all writing program directors, must guard against what Louise Phelps calls "pedagogical imperialism," against the belief that their programs will solve the problems on everyone's political and intellectual agenda: "liberate students from ideology and oppression, single-handedly develop learners into critical thinkers, convert faculty in other fields to their educational philosophies, eliminate sexism and racism, transform the value system of the academy" (168). But the experience of many colleges and universities has shown that quiet revolutions can occur, changing faculty's relationship to students, their relationship with one another, and their relationship to the institution in lasting ways (Fulwiler "Quiet"). If WAC directors move slowly and thoughtfully, with respect for the difference of others, they will be able to use their own difference to bring about meaningful, lasting change.

Notes

1. The members of the Board of Consultants of the National Network of Writing Across the Curriculum Programs are available for such consultation. For further information, contact Prof. Christopher Thaiss, Coordinator, National Network of WAC Programs, Department of English, George Mason University, 4400 University Drive, Fairfax, VA 22030.

2. The term *agent of change* was used in the early 1960s to describe the role that the Peace Corps volunteer was supposed to take; such terminology caused political difficulties for the organization, however, since the host countries for the volunteers didn't always want change (see Hapgood and Bennett).

3. This rationale for writing-intensive courses has been termed *formalist* (Mahala), a term which is misguided at best; a better term would be *rhetorical*. See Maimon for a clear explanation of the rhetorical approach to WAC.

Works Cited

Blair, Catherine Pastore. "Only One of the Voices: Dialogic Writing Across the Curriculum." *College English* 50 (1988): 383–89.

Brooke, Robert E. *Writing and Sense of Self: Identity Negotiation in Writing Workshops.* Urbana, IL: NCTE, 1991.

Crocker, Jennifer, Susan T. Fiske, and Shelley E. Taylor. "Schematic Bases of Belief Change." *Attitudinal Judgment.* Ed. J. Richard Eiser. New York: Springer-Verlag, 1984. 197–226.

Farris, Christine, and Raymond Smith. "Writing-Intensive Courses: Tools for Curricular Change." *Writing Across the Curriculum: A Guide to Developing Programs.* Ed. Susan H. McLeod and Margot Soven. Newbury Park, CA: Sage, 1992. 71–86.

Fullan, Michael G., with Suzanne Stiegelbauer. *The New Meaning of Educational Change.* 2nd ed. New York: Teachers College Press, 1991.

Fulwiler, Toby. "Writing Workshops and the Mechanics of Change." *WPA: Writing Program Administration* 12 (1989): 7–20.

——. "The Quiet and Insistent Revolution: Writing Across the Curriculum." *The Politics of Writing Instruction: Postsecondary.* Ed. Richard Bullock and John Trimbur. Portsmouth, NH: Boynton/Cook, 1991. 179–187.

Glick, Milton D. "Writing Across the Curriculum: A Dean's Perspective." *WPA: Writing Program Administration* 11 (1988): 53–58.

Hapgood, David, and Meridan Bennett. *Agents of Change: A Close Look at the Peace Corps.* New York: Little Brown, 1968.

House, Ernest R. *The Politics of Educational Innovation.* Berkeley, CA: McCutchan, 1974.

Kaufer, David, and Richard Young. "Writing in the Content Areas: Some Theoretical Complexities." *Theory and Practice in the Teaching of Writing: Rethinking the Discipline.* Ed. Lee Odell. Carbondale: Southern Illinois UP, 1993. 71–104.

Magnotto, Joyce N., and Barbara R. Stout. "Faculty Workshops." *Writing Across the Curriculum: A Guide to Developing Programs.* Ed. Susan H. McLeod and Margot Soven. Newbury Park, CA: Sage, 1992. 32–46.

Mahala, Daniel. "Writing Utopias: Writing Across the Curriculum and the Promise of Reform." *College English* 53 (1991): 773–89.

Maimon, Elaine. "Maps and Genres: Exploring Connections in the Arts and Sciences." *Composition and Literature: Bridging the Gap.* Ed. Winifred Bryan Horner. Chicago: U of Chicago P, 1983. 110–25.

Mandler, Jean M. *Stories, Scripts, and Scenes: Aspects of Schema Theory.* Hillsdale, NJ: Erlbaum, 1984.

McLeod, Susan H., ed. *Strengthening Programs for Writing Across the Curriculum.* San Francisco: Jossey-Bass, 1988.

McLeod, Susan H., and Margot Soven. "What Do You Need to Start—and Sustain—a Writing Across the Curriculum Program?" *WPA: Writing Program Administration* 15 (1991): 25–33.

Organisation for Economic Co-operation and Development (OECD). *The Management of Innovation in Education.* Centre for Educational Research and Innovation. Report on a workshop held at St. John's College, Cambridge, June 29–July 5, 1969.

Phelps, Louise Weatherbee. "The Institutional Logic of Writing Programs: Catalyst, Laboratory, and Pattern for Change." *The Politics of Writing: Postsecondary.* Ed. Richard Bullock and John Trimbur. Portsmouth, NH: Boynton/Cook, 1991. 155–70.

Schank, Roger C., and Robert P. Abelson. *Scripts, Plans, Goals, and Understanding.* Hillsdale, NJ: Erlbaum, 1977.

Shue, Larry. *The Foreigner.* New York: Dramatists Play Service, 1985.

Smith, Louise Z. "Why English Departments Should 'House' Writing Across the Curriculum." *College English* 50 (1988): 390–95.

Walvoord, Barbara. "Getting Started." *Writing Across the Curriculum: A Guide to Developing Programs.* Ed. Susan H. McLeod and Margot Soven. Newbury Park, CA: Sage, 1992. 12–31.

Weiss, Robert, and Michael Peich. "Faculty Attitude Change in a Cross-Disciplinary Workshop." *College Composition and Communication* 31 (1980): 33–41.

Witte, Stephen P., and Lester Faigley. *Evaluating College Writing Programs.* Carbondale: Southern Illinois UP, 1983.

Part III

Professional and Scholarly Identities

9

The Scholarship
of Administration

Christine A. Hult
Utah State University

Scene One: a lovely fall day at Miami University in Oxford, Ohio, during a conference optimistically titled, "Composition in the 21st Century." A group of conferees sits in a circle following a stimulating panel, talking over what we have just heard, sharing our reactions and trying to make connections between the speakers' words and our own situations. In quiet tones, a young woman begins to speak; we all lean forward to hear her all-too-familiar story: as a WPA in a large state institution, she had given over her life to build a solid writing program out of the bits and pieces inherited from her predecessors, and she felt positive about what she had accomplished in so short a time. "But I won't be recommended for tenure," she says, looking down at her shoes. "I haven't published enough." The tears well up in her eyes. "Excuse me," she says, standing abruptly and rushing from the room, a tissue pressed to her face. We look at one another in silent communion, our emotions clearly visible: anger, sadness, disgust at the exploitation in the "system."

Scene Two: in a survey on the authority of WPAs as seen through the eyes of English department chairs, conducted by Olson and Moxley, a department chairperson says,

> At one time, the Freshman English Director was always a regular member of the faculty, usually an assistant professor. In recent years, we have appointed a PhD who is not a member of the standing faculty. This has worked well, since it does not destroy the career of an assistant professor. (55)

These two brief scenes pose the same question: Is the position of WPA a career death sentence for its occupant? The subtext of the department chairperson's comment implies that it is all right to "destroy the career" of someone who is not a member of the standing faculty. But the chairperson does not seem to question the system itself, a system that defines an essential position in such a way as to ensure the academic failure of anyone who holds that position. Perhaps it is time to take a hard look at ways the academy traditionally defines administrative work in general and the work of the WPA in particular. Rather than trying to force WPAs into traditional academic molds, institutions of higher education need to acknowledge the changing definitions of scholarship and to legitimize and reward WPAs for the scholarship of administration as reflected in the diversity of our work. By the same token, WPAs need to do a better job of persuading others in the academy of the scholarly merit of the work we are engaged in.

As a long-time member of the Council of Writing Program Administrators and as the editor of the Council's journal *WPA: Writing Program Administration* for six years,[1] I have seen an evolution in our own conceptions of our work and a corresponding professionalization. Just as Ernest Boyer called for a broader definition of "scholarship," in his monograph *Scholarship Reconsidered*, I argue that any definition of scholarship should also include what might be called the "scholarship of administration."

Boyer's monograph blew into the academy like a breath of fresh air at the beginning of the 1990s. The academy, he said, needs to "break out of the tired old teaching versus research debate and define, in more creative ways, what it means to be a scholar" (Boyer xii). To do so, Boyer suggests "four general views of scholarship—discovery, integration, application, and teaching" (xii). In addition to the traditional research and teaching dichotomy, of great interest to WPAs should be the categories of integration and application, for, after all, it is in these realms that the daily life of an administrator is lived.

Boyer defines the scholarship of integration thus: "By integration, we mean making connections across the disciplines, placing the specialties in larger context, illuminating data in a revealing way, often educating nonspecialists, too" (18). And he defines the scholarship of application thus: "the application of knowledge moves toward engagement as the scholar asks, 'How can knowledge be responsibly applied to consequential problems?'" (21). What better way to describe the work of a WPA than making interdisciplinary connections in an effort to solve pressing problems? At this point, I would like to explore the evolution of the research and scholarship by and about WPAs in an effort to define the scholarship of administration more clearly.

It seems to me that changing the conception of writing program administrators' work from "service" to "scholarship" parallels the changing status of the *WPA* journal and its acceptance as a serious publishing outlet for administrators. This change also parallels the growth of the Council of Writing Program Administrators and its enhanced visibility and importance as a professional organization. But, unfortunately, many in the academy, even in our home departments of English, have not significantly changed their attitudes towards writing program administration. Although we see signs of change, currently, in most institutions, work as a WPA does not bring rewards commensurate with the important contributions such work makes to higher education. On the contrary, all too often, to work as an untenured WPA does no less than "destroy the career of an assistant professor."

Traditional definitions of academic work focus on faculty contributions in the areas of teaching, research, and service. Administrative work, such as directing a writing program, has been categorized as "service," along with such often mundane tasks as serving on a university's library committee or a task force on buildings and grounds. But serious administrative work is not the same as the occasional committee service expected of all faculty members; rather, it is a career choice that carries with it a significant commitment to scholarship.

Nor is the administrative work of the WPA the same as other administrative work typical in academe, such as chairing an academic department. The chairperson has a truly professional, credentialed faculty to work with who can be expected to spend several years of their careers at the institution and to function in their classrooms with minimum supervision. The WPA, however, often leads a constantly shifting staff of novices, and hence is perpetually engaged in teacher training and evaluation. (See Ellen Strenski's chapter in this volume for a discussion of the nature of this work.) All too often the WPA may be the only composition scholar, or one of very few, in the department. Whereas a chair can be a scholar *with* the rest of the faculty, many times the WPA must be the scholar *for* the composition "faculty," who may have few chances to travel to conferences or even to read the journals, let alone conduct their own research. In Boyer's terms, when WPAs use their disciplinary knowledge to inform their teachers and improve their programs, they are practicing the scholarship of application.

However, Boyer does take care to distinguish between what may typically be thought of as service activities and what he calls the scholarship of application:

> Clearly, a sharp distinction must be drawn between *citizenship* activities and projects that relate to scholarship itself. . . . All too frequently, service means not doing scholarship but doing good. To be considered *scholarship*, service activities must be tied directly to one's professional activity. Such service is serious, demanding work, requiring the rigor—and the accountability—traditionally associated with research activities. (22)

When we think about the demands of being a WPA, we can see that much of our work revolves around just such scholarship of application: WPAs design curricula, write syllabi, set up placement and evaluation procedures, train and evaluate teachers, assess program outcomes, select and even write textbooks based on sound theory and pedagogy. All of these application activities, as Boyer suggests, "require rigor" comparable to traditional research activities. And they are quite different from the kinds of administrative activities practiced by department chairs.

Other aspects of our work involve the scholarship of integration: reading and interpreting the burgeoning literature from the many fields that contribute to our knowledge (e.g., psychology, learning theory, anthropology, communications, and linguistics), planning and overseeing WAC programs, and integrating technology into the teaching of writing. Similarly, the WPA's work includes the scholarship of teaching: composition theory and methods courses, staff meetings, faculty development seminars and workshops, and so on.

In fact, some WPAs, perhaps at the expense of their personal lives and sometimes their health, practice scholarship in all four of the areas outlined by Boyer, by participating in the traditional academic research and publishing arenas in addition to the application, integration, and teaching activities demanded of them on a daily basis. Writing program administrators often practice the scholarship of discovery, whether or not that research is ever "published" in a traditional sense: We need to stay abreast of all the many developments in the field of rhetoric and composition in order to keep our programs responsive to the changing environment of higher education, and we need to be classroom and program researchers who, through both formal and informal research projects, discover what does and doesn't work in our programs, thus adding to the discipline's knowledge base.

In a recent article in the *Journal of Engineering Education*, Richard M. Felder outlines just such a "universal vision of the professor of the 90s"; this professor does

> pioneering research in a critical area and brings in big bucks to support the research . . . publishes 5–10 papers each year in the most prestigious journals . . . is a dedicated and stimulating instructor and wins teaching awards at her university . . . does more than her fair share of the tedious but vital service chores that no one wants to do and does them excellently. She is mostly imaginary. (105)

Felder points out that most professors are not able to be this "combination of Leonardo, Socrates, and Mother Teresa" (105) and argues that it is unrealistic, and even harmful, to require every new professor to be all things to all people. Rather, he suggests that professors should be allowed to specialize if they wish, with some following a track that is more oriented to research and others following one that emphasizes teaching.

Many times WPAs labor under unrealistic expectations similar to those ascribed to beginning engineering professors. Writing program administrators are, in the main, pragmatists. Their interests, as reflected in articles in the *WPA* journal and in conference presentations, have largely remained focused on how to accomplish effectively the teaching, integrating, and application tasks for which WPAs find themselves responsible: defining and building a coherent writing program; evaluating writing and teaching; training teachers, tutors, and faculty; building liaisons with faculty from across the campus and between campuses; advocating for teachers and lobbying for equitable working conditions; counseling students and staff; adjudicating grade disputes; and so on. (Other chapters in this volume discuss various aspects of the foregoing; for example, Janangelo, Wingate, and McLeod all describe effective ways of building liaisons on campus; Hansen describes how she advocated for part-time teachers.) Despite all this activity, the WPA who is doing her job right will often not draw much notice from other administrators with whom she works. However, the important work she is doing is not accomplished in a vacuum: An effective WPA is a scholar in her own right.

I would like to turn now to a discussion of the evolution of WPA positions over the past twenty years or so. Reviewing changes in the position itself may help us to understand why the academy continues to undervalue the work of writing program administrators.

History of Writing Program Administrators[2]

College English departments have for many decades offered courses to help students become better writers. Since the late 1970s, compositionists have begun to conceive of writing courses, or sequences of courses, as writing programs. Along with attempts at establishing coherent programs, new administrative positions were created to orchestrate and develop these programs, for example, Director of Writing or Coordinator of Composition. The first national attempt to organize those who found themselves in such administrative positions, frequently with little professional training in either composition or administration, came at the 1976 Modern Language Association convention as part of the first meeting of the MLA Teaching of Writing division. Out of this initial meeting, spearheaded by Kenneth Bruffee, grew a fledgling organization and a new journal: The Council of Writing Program Administrators and its journal, *WPA: Writing Program Administration* (with Harvey Wiener as the first WPA President and Kenneth Bruffee as the journal's first editor).

By tracing the progress of the Council of Writing Program Administrators, we can see the professional growth of those individuals serving as writing program administrators. In 1977, the Council outlined its purposes and goals and established its by-laws. Among its lofty goals were "to serve the interests of writing programs by educating the academic community and the public at large about the needs of successful writing programs," and "to promote cooperation among the various writing programs in two- and four-year colleges throughout the country by sharing information and by defining common interests and needs" (Council 61).

The organization took a major step toward achieving its goals by securing an Exxon grant, with which, as Harvey S. Wiener announced in his President's Message in the journal, "WPA has begun on a small scale a successful consultation-evaluation program" (vii). Over the years, the campus visits made by trained consultant-evaluators have had a major impact on the administration of writing programs. (Edward White's chapter in this volume describes why this kind of program evaluation is superior to other models.) One of the current thrusts of the consultation-evaluation service includes designing and implementing a system of peer review to help WPAs define and document their work (Schwegler).

WPA now has a permanent administrative home in the English Department at Miami University in Oxford, Ohio (since 1987), as well as current affiliations with the Association of American Colleges (since 1977), MLA, CCCC, and NCTE. Members participate actively in all of these professional organizations and their conferences. The Council sponsors its own annual workshops and conferences to provide administrators with an opportunity to enhance their professional development. Joint workshops with the Association of Departments of English (ADE) have also been sponsored in an ongoing effort to promote much-needed dialogue between WPAs and English Chairs.

How do WPAs find their way to these positions? One longtime WPA cynically observed that, by tradition, the person in the English department with the neatest desk by default got the job. In 1985, Linda Peterson surveyed WPAs to ascertain and then outline their career patterns. Peterson observed that "most WPAs trace their academic origins to English departments . . . [although] some of the newest WPAs list rhetoric as a specialty" (12). As more and more doctoral programs offer specialties in composition and rhetoric, we will increasingly see a change in the nature of preparation for those holding WPA positions. Similarly, as WPAs and the positions they hold become ever more professional, fewer WPAs will complain of the need to "overcome prejudice against composition [as a] specialty" in English department promotion and tenure decisions (Peterson 14). Unfortunately, the bias against work in composition remains strong in many departments. This general bias by necessity spills over into the academic assessment of WPAs.

In her book *Textual Carnivals*, Susan Miller describes how respondents answered the question "Have recognitions for research and/or publication in composition been equitably visible in your department?" Seventy-one percent answered yes, twelve percent answered no, and sixteen percent judged the question not applicable (209). Although over two thirds of those surveyed by Miller felt their departments were not biased against research in composition, still nearly one third either felt their departments were biased or believed the question did not apply to their situations. As to their uncertain futures, Miller reports that seven respondents had the following to say about the possibility of their being promoted:

> "Not until I have time to write a book" (this person gives workshops and writes pedagogical and administrative documents that are used internally); "the University is debating because I have published a popular composition textbook"; and 3 respondents indicated that they had been kept in their departments without PhDs and would probably not be promoted unless they met "normal" expectations. (158)

Clearly, in many instances, "normal" expectations do not yet include credit for the scholarship of administration. In fact, Miller's very question assumes that scholarship in composition is "research and/or publication," a very traditional, narrow definition of scholarship. Where does this leave administrators whose research may include designs of rising junior writing assessments or calculations of retention rates for freshmen in their colleges? Such important research exemplifies the scholarship of discovery, but it is rarely "published" in the common sense of the term. One of the reasons for beginning the *WPA* journal was to provide administrators with at least one place to publish just such research.

Professionalization of the *WPA* Journal

In 1985, Bruffee published an article reviewing the evolution of the *WPA* journal. He observed that the articles fell into three categories:

1. How-to articles: "Every issue of WPA to date has contained at least one piece intended to explain how to do something."

2. Contextual how-to articles: These articles analyze and evaluate "the way the elements in a program are organized, articulated, sustained."

3. Professional identity articles: "A few articles . . . that address directly or indirectly the issue of professional identity of WPAs and of our national organization." Through these ongoing professional discussions, WPAs are "gradually developing a systematic, generalized core of knowledge of the sort that is basic to any professional practice" (Bruffee 6).

Up until 1985, as Bruffee observed, the preponderance of the articles were of the first type, with fewer of the second, and very few of the third type. Since 1985, that balance has shifted considerably toward the second and third categories as WPAs have striven toward a professional identity. In surveying the journal articles since Bruffee's report, I found that every issue still includes at least one pragmatic, explanatory piece. In fact, in 1991, I instituted a special section of the journal devoted to such how-to pieces, which I called "WPA on Campus." In each subsequent issue, I reserved space for refereed articles that were not necessarily "scholarly" in the traditional sense of the term but rather were intended to help the readers understand the processes WPAs can use to accomplish very specific goals. Recent "WPA on Campus" articles have included guidelines for developing WPA regional affiliates, a discussion of how to improve graduate student status, dissemination of the Portland Resolution describing WPA positions, two reactions to campus visits by consultant-evaluators, and ideas for how to mentor TAs. Publishing such how-to articles, the editorial board hopes, will help to give this kind of pragmatic research a certain legitimacy that is its due.

As WPAs have built a professional knowledge base for the journal, articles of Bruffee's third type have continued to increase. A series of articles that commented on "power and the *WPA*," several articles that incorporated current theories from other disciplines such as speech-act theory or institutional change theory, and many more research-based articles are now finding their way into the pages of *WPA*. In fact, two recent issues published the results of research funded through the Council's research grant program: one article on portfolio assessment and the other on a survey of writing placement practices.

Because *WPA* is the only journal in the profession to feature such articles, it has continued to publish descriptions of significant contributions WPAs have made in program design, implementation, and evaluation at their own institutions. Whatever the topic, authors are asked to be certain that their articles make generalizable connections between their own experiences and larger issues in the profession. Yet, whether or not such descriptions of program innovations are ever published in a journal, the actual work of revising, implementing, and evaluating curriculum is still at the heart of the scholarship that writing program administrators do.

As the *WPA* journal has become more widely known and cited throughout the literature in composition, its circulation has doubled. In the six years of my editorship, it rose from around 400 to nearly 800—still small by most standards, but then the journal appeals to a rather narrow audience of program administrators, of which there are typically only one or two on any given campus. But the journal early on made a decision to focus specifically on administrative issues and not to publish articles discussing composition generally without a clear administrative angle. Keeping this sharp focus has given *WPA* its unique identity.

As circulation has increased, so have submissions. The length of each issue nearly doubled during my editorship, from an average of sixty to one hundred pages per issue, to accommodate the excellent work submitted to the journal. However, in a given year, there is space for only nine or ten articles, about one fourth the number submitted for consideration. These space limitations mean that the journal by necessity must turn away several publishable articles each year. It is also important to realize that many WPAs, who are overwhelmed by the scope of their administrative duties, never have the time to write and submit articles at all. Nor should they be expected to. Their time is no doubt better spent on the writing that is targeted "in-house": that is, the writing used to describe, argue about, justify, and analyze writing programs for specific audiences on specific campuses.

The Scholarship of Administration

Let me return now to the question that I asked at the outset: What is the scholarship of administration? It is the systematic, theory-based production and oversight of a dynamic program (as opposed to traditional scholarship which is generally defined as the production of "texts"). Because it is dynamic, it more nearly resembles the productions of our colleagues in music, theater, or dance, but demands no less "scholarly" expertise than that required by the performance of a Bach cantata.

We see the evidence of the scholarship of administration in the day-to-day written work of the administrator: the guides for students and staff; the program descriptions, curricular outlines, and philosophical statements; the model syllabi and sample writing prompts; the teacher evaluations and hundreds of letters of recommendation for students and faculty; the memos, bulletins, newsletters, news articles, and in-house publications used to communicate among constituencies; and so on. None of these pieces of writing is done in a vacuum; each reflects both the rhetorical skills and the professional knowledge and expertise of its writer. And most of this writing is indeed "published," because it is written, produced, and distributed to a large and diverse audience.

True, such writing is not published or peer-reviewed in the traditional sense of those terms. But surely the impacts and outcomes of such writing are profound for programs and the individuals they serve; in fact, they are often greater and more far-reaching than those of any article in a professional journal.[3] Boyer challenged the academy to allow professors "flexible and varied career paths" (44). Local program demands, as well as personal strengths and preferences, will help WPAs to determine which of the avenues towards the scholarship of administration they choose as a focus: the scholarship of discovery, of integration, of application, or of teaching. But, as WPAs, we shouldn't succumb to the myth of the superhuman professor. Rather we should consciously direct our career paths in the best interest of both ourselves and our campus communities.

With this in mind, we must now ask a related question: How can we describe accurately and evaluate fairly the diverse work of WPAs? Many of us need to share the blame for our currently undervalued work with our higher administrators, since we have too often bought into the hierarchical schemes outlined on our campuses rather than trying to change the premises on which such schemes are based. We need to do a better job of educating our colleagues in academe about the significance of our administrative work and to develop models of evaluation that reflect the complexity of our scholarship. We should get into the habit of forwarding copies of salient documents in our writing programs to department heads, deans, provosts, and so on. And we should initiate dialogues on our campuses with other administrators and faculty to help teach them about what we do.

Tenure and promotion cases also provide us with the opportunity to persuade our colleagues of the value of our scholarship. Every tenure or promotion dossier is an argument for the candidate's effectiveness in the broad categories of teaching, research, and service. We can fold into our tenure and promotion documents explicit arguments for the value of the scholarship of administration, categorizing this work as "scholarly research," not as "service."

For example, found in the revised tenure and promotion guidelines of the Faculty Code at my institution are the following general criteria for research, scholarship, and creative activities:

consultant activities related to areas of research and other scholarly activity
. . . shared presentations or publications with peers and/or graduate students
based on scholarly activities . . . development and dissemination of knowledge, curriculum, innovative strategies or methodologies . . . leadership activities within the university . . . administrative assignments which promote
scholarship; design and use of new and innovative technology. (7)

Within these broad research/scholarship categories or others like them, a
WPA, together with his or her tenure and promotion committee, can make co-
gent arguments for the value of administrative work. To do so effectively requires that the WPA gather all of the artifacts of the job as an ongoing record.
I would suggest that, from the outset, WPAs keep "administrative portfolios"
to record their administrative scholarship, much as teachers have been advised
to build "teaching portfolios" to record their teaching scholarship.

An administrative portfolio should include a representative sampling of
the WPA's written (and oral) work, each of which requires considerable scholarly knowledge to compose and present. Some of the writing placed in the
portfolio, as mentioned earlier, might include program guides for students and
staff; program descriptions, curricular outlines, and philosophical statements;
model syllabi and sample writing prompts; teacher evaluations and letters of
recommendation; memos, bulletins, newsletters, news articles, and in-house
publications used to communicate among constituencies; and speeches, presentations, consulting, workshops, and conference talks.

An important document in any portfolio should be a careful job description that outlines the nature and scope of the position. Anyone entering an administrative position should first negotiate a clear job description and get it in
writing. Of course, the newly appointed WPA would want to keep the document flexible and open to negotiations acceptable both to the WPA and the
institution. The Council of Writing Program Administrators has debated and
discussed in its conferences and journal the equitable treatment of WPAs and
has developed guidelines for writing program administrator job descriptions
(Hult et al.). First dubbed the "Portland Resolution" at the 1990 WPA summer
conference held in Portland, the guidelines are meant to extend the discussion
of professional standards for postsecondary writing instruction, outlined by
CCCC in 1989, to those who administer writing programs and to help new
WPAs define their jobs fairly. The WPA guidelines are in two parts: first, the
working conditions necessary for quality writing program administration; second, guidelines for developing WPA job descriptions. These guidelines can be
useful to those currently in an administrative position as well as to those em-
barking on such a career course. (The Council of Writing Program Administrators will soon issue the guidelines in a pamphlet to be distributed to all
members of the organization.)

As with the teaching portfolio, anyone compiling an administrative portfolio should guide the evaluators through the materials by means of self-reflective
glosses on the contents. A self-reflective overview letter can highlight for read-

ers those items of particular importance, tying documents to their underlying scholarship, for example. Thinking of the entire administrative portfolio as a persuasive document, buttressed by significant evidence (in the form of artifacts) to support the argument, will help the compiler toward a cohesive whole.

These are but a few suggestions, and certainly much more work needs to be done toward fairly describing and evaluating administrative scholarship. The Council of Writing Program Administrators, also recognizing this need, has begun a model project with the aim of "defining, describing, and evaluating the intellectual work of writing program administrators." As a result of the model project, WPA hopes to establish a method for peer review of writing program administrators, perhaps including both site visits by consultant-evaluators and external peer reviews of WPA administrative portfolios. (The guidelines for this method of reviewing a WPA's work are still being drawn up by Robert A. Schwegler, University of Rhode Island, and a committee made up of members of the Executive Board of the Council of Writing Program Administrators. They should be available from WPA sometime in 1995.)

Writing Program Administrators are dedicated to providing for students in colleges and universities the highest quality writing instruction available. They are responsible for defining the philosophical positions upon which their programs rest, for keeping abreast of developments in the field of rhetoric and composition, and for implementing those developments through programmatic and curricular reforms, in addition to their responsibilities for day-to-day program management and implementation. These are all examples of the scholarship of administration, and it is these intellectual challenges that continue to keep WPAs engaged with their work.

Charles Schuster provides us with some suggestions for how we might begin to effect changes in our departments and at our institutions. First, he suggests that, rather than battling for our own departments separate from English, we seek to help English "transform itself in light of recent historical and disciplinary developments . . . becoming departments of rhetoric—or departments of textual studies or departments of discourse" (91). Second, he suggests that English graduate studies, over which WPAs as supervisors of teaching assistants often have considerable sway, should assume a leadership role in transforming English departments.

Schuster points out, and rightly so, that departments need to hire both senior professors in rhetoric and composition and beginning assistant professors, rather than hiring compositionists only as WPAs or temporary staff members. "No departments I know of," he says, "would hire a beginning assistant professor of literature to chair the department or direct the graduate program" (94). And yet, how many WPAs are hired fresh out of graduate programs? Is it any wonder they are doomed to failure? As Schuster writes, "Departments should hire colleagues" whose credentials and scholarship they value, "not administrators" (94). We should all be working together to help redefine our discipline so that it no longer privileges the analysis of texts over the production of them. Only in such a healthy department, suggests Schuster, can specialists in reading and writing, and even administration, be rewarded equally. We need to overcome the second-class status that many writing programs, and by association their directors, have acquired by virtue of their service mission. Through aggressive public relations, thoughtful publication, and careful documentation of our work, as I have suggested in this chapter, WPAs can begin to raise the public image of our programs as sites where significant thinking and research are applied to better instruction in communication skills valued by the entire campus community. Furthermore, it is incumbent upon us to work with our departments and our academic institutions to devise systems of assessment that will more equitably reward writing program administration as a legitimate form of scholarship.

Notes

1. The current editor of *WPA* is Douglas Hesse at Illinois State University.

2. A version of this history of the Council of Writing Program Administrators appears in the *Encyclopedia of English and the Language Arts*, edited by Alan Purves.

3. The ADE also endorses a broadened conception of scholarship in a recent document, "ADE Statement of Good Practice: Teaching, Evaluation, and Scholarship." Among other recommendations, the ADE document states that "scholarship should be defined broadly and not be limited to the academic book or article" (Armstrong 18).

Works Cited and Consulted

Armstrong, Paul B. "Deprivatizing the Classroom." *ADE Bulletin* 107 (1994): 13–19.

CCCC Executive Committee. "Statement of Principles and Standards for the Postsecondary Teaching of Writing." *College Composition and Communication* 40 (1989): 329–36.

Bleich, David. "Evaluating the Teaching of Writing: Questions of Ideology." *Evaluating Teachers of Writing.* Ed. Christine A. Hult. Urbana, IL: NCTE, 1994. 11–29.

Bloom, Lynn Z. "I Want a Writing Director." *CCC* 43 (1992): 176–78.

Boyer, Ernest. *Scholarship Reconsidered: Priorities of the Professoriate.* Princeton, NJ: The Carnegie Foundation, 1990.

Bruffee, Kenneth. "The WPA as (Journal) Writer: What the Record Reveals." *WPA: Writing Program Administration* 9.1–2 (1985): 5–10.

Council of Writing Program Administrators. "Bylaws." *WPA: Writing Program Administration* 4.3 (1981): 61–62.

Dickson, Marcia. "Directing Without Power: Adventures in Constructing a Model of Feminist Writing Program Administration." *Writing Ourselves into the Story: Unheard Voices from Composition Studies.* Eds. Sheryl I. Fontaine and Susan Hunter. Carbondale, IL: Southern Illinois UP, 1993. 140–53.

Felder, Richard M. "The Myth of the Superhuman Professor." *Journal of Engineering Education* 83.2 (1994): 105–110.

Gunner, Jeanne. "Decentering the WPA." *WPA: Writing Program Administration* 18-1-2 (1994): 8–15.

Howard, Rebecca Moore. "Power Revisited; Or, How We Became a Department." *WPA: Writing Program Administration* 16.3 (1993): 37–49.

Hult, Christine. "Writing Program Administration." *Encyclopedia of English Studies and the Language Arts.* Ed. Alan Purves. New York: Scholastic Books, 1994.

———. et al. "The Portland Resolution: Guidelines for Writing Program Administrator Positions." *WPA: Writing Program Administration* 16.1–2 (1992): 88–94.

Miller, Susan. *Textual Carnivals: The Politics of Composition.* Carbondale, IL: Southern Illinois UP, 1991.

Olson, Gary A., and Joseph M. Moxley. "Directing Freshman Composition: The Limits of Authority." *CCC* 40.1 (1989): 51–59.

Peterson, Linda. "The WPA's Progress: A Survey, Story and Commentary on the Career Patterns of Writing Program Administrators." *WPA: Writing Program Administration* 10.3 (1987): 11–18.

Schuster, Charles I. "The Politics of Promotion." *The Politics of Writing Instruction: Postsecondary."* Eds. Richard Bullock and John Trimbur. Portsmouth, NH: Boynton/Cook, 1991. 85–96.

Schwegler, Robert. "Defining, Describing, and Evaluating the Intellectual Work of Writing Program Administrators: A Project Proposal." Adopted by the WPA Executive Committee, March 1994.

Trimbur, John, and Barbara Cambridge. "The Wyoming Conference Resolution: A Beginning." *WPA: Writing Program Administration* 12.1–2 (1988): 13–18.

Utah State University. "Promotion and Tenure (P/T) Guidelines, Activities, and Procedures." 1991.

White, Edward M. "Use it or Lose it: Power and the WPA." *WPA: Writing Program Administration* 15.1–2 (1991): 3–12.

Wiener, Harvey. "President's Message." *WPA: Writing Program Administration* 4.3 (1981): vii.

10

The Rhetorical Problem
of Program Evaluation
and the WPA

Edward M. White
California State University–San Bernardino

Writing program administrators are usually stunned to realize that the job calls for substantial activity in areas they have not even thought about: personnel management, budgets, grade grievances, academic politics, public relations, and so on. Among all these unknowns, program evaluation takes a prominent place. It combines importance—a negative program evaluation can mean the loss of funds or even of the entire program—with an apparently arcane field of study. Program evaluation is often considered to be a subspecialty of fields that most WPAs have consciously or unconsciously avoided for most of their lives: statistics and social science/educational research. The very language of program evaluation often seems forbidding, highly technical, and hostile to humanistic concerns. But there is no escaping the issue. Program evaluation requires the WPA to prove that the expensive writing program works: that it is producing results, fulfilling its goals, and meeting institutional needs.

Program evaluation includes yet an additional problem for WPAs: It seems at the same time so technically remote that it is incomprehensible and so immediate and obvious as to deserve little attention.

"Of course the writing program is successful," the WPA is likely to reply. "Anybody with a brain in their head can see that; look at how hard all of us— teachers and students—are working!"

The interlocutor (a dean, perhaps, or a campus committee seeking new and cheaper models of general education, or a representative of a funding agency) shakes a sage head: "I know you *believe* it is doing your students good; but I need some evidence."

Evidence. That is the issue the WPA needs to confront. Program evaluation is not a technical or statistical problem any more than it is a self-evident
result of hard work. The two propositions that the WPA must accept are that
outsiders have the right to ask and to receive answers to evaluation questions
and that, for once, we do have the training to handle this responsibility, since
it requires the presentation of evidence. The management of evidence to convince an audience is not only the basic stuff of freshman composition instruction but the heart of the heart of composition theory and history: rhetoric.

Program Evaluation and Rhetoric

What kind of evidence will be accepted as real, as convincing, for the particular audience examining our programs? When we frame the question in this way,
as a rhetorical problem, one that we are accustomed to dealing with, the problem of program assessment becomes familiar and manageable. The rhetorical
problem we are faced with is rather like that our freshmen confront as they write
papers for their teachers: What will that unknown audience, in its unfamiliar
discourse community, take to be "evidence" and how can we present that evidence convincingly? Part of the discomfort we feel in this situation results from
the same difficulty our freshmen feel about these same questions.

The audience we confront and must persuade in program evaluation determines other rhetorical decisions. If the report is going to the English department or a humanities dean, we can count on a certain sharing of definitions
and assumptions. We can assume an understanding of the importance of writing for thinking and learning; we need not define our terms, our workload, or,
perhaps, even our goals. A relatively casual survey of students and faculty, a
collection of syllabuses, sample student portfolios, and an appreciation by a
colleague from a neighboring institution might be all we need. But such a be-
nign and undemanding audience is less and less typical. Most of the time we
are dealing with committees or administrators unfamiliar with the teaching of
writing, and sometimes hostile to it. These committees are driven by a need to
demonstrate accountability and by budget cuts; they are likely to be aware of
attempts to replace composition courses at parallel institutions with more economical versions of writing instruction, such as reduced models of writing
across the curriculum or large lectures with lay readers. Our reports may often make their way to trustee or even legislative committees, members of
which may have wholly different agendas from ours.

So the first job in program evaluation is to understand the audience for the
final report, most particularly what that audience's assumptions are and to
what use they will put the report. David Bartholomae has pointed out that the
inexperienced freshman in college must "invent the university" by entering
imaginatively into its discourse community, its language and assumptions. We
have a similar job to do. Just as the freshman must invent the university to
succeed, we must invent a campus committee, a board of trustees, a key ad-

ministrator, or a legislative body. The program evaluation as rhetorical exercise must show understanding of audience and an awareness of its perspective. Anyone taking part in a meeting to parcel out major funding who has been told, as I have been, to "stop talking like an English teacher" will become aware of this necessity, particularly if money flows to programs with a better command of the required rhetoric.

Just as we work with our students to help them see that mere *assertion* is not the same as *demonstration* of what they say, we need to be aware that mere assertion of the value of our programs is not convincing to those outside our discourse community. We need to demonstrate our argument through the use of evidence that will be convincing to the audience for which we are writing. As we have learned from our writing students, that is a much more complicated job than it seems.

If the first task of the evaluation is to understand the audience of the report, the second is to think through the kind of evidence that is likely to fit the assumptions of the audience. Or, if we want to ask our audience to adopt new assumptions about what counts as evidence, we need to know the arguments that may convince them to change.

Positivism and Program Evaluation

The first kind of evaluation of writing programs usually expected (by those not involved with writing instruction) is deceptively simple and based on simple-minded positivism: Writing instruction is designed to improve student writing, so we should measure student writing ability before and after instruction (pre-testing and posttesting), and the measured increase from pretest to posttest (the "gain score") is an indication of how much the program has helped students learn (the "value added"). Like Dr. Johnson kicking the stone to dispose of questions about reality, such positivism dismisses the complexity behind writing instruction. Further, it simplifies and falsifies the issues: Students are not our only "customers" (their parents and children, future teachers, future employers, and society at large are also beneficiaries of writing instruction) and the improvements in writing (not to speak of reading and thinking) that a limited time for instruction can bring about are so complex that they may not show up in first-draft writing samples. We cannot participate in a program evaluation that assumes the entire value of our work can be measured through first-draft essay tests.

Every WPA should be aware that the pretest/posttest method usually fails to obtain statistically meaningful results; it is based on the faulty assumptions I have just described about the nature of writing and writing instruction and, in addition, depends on relatively approximate holistic scoring methods designed primarily to rank papers against each other. This failure to obtain results should not be taken to mean that writing programs are failures, though the evidence can be, and often is, used to draw such conclusions and to damage writing programs. The inability to get results ought, in general, to be seen as a conceptual failure, deriving in part from the naive positivism behind the methodology and in part from a failure to understand the state of the art in the measurement of writing ability. I will deal with the last issue first.

The Measurement Problem in Positivistic Program Evaluation

Positivism assumes that the phenomenon at issue is "out there," is a facet of observable reality, and is readily measurable. Thus positivism reifies the concept of student writing ability and simplifies it, sometimes almost to the point of absurdity. The definition of writing ability emerges from the measuring device used: perhaps some multiple-choice test of usage or spelling; perhaps an impromptu writing assignment. Usually the definition of writing ability that is used is vague and the measurement device is poorly designed. But even when the definition is worked out with some care and actual writing is used in the assessment, the limitations of the assessment design undermine the evaluation, most obviously in the pretest/posttest model.

For example, if you go on a diet and lose ten or fifteen pounds, take in your belt two notches, and fit nicely into an outfit you previously could not button, you have pretty good evidence that your diet has been a success. But suppose that you had decided to employ a more quantitative pretest/posttest model as an added rigorous statistical check, and you used the truck scale beside an interstate highway as your measure before and after your diet. Since the truck scale weighs in hundred-pound increments, it does not register your weight loss. "Alas!" you would say—if you were to follow the usual reductive program evaluation model—"I must have been deceiving myself; I have not lost any weight, since the truck scale does not show I have and the truck scale is, after all, an objective measure."

Strange as it may seem, this truck scale measurement model is still the dominant form of program evaluation and it has led to much absurdity. For example, about thirty years ago, a study of the composition program at Dartmouth College (Kitzhaber) gave much evidence to demonstrate that graduating seniors wrote worse than they did as entering freshmen. The definition and measure of writing skill consisted of an elaborate error count in student prose. The evaluation showed that Dartmouth seniors make more errors in first-draft writing than freshmen do (an unsurprising finding, since many writers who handle complex subjects tend, at least on early drafts, to make more errors than they would if they were writing on simple subjects); but the measure, elaborate though it was, made little attempt to evaluate complexity of ideas, depth of thought, integration of knowledge and opinion, or any of the other higher-order skills that are presumably part of a Dartmouth education. Nor did the study consider other possible program effects beyond the reduction of errors in student prose. The measurement device was the best available at the time and Kitzhaber did the best he could with his data, but they were used to "demonstrate" a finding contrary to much available evidence (and to common sense). Nonetheless, those findings have entered academic folklore, and deans who may know nothing of rhetoric or the writing process may well have heard about studies documenting the decrease of writing ability during the college years—useful if misleading "evidence" to buttress an argument for writing across the curriculum.

Positivism underlies most empirical research designs, those that seek but rarely find statistical evidence for writing improvement. The most dramatic example of this depressing inability of empirical research to provide us with convincing program evaluation is Witte and Faigley's *Evaluating College Writing Programs* (1983). The book has an unintended dramatic structure. In its opening sections, it examines closely a series of empirical program evaluations that failed. The authors select the best empirical precedents and mercilessly detail exactly where these efforts went wrong. At the center of the book is the promise that the authors, who are planning their own program evaluation, will avoid all past errors in their own design. The drama builds as we see the new and more perfect plan they evolve and proceed to implement. And then the denouement, the reward of hubris, the fate of those who challenge the gods: the even more spectacular failure of the new design, with an assessment of the new and more sophisticated errors they committed. It is hard to know which to admire more—the honesty and writing skill of the authors, as they show that they too have failed at empirical writing program evaluation, or the damnable recalcitrance of the problem they tried in vain to solve through empirical methodologies.

The nonfinding of Witte and Faigley's study replicates the nonresults of the well-funded Carnegie Foundation evaluation of the (then) Bay Area Writing Project. That evaluation, headed by Michael Scriven, produced no less than thirty-two separate reports, "none of which," according to the *Carnegie Quarterly,* "was able to present direct cause-and-effect statistics" ("Teaching" 7).

To be sure, if we reduce the scope of the problem sufficiently, we can come up with something. Hillocks (1986) summarizes certain kinds of results and, in his meta-analyses, gives certain kinds of confirmation about effective and ineffective teaching "modes" and "foci" in writing programs. (See White, *Developing,* Chapter Three, for a critical summary and analysis of those findings.) We can take a small part of writing, such as spelling or syntax, and show that some kinds of class work can improve scores on certain narrow kinds of tests. We can imagine that T-units are in fact (as they are in some theories) a way of defining writing quality and then show how to lengthen students' T-units. We can use sentence combining to lengthen sentences, and we can drill on active verbs to shorten sentences. We can use error counts, as Kitzhaber's study at Dartmouth did, to show that freshmen write better than seniors; we can use six-way scoring of complicated essays on three kinds of scales, as the California project (White and Polin) did, to show that weak student writers perform better on campuses where there are upper-division writing requirements. But empirical methods seem always to circle about and get no closer to the "simple" question of whether this or that writing program actually makes students write better or not. Why?

Behind empirical positivism is a simplistic view of reality itself; it is to be expected that writing instruction will be included in that view. To combat uninformed attempts to reduce composition to mechanics or to error reduction in first-draft writing, we need to develop evidence that our composition courses have more complex goals, that the teaching and learning of writing have to do with more than simply observable results on simple tests: teaching revision and writing processes, employing writing as a means of learning, helping students use sources properly to support (not substitute for) ideas, increasing reading ability, enhancing understanding of the self and its relation to society, and so on.

Developing a Goals Statement

A careful statement of the goals of the program is a first line of defense against reductionism as well as an indication of what a responsible program evaluation should ascertain. So the statement must be developed systematically, with participation by a wide span of teachers, and be formally approved by (at the least) the composition program and (usually) the English department. Furthermore, the writer of such a statement needs to show that it is more than a pious hope; the goals need to be distributed to students as well as faculty and to be part of course syllabi. If, as is often the case, the statement is a forgotten document with no real impact on the program, you cannot draw it out of the back of the bottom drawer for use when needed; like an ace from the wrong deck, it will embarrass you when the deception is revealed.

When is the best time to develop a goals statement? Obviously, the sooner the better, since it should be in use long before the program evaluation question arises and since it takes considerable time to bring about the consensus required. A writing program without consensus on goals, typically one in which each teacher is free to do his or her own thing as long as some writing goes on, is particularly vulnerable to reductive program assessment. If the staff cannot agree on goals, then outsiders are perfectly entitled to come up with their own and impose them on the writing program; unlike most other disciplines, writing allows every faculty member, trustee, and politician to feel expert—however uninformed or even unpracticed they may be.

A well-developed and functioning statement of the goals of the writing program is an almost sure defense against reductionist and positivist program evaluation. Unless there is pervasive distrust of writing and writing instruction, no evaluation committee member could effectively argue for a multiple-choice usage test to measure revision skills or for a test of first-draft writing to measure research ability. And if the statement has the breadth to include such effects as improved reading and writing in all courses and continued results ten years after graduation, no one will dare to propose a simple pretest/posttest evaluation design.

But defense is not enough. How do you intend to meet the evaluation questions, now that you have managed to make them sufficiently complicated? It is very good to have complicated and advanced goals, agreed to by all involved; now you must come up with convincing evidence to show that your goals are being met, at least in part. You must come up with some ways to evaluate your efforts.

Since the more sophisticated measurement models I will be discussing frequently seem to be as ineffective as the simple-minded ones, we need to look closely at the usual evaluation models in order to avoid committing the same mistakes. A program evaluation that fails to show results is a damaging document. It is far better to avoid such an evaluation than to engage in one that will seem to demonstrate that no measurable good is being done by an effective composition course, writing-across-the-curriculum program, grant program, or research hypothesis.

Program Evaluation Models[1]

There are five general models of program evaluation that can be applied to writing programs. In the first place, we need to dismiss the norm-referenced pretest/posttest evaluation model, which is certain to show no results. Second, we will look at the criterion-referenced pretest/posttest model, which is much more supportive of the curriculum but also normally is still not sensitive enough to show results. A third model uses a variety of measures, is not irrevocably tied to the narrow and positivist pretest/posttest model, and is very likely to yield results if they are there to be found. The final two models often obtain results, either apparent (by avoiding the gathering or evaluation of data, using instead the impressions of outside experts or of participants responding to survey instruments) or real (by employing well-trained outside consultants).

Certain Failure: Norm-Referenced Testing

The great appeal of a standard norm-referenced test is its supposed objectivity. Some publisher or testing service produces a multiple-choice instrument with an impressive name, such as the Test of Standard English Usage, and, even better, publishes norms and statistical tables along with the test. Furthermore, some local education professor has been heard to say that the test is unexceptionable, or something like it, a kind of confirmation that it must be good. So the college's institutional research office administers the test to students before and after the composition course, only to find that scores do not change. This is the positivist pretest/posttest model I discussed at some length in the previous section, now dependent on an outside test with scores normed on an outside group of students. When the results are published, the composition teachers find themselves in a difficult defensive position.

The basic problem with using someone else's norm-referenced test is that it is probably not the right test for your program. It may define writing as spelling and punctuation, whereas your program defines writing as originality and coherence; it may be normed on a population with characteristics quite different from those of the students in your program. In addition, it has probably been constructed according to the usual procedures for norm-referenced tests—that is, so that it will yield a bell-shaped curve. Such test construction needs a preponderance of questions of middle-range difficulty, since the bell curve is its goal, and hence tends inevitably toward the kind of question suitable for aptitude rather than achievement testing. It is the nature and goal of many norm-referenced tests (the Scholastic Assessment Test—SAT—is the best-known example) *not* to show the effects of short-term instruction.

Thus, the use of a norm-referenced, multiple-choice test, following the pretest/posttest model (the kind of program evaluation that seems to come first to the minds of the uninformed) gives an almost certain negative prognosis. The test is designed not to show what is sought; it will most likely examine something that has not been taught, and it is probably normed on an inappropriate population. Furthermore, it defines the effects of a writing program in the narrowest possible terms. And all this is promoted in the name of "objectivity"! We should certainly demand of any instrument used in program evaluation that it be appropriate to the material and the population in the program and that it be designed to measure the specific kinds of improvement that the program is designed to bring about.

Probable Failure: A Single Essay Test

More sophisticated program evaluation in writing will respond to the problems I have just summarized. Careful WPAs will bring together the faculty responsible for the classes, work out test specifications that correspond to the program goals statement and the writing skills being taught, develop and pretest writing topics, and grade the essay test according to the state of the art of holistic or primary trait scoring. More and more WPAs are following this more responsible model, which they then use as part of a pretest/posttest design in order to show (as they fully expect) that the students' writing performance as they define it has improved as a result of that particular writing program. A particularly ambitious WPA might even substitute portfolios for an essay test, imagining that this more elaborate set of writing samples will yield more conclusive data (which it will not).

Such WPAs deserve applause for their goodwill and effort. The faculty benefit from the discussion of and added sophistication in the assignment and measurement of writing; the students benefit from a consistent emphasis in class and in assessment on actual writing; the program itself benefits from the considerable evaluation of goals and procedures that must take place. Only one important benefit is missing: Normally the posttest shows that no statistically significant improvement has taken place in the students' test scores.

The disappointment brought about by this kind of result, after all the work of the assessment, can be devastating. Sometimes it becomes hard to realize that the fault is still with the evaluation design, since all the problems with norm-referenced multiple-choice testing have been avoided: The essay test or portfolio assessment is a criterion-referenced device, designed specifically for the local population and for the goals of the particular program. Why has it failed to measure the improvement in student writing that every teacher in the program knows has occurred? Or is it (the hidden fear buried in every American intellectual) all a delusion that education has an effect, that students can be taught to write, that we have really earned our salaries, such as they are?

No, the problem remains with the evaluation model—the pretest/posttest model, to be precise—with its assumption that the only program effect worth measuring is the short-term learning that may show up in first-draft products on a writing test or the other products in a portfolio. Although such a model may well be effective for lower-order skills, such as counting or spelling, or for limited kinds of learning, such as the declensions of Latin nouns or theorems in geometry, writing instruction and learning are too complex and multifaceted to be measured in such a way. The amount of improvement in first-drafting that can occur as part of so complex a skill in a few months is likely to be submerged by such statistical facts as regression to the mean (on retesting high scores move down while low scores move up) or less than ideal reliability (consistency of scoring). The amount of improvement in writing shown by portfolios will be obscured by the many measurement problems that make the scoring of portfolios difficult and expensive.

A carefully designed essay test is an appropriate part of many composition programs' evaluation designs. The more careful it is, the more likely it is to show the effects of instruction (Sanders and Littlefield). But everyone involved in the evaluation should be aware of the strong odds against obtaining statistically meaningful results from this one instrument. Therefore, a simple pretest/posttest model using actual writing scored holistically should never be the entire evaluation design. As part of the design, such a test has many beneficial effects and just might document some of the improvement that has taken place; as the whole design, the test is asked to carry more weight and more responsibility than it can well bear.

Those using a writing sample as part of the evaluation design should attend to the following procedures, in order to give themselves the best chance of obtaining results:

1. Those teaching the classes must be involved in developing the test specifications, and at least some of them should take part in selecting or creating the writing topics. If the test is to be truly criterion-referenced, energy, time, and money will have to be spent on test development. A primary-trait scoring guide (focusing on specific matters in the curriculum, such

as paragraph development or use of detail, rather than overall writing ability) will help those scoring the test focus on the aspects of writing that are being taught in the program.

2. Unless the program being evaluated teaches only one mode of discourse (as some business or research-writing courses do), the test should give all students an opportunity to do their best by requiring at least two different kinds of prose, for example, a personal experience essay and an analytical essay. The test should recognize that some students learn some kinds of writing much more quickly than others.

3. Two separate forms of the test should be prepared, so that each half of the student group can take different forms as pretest and posttest. Thus, half the group will take Form A as the pretest and Form B as the posttest, whereas the other half will take Form B as the pretest and Form A as the posttest. Raters will then be unable to distinguish pretests from posttests by topic.

4. After all tests have been coded, all identifying marks should be removed from them, and all the tests (pretests and posttests) should be scored at the same controlled essay reading. After the scoring has been completed, the tests should be grouped once again by test date, campus, class, and so on, so that statistical processing can take place. Pretests should never be scored separately from posttests.

5. The test needs to have enough administrative, clerical, statistical, and computer support so that its various components can be carried out professionally. It is a foolish economy to ask an English professor to do statistical work or to ask secretaries to grade compositions. In testing, as in life, we are likely to get what we ask for and usually what we pay for. Those elected or chosen to direct this limited evaluation design need to recognize the strong odds against achieving results and to resist the kinds of economies that lower reliability (consistency and fairness) and validity (actual measurement of what you intend to measure).

Probable Results: Evaluation by Varied Measures

Writing programs have many goals, all of which have something to do with improving student writing. An evaluation design that attempts to define and acquire information about a wide range of these goals—such as those discussed in the following sections—will be more responsible and much more likely to identify measurable results.

Student Outcomes

Even though the quest for demonstrable improvement in student writing is usually futile, no instructional program evaluation will be taken seriously if it does not attempt to identify the benefits to students—either by coming up with "gain scores" or by devising some other measure, such as a portfolio assessment. Despite all the limitations of the pretest/posttest model, the rhetorical value of measuring student writing skills by means of several holistically graded writing samples or by portfolios is beyond question; yet this type of assessment rarely produces a "gain score," since only a fairly narrow improvement can be expected as a result of a relatively short writing program. Another approach to student outcomes through direct measurement would be to set program goals and seek to measure the proportion of students who reach them as time goes by; if an increasing percentage of students achieve these goals each year, the program is clearly attaining success, even if individual gain scores cannot be obtained.

An early indication of improvement to come is an attitude change. Measures of student attitudes may show that students have more positive feelings about writing after they complete the program, even if their first-draft writing skills have not yet improved very much. Other desirable student outcomes might be improved grades in some or all other classes that require writing, a lower dropout rate, or a willingness to take other courses requiring writing. Long-range outcomes, such as changed attitudes and behavior years after the program has been completed, have not been much attended to, but they offer real possibilities for demonstrating program effectiveness under the right circumstances.

Faculty Effects

Although the effects of a program upon teachers are generally ignored, programs that value and challenge the faculty, that make them feel efficacious and appreciated, usually are successful programs. Teachers' feelings about a program can be discerned in their attitudes toward the subject and the students, morale, conference attendance, pedagogical research and publication, classroom assignments, syllabi, and exams.

Faculty effects have received the most attention in writing across the curriculum (WAC) programs, which encourage faculty in all areas to use writing as part of their teaching. As Gail Hughes has shown, WAC programs proceed in three stages: In the faculty development stage, faculty are shown how to use writing in their courses; in the classroom implementation phase, faculty attempt to increase or improve their writing assignments in the classroom; and in the student impact phase, students improve their attitudes about and skill in writing and increase their learning in all their classes through writing. Hughes argues that program assessments cannot stop with the first phase, since faculty may be delighted with the faculty development workshops or retreats but may fail to change their teaching in any way; an evaluation of classroom implementation is therefore crucial. If the first two phases are taking place successfully, the third phase can be shown to occur.

According to Hughes, program evaluation for WAC does not address the apparent question "Does it work?" Rather, it seeks to deal with two more relevant questions: "Can it work?" and "How can I get it to work at my college?"

To answer these questions, a program evaluation must be highly detailed and descriptive, using an "eclectic, multi-method, and multidisciplinary approach" (Hughes-Wiener and Jensen-Cekalla; Hughes, forthcoming).

Spread of Effect

Writing programs, particularly the most successful ones, may have a wide circle of effects beyond the immediate impact on students and faculty in the program. Sometimes faculty outside the program show their support by adding writing assignments, essay tests, or writing portfolios to their own curricula. Perhaps a special college writing program at the freshman level calls forth other programs at the upper-division level, or an extraordinary program at a junior high school elicits changes in the school district's elementary schools and high school. Sometimes writing programs lead to changes in the way that students, or even their parents, deal with writing or reading outside the classroom.

A further advantage to an evaluation design not limited merely to a pretest/posttest model is the formative effect the evaluation itself can have. The very act of gathering information from a variety of sources leads to new lines of communication and new thinking about the program. There is no need to wait years for data analysis; some findings result directly from the evaluation activity. The department head discovers that the new creative software he or she proudly ordered is still not in use; the freshman composition director is dismayed to find out that half the staff are teaching literature instead of writing; the English teachers are amazed to hear that they are held in high esteem by their colleagues in the sciences, many of whom require writing in their classes.

Anecdotal Results: Outside Experts and Opinion Surveys

Just as the pretest/posttest model seems to come readily to the minds of those with little assessment experience, so do two other means of simplifying the complex questions of program evaluation: hiring a sympathetic outside evaluator and administering an opinion survey. Although these procedures are not improper in themselves as part of an overall evaluation plan, they are sometimes adopted as substitutes for an evaluation plan. They usually will produce positive results, whether the program is an effective one or not. For this reason, the results may not be convincing to some important audiences, particularly those looking for data rather than opinions.

Surveys of faculty and students about writing programs are often part of responsible program evaluations, but they cannot substitute for such evaluation. Those without much experience at conducting such surveys imagine them to be much easier to prepare and analyze than they in fact are and often will ask local faculty to prepare one on short notice. Such quick and cheap surveys are almost sure to have numerous flaws; most prominently, the wording of the questions will lead respondents to give answers that the evaluators are hoping to obtain. It is relatively easy to accumulate favorable opinions of a writing program from those teaching in it and from the students who have invested time and labor in it; even faculty and administrators who have little contact with the program are often ready to say positive things about their friends and colleagues if a questionnaire urges them to do so.

Those who develop questionnaires and surveys professionally have learned how to protect such instruments from the usual abuses: ambiguity, suggested or even forced choices, oversimplification, and so on. They develop the instruments over a considerable period of time—pretesting, evaluating, and revising them—and subject the results of the drafts to intense analysis for reliability and validity. Even after such labor, however, the data produced by surveys must be regarded only as statements of belief, not as program descriptions or program effects, although opinions sometimes may reflect or anticipate behavior.

Outside experts and surveys of opinion do not, in themselves, solve the problems of program evaluation. Indeed, since they are easy substitutes for a program evaluation, and since they are even occasionally used as if they were program evaluation, they may be even more deceptive than the pretest/posttest models. The worst one can say about these latter models is that they generally do not live up to the expectations of those who employ them, whereas experts and surveys are often sympathetically misleading.

Outside experts are often chosen rather haphazardly, sometimes by a chair or a departmental committee without much awareness of assessment issues. The experts are often long-time English faculty who may have some expertise (or may not) in some aspects of composition and may even have some experience in evaluation. But all too often the outsider has less expertise than good will. (Some genuinely knowledgeable and experienced evaluators are available, such as those trained by the Council of Writing Program Administrators; they have some systematic questions to ask and will require substantial in-house evaluation work to precede a visit. I will detail this use of more expert evaluators in the last section of this essay.) But, although training and qualifications may or may not matter to those selecting the expert, two characteristics are almost invariable: the expert must be from out of town, preferably out of state, and the expert must be friendly to the program being evaluated.

The outside expert, for a nominal fee, is usually expected to spend a day or two on campus and to write a brief report about the program in question. An astute and experienced visitor can discover a great deal about a program even under such disadvantageous circumstances and can prepare a modest document for the use of the program administrators. Such documents usually take two forms: The first is highly laudatory of the professionalism of the program, citing its best features and most qualified personnel. Negative matters, if reported at all, are likely to be only hinted at—buried in the praise and covered with qualifiers—unless these items can be used by program administrators to gain more funds or other advantages in future negotiations with campus officials. In the other form, the reports use the evaluator's home campus as if it were the best model to be followed, a sure irritant to the campus that asked for a responsive evaluation of its own circumstances. Whatever form they take, the reports produced by most outside evaluators, particularly by those without discernible expertise, should really be called subjective impressions of a program rather than program evaluations. But no one expects to take such reports too seriously. Since the person is making a brief visit from out of town, he or she can hardly be expected to understand the program in detail in the time allowed; so recommendations can easily be ignored if they are not convenient.

Authentic Assessment by Genuine Experts: Consequential Validity

It is possible, of course, to contract for a serious evaluation by an experienced evaluator or evaluation team, and the WPA consultant-evaluator service is the most prominent source for such evaluations.[2] But even the WPA team, which brings a national perspective and regular training to the job, in the interests of economy will produce only one report, usually relying on the materials that the campus supplies and a day or two of campus interviews. More elaborate evaluations will generate their own studies and data over a period of months or even years, but few institutions are willing to find the large amount of money such an evaluation team demands (running into the tens or even hundreds of thousands of dollars) or the time such an effort would take. Those seeking serious but economical evaluation prefer to use evaluators who already know the program and its context and who can find legitimate evaluation devices at modest cost.

For this reason, the most practical and effective of all program evaluations, to my admittedly prejudiced knowledge as former director, remains those done by the WPA Consultant-Evaluators. The strengths of this program are notable:

1. The two visitors on the team are assigned by the director of the consultant-evaluator program, in consultation with the local WPA, from the highly selected national panel. Thus the campus can be assured that the visitors are highly professional, experienced and trained in program evaluation, and that they have national reputations. Their report will have greater credibility than one produced by the friendly colleague from out of state.

2. Before the visit, the campus must prepare an elaborate self-study, following national guidelines (see "Guidelines" or the reprint in White *Teaching*, 304–313). This self-study is a powerful document on campus, since it is produced by local faculty and administrators. Because of the investment of time and effort they make in completing the self-study, they have some stake in it and are thus far less likely to ignore the WPA Consultant-Evaluators' final report. The self-study also means that the evaluation team arrives on campus already much better informed than the friendly out-of-state consultant.

3. The report filed by the Consultant-Evaluators has rhetorical power, both

from its basis in documents and interviews and from its high-profile prov-
enance. It also tends to be well written, which is a welcome surprise to
those accustomed to reading program evaluations.

4. The campus commits itself to a follow-up report within a year, detailing
   its action in relation to the recommendations of the report.

The strengths of the program derive in large part from the qualifications
of the consultant-evaluators themselves, most particularly the knowledge and
experience they can bring to bear on campus issues:

1. Knowledge of and experience with various institutional contexts, derived
   from participating in and discussing other visits. The visitors can provide
   multiple models for coping with campus problems.

2. Knowledge of and experience with composition programs themselves,
   derived from teaching in and administering such programs. Thus the visitors can be expected to understand the questions and concerns of part-timers, adjuncts, graduate students, beginning and experienced WPAs, writing faculty, literature scholars, and central administrators.

3. Knowledge about current theoretical, pedagogical, and curricular issues
   that comes from being in the forefront of the profession, being involved
   in the leadership of national organizations, and being published scholars
   in the field.

4. Knowledge about the labor issues in writing programs—what course
   loads, number of students in a course, number of assignments per course,
   and the like mean for the teachers and the program. The visitors have the
   unique opportunity to enlighten administrators about the ramifications of
   increasing work loads and of other budgetary measures, in comparison to
   like institutions.

5. Knowledge of the emotional and personal issues that writing programs
   excite—and of the need for consultants to maintain distance from them.
   The visitors have no local agenda and are interested only in improving the
   institutional fit of the writing program for the students, the faculty, and
   the institution as a whole.

While the WPA program is not a data-based, empirical evaluation, and
hence may not be convincing to those for whom statistical findings are required, it does avoid most of the problems of the usual "outside expert." In
addition, it seems to be the single evaluation program that fosters genuine
change on campus, no doubt because it involves key campus people so heavily
in preparing for the evaluation.

For recent examples of ways the WPA service initiated genuine change at
two institutions, see "WPA on Campus," in which the WPAs of Lehigh and
Washington State Universities describe the effects of visits by teams of consultant-evaluators. In both cases, newly appointed WPAs called for the visits

in order to deal with problems they saw in their programs, as well as with their administrations. The outside consultants helped magnify the voice of the profession, which was not likely to be heard if articulated only by the new WPA, and their reports led to major improvements in facilities, curriculum, assessment, and—in the Lehigh case—faculty (an endowed chair in composition).

I do not mean to suggest that the WPA consultant-evaluator program is without problems. The visiting team members may not be paragons of evaluative clarity or neutrality; the program might be in such disarray that the report turns out to be so negative—or so non-judgmental—that it is dismissed by the campus; administrators may feel that the visitors are too implicated in writing instruction to be disinterested observers; and so on. I have been asked during a campus visit by a university president (behind closed doors) if the WPA should be fired or promoted, an improper question a visitor must avoid answering (as I did), but an example of how outside evaluators can be misused on campus. Further, campus follow-up reports are usually late or non-existent, presumably because institutional change is so difficult to implement that the reports would have little to present. In addition, the report filed by the visiting team must be integrated into a campus program evaluation; the report cannot accomplish the entire job by itself.

Nonetheless, in an area where even a little evidence and even an attempt at program improvement have usually been anomalies, the consultant-evaluator service offers an important opportunity to the WPA. Under the right circumstances, as the Lehigh and WSU examples show, a report can serve as springboard for massive overhauls of writing programs, for changes that sometimes have been needed for generations but could never quite get off the ground. The report sets a rhetorical frame for the larger program evaluation of which it is a part, giving the WPA an approach to gathering evidence and addressing an audience that has not otherwise been available.

Moreover, the report of the evaluation team can be considered to have a kind of validity that is lacking in the other forms of evaluation described earlier. The concept of measurement validity has recently been enriched by consideration of the results of measurement (Moss). That is, a valid measurement must not only demonstrably evaluate what it sets out to measure (writing, for instance, not parental income), but also have appropriate effects and consequences. Thus, a writing measure that winds up diminishing the quantity and quality of writing instruction (such as some multiple-choice tests) cannot be valid, whatever data it may produce. If we follow this new concept of "consequential validity" for program assessment, we must include the degree to which it brings about positive change in the program. On these grounds, the WPA Consultant-Evaluator program becomes one of the more valid program assessments.

The value of the WPA program lies in its sensitivity to the uniqueness of local situations and its resistance to oversimplification. The highly visible scholars on the WPA panel have learned the rhetoric of program evaluation, which calls for awareness of multiple, differing audiences and for a variety of kinds of evidence. In program evaluation, as in all other aspects of writing programs, we need to avoid using or accepting simple and reductive definitions, procedures, tests, and inferences. It is surely a wise instinct that leads us to trust writing instruction and administration more to poets than to scientists, or even to logicians. The resistant reality of learning to think, to write, to create, to revise and recreate, and to understand, does not yield its secrets readily. Our primary job, in program evaluation as in many other aspects of our work, is to help others see the complexity and importance of writing, to distinguish between the simple and the not so simple, to be willing to accept the evidence of many kinds of serious inquiry into the nature of creative thought.

The Value of Evaluation

While a negative program evaluation or a badly done evaluation report can be most damaging, a well-handled evaluation has many advantages. The sheer consideration of goals and ways of approaching those goals that evaluation demands is a formative activity; it asks those who teach writing to consider what they are doing and why—questions that need to be asked far more often than they usually are. The gathering of information for an evaluation is itself a constructive activity; it not only forces those producing the information to see it with new eyes but makes statements about the importance of the information being collected. Imagine, for example, an item on a faculty questionnaire asking about the number of professional conferences the professor has attended on the teaching of writing or the number of papers he or she has read at conferences on pedagogy; merely requesting such information elevates its importance.

The rhetorical problem of writing program assessment requires us to gather and then present appropriate information about the program to an audience—usually a skeptical audience expecting empirical evidence. But we must take the position that other kinds of evidence are more in keeping with the goals of our programs and the nature of our discipline. As writing teachers and writers, we need to recognize that we have a wide range of options and that all of our training and skill can be brought to play on the task.

Finally, of course, a careful evaluation leads to a reexamination of the way things are being done, the way human and financial resources are being spent. It may suggest that some of us have found more successful ways of doing our jobs than did our predecessors. It may even suggest that we are so enormously effective at what we do that we should spend rather more time than we do at self-congratulation. Or it may suggest that we are not very effective at all. In any case, the evaluation of writing programs need not be threatening or destructive; if it is done in a sensitive and intelligent way, using a wide range of measures and involving those teaching in the program in the substantive issues of the evaluation, it can be a valuable experience for everyone.

Whenever writing teachers involve ourselves, as we should, with program evaluation, we must be fully alert both to the dangers of oversimplification and to the large possibilities for constructive change offered by any evaluation program. Program evaluation ought never to be seen as a mere measurement issue, unrelated to conceptual, contextual, and curricular issues that define the writing program. Behind program evaluation lies our responsibility to our students and to the central role of writing, in all its complexity, in education. Behind our reports lies our rhetorical skill, attending to the expectations of our audiences, yet demonstrating that we have other kinds of convincing evidence to offer than they might have expected to receive.

Notes

1. This discussion of program evaluation models is adapted from my *Teaching and Assessing Writing*, 2nd ed., San Francisco: Jossey-Bass, 1994, pp. 248–269.

2. The current director of this program is Ben McClelland, English Department, University of Mississippi. The organizational headquarters of WPA is located at Miami University, Oxford, Ohio.

Works Cited

Bartholomae, David. "Inventing the University." *When a Writer Can't Write*. Ed. Mike Rose. New York: Guilford, 1985. 134–165.

"Guidelines for Self-Study to Precede a Writing Program Evaluation." *WPA: Writing Program Administration* 17.1–2 (1993): 88–95. Reprinted in White, *Teaching*, 304–313.

Hillocks, George. *Research on Written Composition: New Directions for Teaching*. Urbana, IL: NCTE, 1986.

Hughes, Gail. "The Need for Clear Purposes and New Approaches to the Evaluation of Writing Across the Curriculum Programs." *Writing Assessment: Politics, Policies, Practices*. Eds. Edward M. White, William Lutz, and Sandra Kamusikiri. New York: MLA, in press.

Hughes-Wiener, Gail, and Susan Jensen-Cekalla. "Organizing a WAC Evaluation Project: Implications for Program Planning." *Writing Across the Curriculum in the Community College*. Eds. L. Stanley and J. Ambron. San Francisco: Jossey-Bass, 1991. 65–70.

Kitzhaber, Albert R. *Themes, Theories, and Therapy: The Teaching of Writing in College*. New York: McGraw-Hill, 1963.

Moss, Pamela A. "Shifting Conceptions of Validity in Educational Measurement: Implications for Performance Assessment." *Review of Educational Research* 62 (1992): 229–258.

"Teaching and Learning the Art of Composition: The Bay Area Writing Project." *Carnegie Quarterly* 27.2 (1979): 4–7.

White, Edward M. *Developing Successful College Writing Programs*. San Francisco: Jossey-Bass, 1989.

———. *Teaching and Assessing Writing*. 2nd ed. San Francisco: Jossey-Bass, 1994.

———. and Linda Polin. *Research in Effective Teaching of Writing: Final Report*. NIE-G-81-0011 and NIE-G-82-0024. Washington, DC: National Institute of Education, 1986.

"WPA on Campus." *WPA: Writing Program Administration* 14.3 (1991): 69–77.

11

From Icon to Partner
Repositioning the Writing Program Administrator

Barbara L. Cambridge
Indiana University Purdue University Indianapolis
Ben W. McClelland
University of Mississippi

The authors of this chapter have both led large writing programs, served as president of the largest national professional association of writing program administrators, led together for two years the annual Summer Workshop for new and veteran WPAs, and served and continue to serve as consultant-evaluators for writing programs of many kinds. Yet, with all our experience and knowledge of writing programs, we had not until recently challenged a basic assumption of the self-study document that guides evaluation of writing programs by the National Council of Writing Program Administrators. That assumption was that a writing program should have a director.

We should have listened to our own theory of social construction. Theorists and practitioners in composition have insisted that all complex social phenomena are strongly influenced by social, cultural, and historical context. Awareness of the influence of context has changed reading theory to include the reader as a maker of meaning, has mandated collaborative learning during the writing process, and has challenged our definitions of texts worthy of being written and read. Our epistemology has changed our pedagogy and even our assessment as more and more faculty and students value the instructional and evaluative potential of performance assessments like portfolios. Similarly, we have mounted team efforts in our scholarly pursuits, despite disapprobation by traditionalist colleagues. In "The Case for Collaborative Scholarship in Rhetoric and Com-

151

position," Geraldine McNenny and Duane Roen argue for scholarly collaborations, "dialogic models [that] promote the understanding of knowledge as
jointly constructed and negotiated" (305). Our recognition of the social construction of reality, nonetheless, has not led to an examination of the ways that
we structure the leadership roles involved in administering writing programs.

Pyramids of Power

The recognition of social context *does* help explain our assumption about a
single writing program administrator. Colleges and universities are typical
administrative structures with a hierarchy of administrators: presidents, vice-
presidents, chancellors, vice-chancellors, deans, associate deans, directors,
assistant directors, chairpersons, assistant chairpersons, and so forth. Within
that vertical structure diagrammed on organizational charts, one rarely sees a
tree that indicates partnership or a schema that has more horizontal than vertical lines. While some interdisciplinary programs featuring "studies" or "center" in their titles may operate internally on non-hierarchical bases, they are
still situated within the university's larger vertical construct. Although the
business world has been moving, sometimes dramatically, to a flattened administrative structure, universities have persisted in adhering to a traditional
pyramid of power. A writing program administrator position, in fact, creates a
space in that pyramid of power, acknowledging that faculty and students need
leadership as they engage in teaching and learning writing.

In his book *On Leadership* John W. Gardner describes large-scale organizations. "Predictable characteristics of large-scale organizations include a
complex division of labor, specialization, fixed roles, and careful definitions
of rank and status. Equally predictable are the proliferation of defined subsystems, increasingly rigid boundaries between subsystems and emergence of
the turf syndrome" (84). That turf syndrome has been actively chronicled in
publications about English Departments in North American colleges and universities. The turf battles between literature and composition, as composition
has emerged as a discipline, have foregrounded specialization disputes, overt
status issues, and the relative positions of department chairperson and writing
program administrator. To engage successfully in turf battles, the WPA has
needed to operate from a position of strength, however low on the pyramid of
power. Much emphasis has been placed on drawing to the WPA position someone who can fight well the necessary battles for composition.

In fact, many WPAs do feel embattled. When the Association of Departments of English of the Modern Language Association and the National Council of Writing Program Administrators held a joint conference in the summer
of 1994, planners of the conference worked to foster interactions between
chairpersons and WPAs that would lead to mutual understanding and action.
The extent of vocal angst of WPAs, however, was surprising to both planners
and to chairpersons, many of whom were made aware of the defensive stance

which so many WPAs felt they had to maintain in their departments and colleges. New WPAs, in particular, wished to be proactive in implementing emerging theories of composition, connecting teaching and learning for faculty and students, and affirming disparate modes of discourse. Yet these WPAs found entrenched canons, practices, and attitudes which kept them from moving forward. Their place in the pyramid of power meant that they had continually to be defending their territory within the academic terrain.

Webs of Relationships, Clusters of Roles

And that territory is vast. At each of the WPA Summer Workshops which we facilitated, we asked participants during the first hours of the multi-day meetings to write a cluster around "Myself as WPA." The results dramatically demonstrate the complexity of the role of writing program administrator. Low on the pyramid, WPAs are therefore close to the many full- and part-time faculty and graduate students who teach writing. Because writing is often a university-wide requirement, WPAs also relate to faculty in all disciplines, to learning or writing center directors, and to faculty development officers. In the administrative hierarchy WPAs report to chairpersons, deans, and chief academic officers, all of whom may view writing as part of their charge. In addition, with emphasis on a seamless move from secondary school to college, WPAs have connections with K–12 educators. WPAs in universities may also have relationships with adminstrators in nearby two-year colleges whose students transfer to the four-year institution. More than most administrators of campus programs, WPAs interact directly with a multitude of constituencies.

In addition, WPAs have responsibilities for teaching and for research. In their book *Women of Influence, Women of Vision: A Cross-Generational Study of Leaders and Social Change*, Helen Astin and Carole Leland identify two kinds of leaders, positional and nonpositional. They identify a positional leader as one who provides leadership within an organization and a nonpositional leader as one who produces knowledge as a scholar. The position of WPA demands that one be both a positional and nonpositional leader, existing in a wide network of administrators, scholars, teachers, students, and other publics who expect excellence in both kinds of leadership.

The positional and nonpositional aspects of the WPA position are illustrated in clusters drawn by our workshop participants. A new WPA included on his cluster the roles of teacher, coach, innovator, researcher, observer, administrator, supervisor, advisor, writer, colleague, and resource person, concluding that he was "uptight, lost, and anxious, trying to find a niche." Another new WPA drew arrows to himself with the descriptors "person who has learned to like politics, person who has discovered how to have conversations with those he disagrees with, pragmatist, problem solver, teacher, and linguist who is a student of language." Around the center "my role as WPA," a third person wrote, "administrator, efficiency expert, creator, risk taker, problem solver, writing project director, and struggling writer." Imaginatively, another workshop participant placed these descriptors around the center circle "Blakean prophet": innovator, tester, visionary, arbitrator, guide, Ghandian follower, and conservator. The title of his cluster was "Reconciling Opposites."

The complexity of the writing program administrator's position, often the most complex on the institutional hierarchy because of its place near the bottom of the pyramid and because of the nature of the discipline and whom it affects, is apparent in the Portland Resolution, a position paper of the National Council of Writing Program Administrators. At the 1990 WPA Summer Workshop when a group of WPAs were discussing the difficulty of WPAs at tenure and promotion time, they decided to list the various duties of the WPA. Their purpose was partly to provide about-to-be-hired WPAs a rather complete list of possible duties from which their institution and they could choose. The priority duties could then be agreed upon and put into writing, so that the institution would have reasonable expectations and the WPA reasonable responsibilities. An initial draft naming all the duties a WPA might conceivably perform was widely circulated.

The outcome, as you may guess, was that some institutions liked the list so well that they decided the WPA should fulfill all the duties on the list. After all, the institution needs all those jobs undertaken and completed well. Instead of making the job of the WPA more feasible, however, these institutions made it impossible. Even with their most conscientious efforts, WPAs in these positions could not meet all the expectations. For example, at one state university campus, a new WPA was asked to develop a comprehensive program, including a freshman composition program, a writing center, and a writing project for public school teachers. When the programs grew in size and complexity after a few years, the WPA asked for others to share the administrative duties. The request was denied and the WPA was informed that he could expect to be responsible for oversight of all of the campus writing programs now and in the future. Fortunately, other institutions have used the final draft of the Portland Resolution (Hult et al.) to create more feasible positions. Several new members of the Council of Writing Program Administrators have reported that their positions are more focused and expectations clearer because they used the Portland Resolution in negotiations before accepting their positions.

Administrators as Scholars

Another conceptualization which speaks to the complexity of the WPA position is Ernest Boyer's redefinition of scholarship in *Scholarship Reconsidered*. Persuaded that the traditional definition of research as the primary mark of intellectual vitality privileges only one kind of scholarship, Boyer offers four categories of scholarship which we can use to describe our work: the scholarships of discovery, teaching, application, and integration. Each of these kinds of scholarship involves intellectual work which creates and uses knowledge. For example, administrative work, which has traditionally been viewed as service, can be analyzed to reveal its conceptual basis. Richard Bullock argues persuasively that the WPA's "activities—from articulating the program's guiding principles, suggesting syllabi, and recommending textbooks to interviewing prospective faculty and arbitrating students' grievances—aim toward the construction and implementation of a program that embodies the key elements of the administrator's knowledge and expertise" (15–16). Citing the "dynamic nature" of the WPA's work, which requires innovative problem-solving that involves "implementing general principles in specific situations," Bullock suggests a simile: "Like the literary scholar applying theoretical critical principles to a specific text, the writing specialist's arena is the writing classroom and program" (16). Administrative work can involve all categories of scholarship; however, the scholarships of integration and of application are central. (See Christine Hult's chapter, this volume, for suggestions of how the WPA can use Boyer's categories to describe administrative scholarship.)

The Modern Language Association Commission on Service offers an insightful new look at the definition of service which can help us describe the way in which service can demonstrate intellectual work. The committee's schema posits a continuum of service that begins with description of action, leads through analysis of change based on action, and culminates in identification of conceptual leadership (Phelps and Slevin). With such a continuum it is possible to assess the excellence of all kinds of scholarship. Because WPAs usually engage in all four categories of scholarship, this continuum enables them to describe and document their work for evaluation, both for low stakes, such as yearly review, and for high stakes, such as promotion and tenure.

Russell Edgerton, President of the American Association for Higher Education, has reviewed the use of Boyer's categories across the country. Noting that some colleges and universities have adopted the four categories, he indicates that many sites have used the categories as a heuristic to examine the problematic nature of the categories of teaching, research, and service and our limited development of means to document and evaluate each of the traditional categories (Edgerton). WPAs would benefit from the use of Boyer's categories as heuristic but more from adoption because the leadership work of the WPA spreads across all categories. Until the intellectual nature of each part of the position is described and evaluated, WPAs will remain underacknowledged and undervalued.

In this essay, however, we will suggest a more radical redefinition of the WPA, a redefinition that involves changing the basic architecture of leadership and the responsibilities of the WPA.

Toward a Multitude of Partnerships

Because the position of WPA has often been overloaded, both in expectation and in actuality, the first change needs to be in the conceptualization of the position. In *The Age of Paradox* Charles Handy explains that organizations now and in the future need to operate on a federalist model. Federalism, as defined

by Handy, "endeavors to maximize independence, provided that there is a necessary interdependence; to encourage difference, but within limits; it needs to
maintain a strong center, but one devoted to the service of the parts; it can, and
should, be led from that center but has to be managed by the parts" (110). Two
concepts are central to this federalism: twin citizenship and subsidiarity. In a
federation a person belongs to his or her own state but also to the larger federal
union of states. Identification with the larger group is more difficult, demand-
ing trust among groups, cross-fertilization among groups, a common set of principles, and a common information system. Subsidiarity requires "leaving power
as close to the action as possible. . . . The center's role is to orchestrate the broad
strategic vision, develop the shared administrative and organizational infrastructure, and create the cultural glue which can create synergies" (135).

If power is left as close to the action as possible, the writing program administrator will be part of a multitude of partnerships. The WPA will work with
teaching faculty, departmental administrators, deans, and all the other constituencies which are currently in the relational network; however, the nature of the
relationships will be changed. As Peter Block points out in *Stewardship: Choosing Service Over Self-Interest*, leadership in the past has been associated with
"control, direction, and knowing what is best for others." But "the act of leading cultural or organizational change by determining the desired future, defining the path to get there, and knowing what is best for others is incompatible
with widely distributing ownership and responsibility in an organization" (13).
It is not the fault of people in leadership positions that we are not operating well;
rather it is the problem of the way we have framed the role of leader.

Block reminds us that "governance structures and strategies aimed at control, consistency, and predictability work well in stable, predictable environments. . . . It is these patriarchal beliefs, though, that form the operating reality
for most of our institutions with power, privilege, and rewards concentrated at
the top" (26). Colleges and universities are certainly not stable, predictable
environments during these times of fiscal and attitudinal change. As the context changes for educational institutions, we must rethink our structural leadership model. This rethinking is particularly needed for WPA positions, many
of which are readily described as dysfunctional for those who hold them. Rethinking and re-creating dysfunctional positions ought to be done collectively
by all interested parties, for, as John Trimbur points out, "it is through the social interaction of shared activity that individuals realize their own power to
take control of their situation by collaborating with others" (604).

In a partnership, Block points out, four conditions are required. First, each
person involved is responsible for defining vision and for enacting that vision.
Second, each person has a voice, even if there are different levels of authority.
Third, each person is responsible for outcomes of the unit or community.
Fourth, each person is honest: In this redistribution of power, persons are less
vulnerable so they can be more honest (30–31). Block emphasizes that "the
difficult part is to maintain contact without control" (31). In other words, when

dominance is not the cultural glue mentioned by Handy, we have to create another cohesive device.

In the past the WPA has attempted to be the cohesive device which connects the multiple functions of writing within the university. Responsible for the writing center, writing across the curriculum, basic writing courses, assessment for graduation, faculty development, and running a program, the WPA in himself or herself became the hub. When David Bartholomae decided to leave the WPA position at the University of Pittsburgh, he told an audience of WPAs that he would be glad to give up being the writing icon on his campus (Bartholomae). WPAs often become the central symbol of writing on a campus. Worse, they are expected to be the actual glue that holds it all together.

If WPAs indeed should not and cannot be expected to be the glue, what is their role in the modern university? That question is impossible to answer categorically for all situations because each university will have different needs: in market terminology, each university is a different customer whose needs will be differently met. But WPAs can in most cases fulfill the role of the "center" as set forth by Handy: "[1] orchestrate the broad strategic vision, [2] develop the shared administrative and organizational infrastructure, and [3] create the cultural glue which can create synergies" (135).

Writing program administrators are often in an ideal spot to engage all parties in strategic planning. Because they have contact with so many stakeholders in the university, they can contribute to circumstances that elicit engagement in and commitment to envisioning the future by all parties. For example, if a college decides that a certain level of writing competency will be a student learning goal, the WPA can enter into the joint-decision making about how each faculty member will enact that goal. No longer is the WPA primarily responsible for the program but remains intimately involved in coordinating the faculty who decide what they are able to do and for what they will be accountable. The value of the WPA's coordination and of the faculty members' pedagogical success are both measured by the student learning outcomes. The partnership implicates both the WPA and faculty in joint responsibility.

The second mark of the center is developing a shared administrative and organizational infrastructure. Tricky business, this. Other than Michigan's composition board, there is little historical record of our experimenting with shared governance. One large northeastern university annually rotated three WPAs through two administrative positions in a form of musical chairs. One person directed the composition program, while a second directed the writing center. Meanwhile, the third, who was without administrative duties, taught graduate courses and conducted research. However, this longstanding arrangement was devised for the professional development of the WPAs, rather than as an innovation in administrative structure. In fact, each position retained its traditional, discrete institutional form. With the wide client base of writing students and the multiple levels above them in the administrative hierarchy, WPAs may have trouble imagining how to achieve a shared infrastructure.

WPAs, however, can start with their own positions. At the beginning of this essay, we admitted that we had only recently questioned the assumption that a writing program should have a director. Perhaps models like the Writing Co-ordinating Committee at Indiana University Purdue University Indianapolis or another configuration that spreads power and authority should be studied by individual WPAs, by institutions, and by professional associations. Concurrently, we can ask those whom we serve how best to serve them. Are students being best served by WPAs who are assuming too many tasks for one individual and too much authority for a successful partnership? What do students in our contexts need? What relationships need to be developed with units and administrators of those units to answer the needs of students? If WPAs research such questions, they will be in a position to negotiate change in the pyramidic structure of their institutions.

Thirdly, WPAs can help "create the glue which can create synergies." John Gardner establishes that an interdependent world requires leaders who can "manage interconnectedness" (118). He lists five skills that are critically important for this task: (1) agreement building, including skills in conflict resolution, mediation, compromise, and coalition building; (2) networking, building the linkages needed to get things done; (3) exercising nonjurisdictional power, relying not on position but on the power of ideas, the power that belongs to those who understand systems; (4) institution building, including building systems that institutionalize problem solving; and (5) flexibility, including willingness to redefine one's own role at any time (119). Creating the glue, in other words, does not mean being the glue. The WPA must contribute to the community of people who care about students learning to write.

Community does not, however, relate only to the positional role of the WPA; it is essential in the WPA's nonpositional role as well. In *To Know As We Are Known* Parker Palmer describes community as "central to four issues that have long been basic to the life of the mind: the nature of reality (ontology), how we know reality (epistemology), how we teach and learn (pedagogy), and how education forms or deforms our lives in the world (ethics)" (xiii). We return to scholarship and the purposes of scholarship. Why do we put ourselves in relationship to discover, teach, integrate, and apply knowledge? How is the nonpositional work of the WPA related to the positional work? If we now know that chaos theory posits infinite interrelationship (ontology), that we know because we agree to know (epistemology), that if reality is communal, we learn best by interacting with it (pedagogy), and that learning can lead to communal as well as personal standards (ethics), how can we return to a single writing program director?

The hidden curriculum of a university includes the lessons of the administrative structure. If our positional and nonpositional values are to be consonant, we must reexamine the ways in which we administer the university, including the ways that we administer writing programs. Resulting changes will reposition the WPA from icon to partner but, more importantly, will model for students the ways in which we all can learn, know, and live as responsible, decision-making partners in the work and life of the academy and of the world.

Works Cited

Astin, Helen S., and Carole Leland. *Women of Influence, Women of Vision: A Cross-Generational Study of Leaders and Social Change.* San Francisco: Jossey-Bass, 1991.

Bartholomae, David. Plenary speech. Annual Conference of the Council of Writing Program Administrators. Oxford, Ohio. July 1989.

Block, Peter. *Stewardship: Choosing Service Over Self-Interest.* San Francisco: Berrett-Koehler Publishers, 1993.

Boyer, Ernest. *Scholarship Reconsidered: Priorities of the Professoriate.* Princeton: The Carnegie Foundation, 1990.

Bullock, Richard H. "When Administration Becomes Scholarship: The Future of Writing Program Administration." *WPA: Writing Program Administration* 11.1–2 (Fall, 1987): 13–18.

Edgerton, Russell. Speech. "National Perspectives on Faculty Roles and Rewards." Indianapolis, Indiana. October 14, 1994.

Gardner, John W. *On Leadership.* New York: The Free Press, 1990.

Handy, Charles. *The Age of Paradox.* Boston: Harvard Business School Press, 1994.

Hult, Christine, et al. "The Portland Resolution: Guidelines for Writing Program Administrator Positions." *WPA: Writing Program Administration* 16.1–2 (1992): 88–94.

McNenny, Geraldine, and Duane Roen. "The Case for Collaborative Scholarship in Rhetoric and Composition." *Rhetoric Review* 10.2 (1992): 291–310.

Palmer, Parker J. *To Know As We Are Known: Education as a Spiritual Journey.* San Francisco: HarperCollins, 1993.

Phelps, Louise, and James Slevin. Discussion Group. "Professional Service and Rewards." Annual Conference of the Council of Writing Program Administrators. Oxford, Mississippi. July 1994.

Trimbur, John. "Consensus and Difference in Collaborative Learning." *College English* 51.6 (1989): 602–16.

Notes on Contributors

Lynn Z. Bloom is Professor of English and Aetna Chair of Writing at the University of Connecticut, Storrs, and serves on the Board of Directors, National Archives of Composition and Research. Past President of the Council of Writing Program Administrators, she has led Summer Workshops and co-organized the 1993 conference, "Composition in the 21st Century: Crisis and Change," the proceedings of which are forthcoming from Southern Illinois University Press in 1995.

Barbara L. Cambridge is Associate Dean of the Faculties and Professor of English at Indiana University Purdue University Indianapolis. Past President of the Council of Writing Program Administrators, she is interested in administrative structures, the intellectual work of administrators, and collaborative decision making within institutions. Cambridge edits the *Journal of Teaching Writing*, is active in the Peer Review Project of the American Association for Higher Education, and teaches gateway and capstone courses for English majors. Her current administrative work focuses on documenting and rewarding undergraduate teaching and redefining general education to enhance both student learning and the academic environment.

Lester Faigley is Professor of English and Director of the Division of Rhetoric and Composition at the University of Texas at Austin. The author of numerous essays in composition journals and books, he most recently published *Fragments of Rationality: Postmodernity and the Subject of Composition* (Pittsburgh UP, 1992), which was awarded the MLA Mina P. Shaughnessy Prize. He is the 1995–96 Chair of the Conference on College Composition and Communication.

Kristine Hansen is Associate Professor of English at Brigham Young University, where she is past Coordinator of Composition. She has published essays in *CCC, English Journal, Advances in Writing Research: Writing in Academic Disciplines* (Ablex, 1988), and *The TA Experience: Preparing for Multiple Roles* (New Forums Press, 1993). She serves on the Executive Board of the Council of Writing Program Administrators.

Christine A. Hult is Professor and Assistant Department Head in the English Department at Utah State University. She served as the editor of the *WPA: Writing Program Administration* journal from 1988–1994 and is currently on the WPA Board of Consultant-Evaluators. Her research interests include computers in writing and program and teacher evaluation, as reflected in recent publications in *Computers in Composition* and the *Journal of Advanced Composition*, as well as in her textbooks, which include *Researching and Writing Across the Disciplines* (3rd edition in press) and a series of writing-in-the-disciplines research texts with Allyn & Bacon publishers (forthcoming 1995). She recently edited a collection for NCTE called *Evaluating Teachers of Writing* and is the guest editor (with Joyce Kinkead) of a special issue of *Computers and Composition*, addressing computers and writing centers, that will appear in 1995.

Joseph Janangelo is assistant professor of English at Loyola University–Chicago. He serves on the editorial boards of *Dialogue: A Journal for Writing Specialists* and *Teacher Research: The Journal of Classroom Inquiry*. Having published essays in CCC, *Computers and Composition, English Education*, and *WPA: Writing Program Administration*, he recently co-edited *Theoretical and Critical Perspectives on Teacher Change* (Ablex, 1993).

Ben W. McClelland is Professor of English and Holder of the Ottillie Schillig Chair of English Composition at the University of Mississippi, where he directs the comprehensive writing program and the University Writing Project. Among his many publications are *Perspectives on Research and Scholarship in Composition* (MLA, 1985) and *Eight Approaches to Teaching Composition* (NCTE, 1980), both co-edited with Timothy Donovan, and a textbook, *The New American Rhetoric* (HarperCollins, 1993). He is Past President of the Council of Writing Program Administrators and currently directs its Consultant-Evaluator Service.

Susan H. McLeod is Associate Dean of the College of Liberal Arts at Washington State University, and a member of the Board of Consultants of the National Network of Writing Across the Curriculum Programs. Her publications include *Writing Across the Curriculum: A Guide to Developing Programs, Strengthening Programs for Writing Across the Curriculum, Writing About the World*, and articles on writing across the curriculum, writing program administration, and the affective dimension of the writing process.

Elizabeth A. Nist has taught for twenty-five years in two-year colleges and is currently an English instructor at Anoka-Ramsey Community College in Coon Rapids, Minnesota. The founding chair of the Western Regional Conference of Two-Year Colleges, she is now on the advisory board of the Minnesota Writing Project and serves as President of the Minnesota Council of Teachers of English. She has published essays in *College English, Teaching English in the Two-Year College*, and *Minnesota English Journal*. With Helon Raines, she also co-authored an essay in *Writing Ourselves into the Story: Unheard Voices from Composition Studies* (SIU Press, 1993).

Helon H. Raines taught writing for eighteen years at Casper College and the University of Wyoming, where she created and directed the UW/CC Writing Center. In 1992–1993, she chaired the National Two-Year College Council during the restructuring of two-year college programs in NCTE. She has published essays in professional journals such as *CCC, WPA*, and *The Writing Center Journal*. In the fall of 1994 she assumed duties as Director of Composition at Armstrong State College in Savannah, Georgia.

Susan Romano is a doctoral candidate in English at the University of Texas at Austin. She has served as the Assistant Director of the Division of Rhetoric and Composition and as program coordinator for the 1995 CCCC Convention. Her essay, "The Egalitarianism Narrative: Whose Story? Which Yardstick?" received the 1994 Ellen Nold Award for best article in computers and composition studies.

Charles I. Schuster is Professor of English at the University of Wisconsin–Milwaukee and President of the Council of Writing Program Administrators (1995–97). His publications include *The Politics of Writing Instruction: Postsecondary*, which won the CCCC Outstanding Book Award in 1993, and *Speculations: Readings in Culture, Identity, and Values.* He has published essays and reviews in *College English, CCC, Rhetoric Review,* and many anthologies. He is currently editing *CrossCurrents,* a series published by Heinemann–Boynton/Cook, and he is General Editor of *Literature and Culture,* a series of anthologies to be published by HarperCollins.

Ellen Strenski, now Assistant Writing Director in the Department of English and Comparative Literature at the University of California, Irvine, has been a WPA in the University of California system since 1983, a turbulent time during which nontenurable lecturers unionized, achieving through collective bargaining the possibility of renewable appointments after rigorous review. As Assistant Director in the UCLA Writing Programs, the University of California program with the largest number of lecturers, she helped design and implement policy and procedures for reviewing teachers, work that is reflected in various of her publications. She has published in a range of disciplinary journals, including *The History Teacher, Media and Methods,* and *Doctor-Patient Studies,* as well as in journals and collections of essays about composition. She has also co-authored several textbooks, including *The Guide to Writing Sociology Papers* (St. Martin's, 3rd ed., 1994) and *The Research Paper Workbook* (Longman, 4th ed., 1996).

Edward M. White is Professor of English at California State University, San Bernardino, where he has served prolonged periods as English department chair, English graduate coordinator, and coordinator of the upper-division university writing program. He directed the Consultant-Evaluator Service of the Council of Writing Program Administrators from 1988–1994 and in 1993 was elected to a second term on the Executive Committee of CCCC. He has written several influential books, including *Teaching and Assessing Writing* (Jossey-Bass, 2nd ed., 1994), *Developing Successful College Writing Programs* (Jossey-Bass, 1989), and *Assigning, Responding, and Evaluating: A Writing Teacher's Guide* (St. Martin's, 3rd ed., 1995). He is co-editor of *Composition in the 21st Century,* forthcoming from Southern Illinois University Press in 1995.

Molly Wingate has worked in writing centers since 1981 and presently directs the Writing Center at Colorado College. She is a regular presenter at CCCC and co-chairs CCCC's Task Force on Curricular Principles. She is a charter member of the steering committee for the National Conference on Peer Tutoring in Writing. She received her BA and MA in English from Bucknell University.